Every Californian's Guide to
Estate Planning

Wills, Trusts, and Everything Else

Attorney Liza W. Hanks

FIRST EDITION	JANUARY 2018
Editor	MARCIA STEWART
Book Design	SUSAN PUTNEY
Proofreading	SUSAN CARLSON GREENE
Index	RICHARD GENOVA
Printing	BANG PRINTING

Names: Hanks, Liza Weiman, 1961- author.
Title: Every Californian's guide to estate planning : wills, trusts, and
   everything else / Attorney Liza W. Hanks.
Description: 1st edition. | Berkeley, CA : Nolo, 2017. | Includes index.
Identifiers: LCCN 2017026770 (print) | LCCN 2017027092 (ebook) | ISBN
   9781413324693 (ebook) | ISBN 9781413324686 (pbk.)
Subjects: LCSH: Estate planning--California. | Wills--California. | Trusts
   and trustees--California.
Classification: LCC KFC195 (ebook) | LCC KFC195 .H36 2017 (print) | DDC
   332.024/01609794--dc23
LC record available at https://lccn.loc.gov/2017026770

Please note

We believe accurate, plain-English legal information should help you
solve many of your own legal problems. But this text is not a substitute
for personalized advice from a knowledgeable lawyer. If you want the
help of a trained professional—and we'll always point out situations
in which we think that's a good idea—consult an attorney licensed to
practice in your state.

Acknowledgments

I would like to give my heartfelt thanks to:

My family: Steven, Kate, and Sam Hanks, for their support, patience and collective sense of humor.

My editor: Marcia Stewart, for working hard to make this book inclusive, readable, accurate, and just plain better.

My former editor, friend, and fellow writer, Mary Randolph, (author of *The Executor's Guide* and *8 Ways to Avoid Probate*) for initially encouraging me to write books about estate planning and for always setting the bar high.

My estate planning friends and colleagues: Tish Loeb and Barbara Small at GCA Law Partners LLP, in Mountain View, California; Barbara Wright at Finch Montgomery Wright PC in Palo Alto, California; Carol Elias Zolla, at Zolla Law Firm, in Los Gatos, California; Einat Arbel at Law Office of Einat Arbel, Palo Alto, California; and all of the members of the Bay Area Estate Planning study group for keeping me honest, answering my endless questions, and inspiring me, always, to do my best job for clients. And finally, Barbara Krimsky Binder, CFP, BKB Financial Advisors, Menlo Park, California, for making sure my numbers add up.

About the Author

Liza Hanks is a partner at GCA Law Partners LLP in Mountain View, California, where she practices estate planning, trust administration, and probate law. She is a certified specialist in Estate Planning, Trust and Probate Law by the State Bar of California Board of Legal Specialization and taught Estate Planning and Taxation at Santa Clara University Law School as an adjunct lecturer. She is a graduate of Stanford Law School, a former magazine editor, and the mother of two children (neither of whom has any interest in becoming an attorney). She's also the author of *The Trustee's Legal Companion* (with Attorney Carol Elias Zolla).

Table of Contents

Introduction:
What's So Special About Estate Planning in California? 1

Why Is This Book Just for Californians? 3

What Will I Get Out of This Book? 5

1 What's in an Estate Plan and Why Do You Need One? 9

Getting Started 11

Understanding Probate 13

The Workhorses: Wills and Trusts 22

Preparing a Personal Inventory and a List of Beneficiaries 27

Special Estate Planning Issues When You Own Real Estate 34

2 Wills 41

Making It Legal 44

A Will Is Just One Part of Your Estate Plan 45

Right of Survivorship: Property You Own With Others 47

Choosing an Executor 49

Choosing Guardians and Managing Money For Children 55

Planning for Pets 55

Preparing a Will Worksheet 58

Making a Will: A DIY Project or Not? 60

Once You've Done Your Will 62

What Happens If You Don't Make a Will? 63

3 Living Trusts 65

What Is a Living Trust? 67

Creating a Living Trust: The Settlor's Job 72

Casting the Play: Selecting Trustees and Beneficiaries 74

Preparing a Trust Worksheet 78

Creating a Living Trust: DIY Project or Not? 80

Transferring Assets Into the Trust 84

Pour-Over Wills 87

4 Estate Planning for Minor Children: Choosing a Guardian 91

Get It Done 93

What Guardians Are (and Are Not) Responsible For 94

Court Approval and Oversight of Guardians 96

Picking the Right Guardian 97

Common Problems and Some Solutions 106

After You've Chosen a Guardian: Talking It Over 113

Giving Guardians Some Written Guidance 115

Congratulate Yourself on Choosing a Guardian! 117

5 Leaving Money to Children 119

Money and Kids: The Basics 121

Custodial Accounts 125

Children's Trusts 131

Your Backup Plan: Appoint a Property Guardian 149

Pull Your Plan Together 151

Life Insurance Primer 153

6 Estate Planning Across Borders 163

Resident and Nonresident Aliens for Tax Purposes 165

Estate and Gift Taxation of Non-U.S. Citizens
(Resident and Nonresident) 167

How Assets Are Taxed Worldwide for U.S. Taxpayers 169

Naming International Trustees and Executors 171

Naming Guardians for Minor Children Who Don't Live in the U.S. 174

Estate Planning for a Noncitizen Spouse 175

7 Yours, Mine, and Ours: Estate Planning for Blended Families 179

Community Versus Separate Property.. 182

Community Property and Taxes... 190

Planning Strategies for Blended Families...192

Planning for Children of Different Ages.. 199

Putting It All Together 200

8 Estate Planning and Property Tax: What You Need to
Know About Prop 13 201

Property Taxes in California and Prop 13... 203

What Really Matters: Change in Ownership of Your Home.................... 206

Exclusions From Reassessment That You Have to Request...................... 209

Automatic Exclusions from Reassessment 216

Reporting a Change of Ownership... 220

9 Death and Taxes: Income, Gift, and Estate Taxes 223

Some Background on Death and Taxes.. 225

Income Taxes.. 226

Gift Tax 236

The Estate Tax..243

Estate Tax Planning Strategy If You Are Single: Philanthropy 247

10 Naming the Right Beneficiaries: Retirement and Life Insurance 249

Alphabet Soup: Retirement Plans Explained 252

What Beneficiaries Have You Already Named? 255

Retirement 101: The Basic Rules of Choosing Beneficiaries
and Withdrawing Money.. 258

Naming Beneficiaries for Retirement Plans 263

A Little Housekeeping: Cleaning Up Your Retirement Plans.................271

Filling Out the Forms Naming Beneficiaries... 272

Naming Beneficiaries for Life Insurance 274

11 Advance Health Care Directives & Powers of Attorney for Finances 279

　Health Care Directives 281

　Durable Power of Attorney for Finances 298

12 Managing Your Plan and Keeping it Current 307

　What's in Your Plan 309

　Storing Your Estate Plan 310

　Digital Estate Planning Issues 310

　Whom to Give Copies of Your Estate Planning Documents To 312

　Keeping Your Plan Current 313

　How to Make Changes to Your Estate Plan 317

13 Finding a Lawyer and Help Beyond the Book 321

　Start With Referrals 322

　Do Some Research 323

　Make Contact 324

　Ask Questions 324

　Trust Yourself 325

Appendix

　How to Use the Downloadable Forms on the Nolo Website 327

　Editing RTFs 328

　List of Forms Available on the Nolo Website 329

Index 331

Introduction:
What's So Special About Estate Planning in California?

Why Is This Book Just for Californians? 3

    Our Families 3

    Our Homes and Property...4

    Our (Personal) International Relations 4

What Will I Get Out of This Book?...5

Almost every single call that I get from a new client begins with someone apologizing for the fact that they don't have an estate plan yet or that it's been many years since they updated it. And I always tell them the same thing, "Don't apologize! Give yourself credit for making this call and getting the ball rolling." For the last 17 years, my motto has been, "Feel good, not guilty!" And you, reader, are way ahead of most people, too, just by reading this book.

The truth is that more than half the people in the United States die with no estate plan in place at all—not even a will. And believe me, I get it. The details of day-to-day life in California can be all consuming—finding a job that allows you to live here, sitting in bumper-to-bumper traffic to and from that job, driving kids to and from activities, searching for a house or an apartment in our pricey real estate market, taking care of elderly parents, and on and on. Finding the time to create an estate plan is frankly heroic given the pace of life here.

But estate planning is also important—and doesn't need to be an onerous task. Whether you are young or old, rich or poor, married, single, or living with someone, and whether you have children or not, making an estate plan should be on your agenda. Your plan might be as simple as naming your favorite charity as a beneficiary of your IRA, or as complex as creating a multigenerational trust, or something in between, such as writing a will and leaving all your assets to your spouse or partner. The specifics don't matter. What does matter is that you take some time to make a plan before it's too late.

Estate planning starts with asking yourself some fundamental questions about the people you love, your goals, and your assets. Who do you want to give your money and property to when you die? If you have minor children, who would raise your kids if you couldn't? What assets do you actually have, anyway? How would you feel if your spouse remarried after your death or your partner got involved in a new relationship? Who should take care of your beloved pet? What nonprofit organizations do you want to support? What kind of legacy do you want to leave behind? What's the best way to avoid the cost and delay of probate?

You are the best person to answer all of these questions. Putting an estate plan in place now means that you keep control over critical decisions that will need to be made when you die, or if you get sick—especially if one of these things happens unexpectedly.

Unless you are very wealthy (as in the top 1% of the population), the actual estate planning tasks aren't that hard. You don't need to create lots of complicated legal documents to avoid paying taxes or to structure complex trusts for children. For most people, estate planning is straightforward and this book explains what you need to know to move forward, whether you choose to do it yourself or work with an attorney.

Why Is This Book Just for Californians?

I wrote *Every Californian's Guide to Estate Planning* because there are a lot of us—California is the largest state in the country, with more than 37 million people, and is the sixth largest economy in the world, ahead of France and Brazil. I also wrote this book because Californians have some special issues to deal with that no other estate planning book addresses.

Our Families

- Less than 25 percent of Californians live in traditional "nuclear" families with two parents raising mutual children. The majority of us live in nontraditional families: same-sex, blended, or headed by single parents. In fact, more than one-third of children in California are raised in single-parent households.
- The number of California adults who have never married has doubled since 1969 (it's now 34%).
- Many of us are single and we consider our friends (and pets) to be our family.

Our Homes and Property

- California is one of a few states where property is subject to community property rules.
- Our houses have appreciated so dramatically that middle class Californians face capital gains tax issues that only the very wealthy must think about in every other state.
- Our property tax system means that property tax rates go up only when a property changes hands, so we want our estate plans to try and maintain our lower property tax rates if we can.
- Our houses cost so much that many of us want to help our children buy homes so that they don't move far away.

Our (Personal) International Relations

- More than one-quarter of Californians were born abroad, which is more than twice the national average.
- Foreign-born residents represent more than 30% of the population in eight of California's largest counties: Santa Clara, San Mateo, Los Angeles, San Francisco, Alameda, Imperial, Orange, and Monterey.
- Half of Californian children have at least one immigrant parent, compared to 26% nationwide.
- Many Californians also own property abroad or are married to noncitizen spouses.
- Between 2000 and 2015, California (tied with Texas) had the largest absolute growth of their immigrant population (1.8 million), followed by Florida (1.4 million), New York (662,000), and New Jersey (501,000).

What Will I Get Out of This Book?

This book will help you make the key decisions you'll need to get your estate plan done and understand basic estate planning concepts and rules so that your plan will be smart and effective, including:

- whether you need a will or a trust
- how to avoid probate in California and why that's a good idea
- how to preserve and protect low property tax rates for your family and heirs under Prop 13
- how California defines community and separate property and why it matters
- how to make an estate plan when you are in a blended family and want to balance loyalty to your new family with loyalty to children from prior marriages or relationships
- how to choose guardians for minor children and make a plan to manage children's assets
- how international issues affect your estate plan, including owning property abroad and being married to a noncitizen spouse
- how gift, estate, and income taxes are calculated and how to plan for them
- how to structure your living trust to minimize capital gains taxes for your children and heirs
- how to review and update your retirement plans and life insurance policies to make sure you are leaving enough money and leaving it to the right people
- how to choose the best people to make critical health care and financial decisions for you if you can't make them yourself, and
- what happens if you do nothing.

As an estate planner who has worked with many individuals, couples, and families who grapple with these issues, I'm certain that this book will help you get your estate plan started or updated—whether you're:

- a young married couple in the East Bay with a newborn
- a middle-aged woman caring for your elderly mother in San Diego and eyeing retirement
- an unmarried couple in San Jose who want to take care of children from both your current and previous relationships
- a single mother with children living in Los Angeles
- a divorced man in the Central Valley who wants to leave money to your favorite nephew
- an older couple in Sacramento wanting to put your affairs in order,
- or anyone who wants to benefit charity or make sure your beloved pet is taken care of.

I've tried my best to cover the interests of all Californians in this book. I'll give you the benefit of real-life examples that come from the clients I've had the privilege of working with, my most illuminating war stories, and what I consider best practices so that you can feel empowered and confident as you put your plan together.

Most lawyers think estate planning is only about creating legal documents. I don't. This book *will* help you understand what kind of legal documents you'll need to make your plan (plus I provide lots of helpful forms to help you get organized to prepare key estate planning documents).

But I hope this book will also prompt you to think about things that you may not have considered before, such as preserving your low property tax rate when you leave your house to your family, owning assets in other countries, how you own property during a marriage, how divorce affects your retirement and life insurance beneficiary designations, how to make gifts to kids, how to plan for incapacity, and what kind of care you want at the end of your life.

But don't worry. It's not as bad as it sounds. Many of my clients find, to their surprise, that they've enjoyed the process by the time they're done and I hope you will, too. It's rare to sit down and think about life and death issues and the people, organizations, or animals that you love the most. But it can be deeply meaningful.

For some reason, we all seem to think that death happens to everyone else. My clients often use the phrase "If I die," not "when." By taking the time to get real for a little while, you might rediscover core values, remember organizations and friends that you want to support, and find unexpected patterns and hidden meaning in the journey your life has taken so far. Don't take death so personally—lighten up. We are all in the same boat and getting real about this can be a relief. I once had a colleague ask me, after she overheard an estate planning meeting in my office, "What are you *doing* in there? Why are you all laughing?" I told her, "Oh, you know, talking about death."

You can read this book from beginning to end or skip to the specific chapters that are relevant to you. You can use it as a guidebook for do-it-yourself resources or to make sure that your meetings with an attorney are efficient and productive. However you choose to use it, I hope you will find it helpful and illuminating.

Check Out My Estate Planning Blog and Podcast!

Please read my blog, Life/Death/Law, www.lifedeathlaw.com, to keep up to date on new estate planning laws and issues in California and listen to my podcast, Life/Death/Law (https://soundcloud.com/lifedeathlaw) to hear stories about real people's estate planning experiences that I hope you'll find inspiring, illuminating, and interesting.

Get Useful Estate Planning Forms, Worksheets, Legal Updates, and More on This Book's Companion Page on Nolo.com

This book includes several useful forms, including

- a **Personal Inventory** you can use to gather all of your important financial information in one place
- a **Fiduciary Worksheet** to record your choices for trustee, executor, and agents for health care and power of attorney for finance
- a **Net Worth Calculation Worksheet** so you can see for yourself how much you have to give away
- a **Current Beneficiaries List** to list your beneficiaries for your retirement plans, life insurance policies, and other beneficiary-designated accounts
- a **Planning for Minor Children Worksheet** to help you select guardians
- a **Managing Money for Minor Children Worksheet** to help you decide how to manage money for minor children
- **Will and Trust Worksheets** that you can use to structure a will or a trust, and
- an **Interviewing Professional Trustees Worksheet** that you can use to find a professional trustee.

You can download all the forms in this book at:

www.nolo.com/back-of-book/ESCA.html

See the appendix, "How to Use the Downloadable Forms on the Nolo Website," for a list of all forms available on what we call this book's companion page on Nolo.com.

You'll find other useful information on this companion page, too, including legal updates on estate planning, such as changes to California's probate code or the federal estate and gift tax laws.

What's in an Estate Plan and Why Do You Need One?

Getting Started 11

The Key Estate Planning Documents 12

Will or Trust? 13

Understanding Probate 13

How Long Does Probate Take and What Does It Cost? 15

What Property and Assets Must Go Through Probate 16

Why Avoid Probate? 20

How to Avoid Probate 21

The Workhorses: Wills and Trusts 22

Wills 22

Who Should Do a Will 23

Living Trusts 24

Who Should Do a Living Trust 25

Preparing a Personal Inventory and a List of Beneficiaries 27

Why Do an Inventory? 27

How to Complete an Inventory 33

Special Estate Planning Issues When You Own Real Estate 34

How to Order a Copy of Your Deed 35

Forms of Property Ownership 35

Transfer-on-Death Deeds: How to Keep Your House
Out of Probate 37

Other Real Estate Issues Related to Estate Planning 39

Read this chapter if:

- You have been procrastinating for years and need to get started on your estate plan.

- You want to learn about probate and how to avoid it.

- You don't know whether you should use a will or a living trust to create your estate plan.

- You want to create a personal inventory of your assets and a list of your beneficiaries for retirement plans, life insurance, and any other beneficiary designated accounts that you own.

If you've picked up this book, I'm assuming that you want to get your estate plan started, or update an existing one. If you don't know quite where to start, just start here. Your will (or trust) is like the center of a wheel. The specific issues that you'll have to consider as you make your will or trust are like the spokes coming out from that center. This chapter is meant to give you an overview of the territory before you get into the details of navigating your way from start to finish. You might not read this book in order. That's fine. When you need to, take the time to explore a particular topic in depth, and then come back to Chapter 2 (if you decide to create a will) or Chapter 3 (if you decide to create a trust) and fill in another blank on the worksheets that accompany each chapter. After you've worked your way through the entire book, you can use the Fiduciary Worksheet (included in Chapter 11) to capture your choices for all of the jobs you'll need people to fill in your plan: trustees, executors, and agents for health care and power of attorney for finance. And, even if you don't actually want to make your own will or trust, working through those worksheets (and reading this book) will help you be prepared to work with an attorney more efficiently and effectively.

Getting Started

Estate planning boils down, really, to three things: who gets what, who does what, and how you are going to get those things to those people:

- First, you have to identify your assets.
- Second, you have to decide who you want to give these assets to.
- Third, you have to decide how you want to accomplish the transfer of your assets to your beneficiaries after you die.

This chapter will help you get started with all three of these tasks. But not in this order.

I know it's important to figure out what you own and how you own it. But, let's face it, that's also a chore, and I want you to be motivated, not dispirited. To put it another way, I want you to imagine your destination before you pack your suitcase. I think it makes the most sense to get started with your estate plan this way: First, I'll give you an overview of how probate works in California so that you can decide the "how" question—whether it makes the most sense for you to build your plan around a will or a trust. After that, you can work on the "what" part by preparing an inventory of what you've got and creating a list of your key beneficiaries.

For most people, an estate plan consists of three or four main documents: a living trust, a will, a durable power of attorney for finance, and an advance health care directive. Your plan also includes the transfer of your retirement assets and life insurance, which pass to the beneficiaries named on your beneficiary forms for each such account or policy. This book explains why each of these four documents is important, what you'll need to think about to create each one, and how to name the right people as beneficiaries for your retirement plans and life insurance policies.

But before we get started, let's consider the word "plan." It's important because the alternative to making a plan, is, of course, not having one at all. People who die with no plan in place will have their property distributed according to California intestacy law; will have to go through a probate proceeding if their estate is big enough;

and, if they have minor children, will have those children placed with adult guardians after a court investigation and hearing. It might work out just the way you hoped it would—but, really, what are the odds?

California's intestacy laws leave property belonging to people who die without a will or trust to surviving spouses, children, parents, and siblings—and more distant relatives after that. (See Chapter 2, "What Happens If You Don't Make a Will," for more on the subject.) But if you aren't married or don't want your assets distributed to your family, the only way to make your wishes known and legally binding is to make a will or a trust. If you want to nominate guardians for your minor children, you have to do that in writing, too. There's just no other way to make it clear to a judge that your partner is the best choice and that your former mother-in-law is not. Given the alternative, it's hard to justify *not* putting at least a simple plan in place, isn't it?

The Key Estate Planning Documents

Wills are the simplest estate planning tools. They are extremely flexible and provide for appointment of executors, guardians, tax savings trusts, and trusts for children. If your estate plan uses a will as its central document, your estate will usually have to go through probate before it can be distributed to your heirs. (Read more about wills in Chapter 2, choosing guardians for minors in Chapter 4, and leaving money to minors in Chapter 5.)

Living Trusts are legal entities that hold property during a person's life and provide for a distribution plan after death. All assets in the living trust avoid probate. Living trusts are coordinated with pour-over wills to appoint guardians (if necessary) and tie up loose ends. (Read more about living trusts in Chapter 3, and about using trusts to plan for blended families in Chapter 7.)

Durable Powers of Attorney for Finance allow someone to make decisions and to manage your financial affairs for assets outside of a living trust if you become incompetent or incapacitated. (Read about durable powers of attorney in Chapter 11.)

Advance Health Care Directives allow you to name an agent to make health care decisions for you and state your wishes for end-of-life care. (Read about advance health care directives in Chapter 11.)

Retirement Plans and Life Insurance Policies are distributed to named beneficiaries and pass outside of your will or trust. (Read about naming beneficiaries for retirement plans and life insurance in Chapter 10.)

Will or Trust?

If you're going to make a plan, your first decision is going to be what kind of plan you need to make—one that uses a will as the central organizing document, or one that uses a living trust to manage your property and distribute it at your death. Think of this choice as a fork in a road. Either kind of estate plan will get you where you want to go. Doing either one is far superior to doing nothing at all.

Both wills and trusts are perfectly effective, legal ways to manage and distribute what you own at death. But they differ in how long it will take to settle your estate and how smooth the road will be between where you are now and that ultimate destination. They also differ in their initial cost to set up and in the time and energy they take to maintain during your lifetime. The biggest difference of all is whether or not you want to plan to avoid probate in California—for most people that's the determining factor in choosing a will or a trust.

Understanding Probate

Probate isn't inherently evil. Actually, it was created with the best of intentions—to make sure that, after a person dies, their assets get distributed according to their will and that all of the estate's creditors are paid.

A probate proceeding is a judicial process where a judge supervises the settling of an estate. After a will is submitted to the court, and determined to be valid, an executor is appointed—that's how probate begins. The probate ends when the court issues an order detailing how the estate's assets are to be distributed. No one gets anything until that order is issued.

If you die in California with an estate worth more than $150,000 (counting only those assets that must go through probate, which I'll explain in a moment), your estate must go through probate, which takes place in the probate division of the superior court located in the county where you died.

Simple California Court Procedure for Small Estates

If the value of your probate assets is below $150,000, those assets can transferred outside of probate by using a simple affidavit procedure. For a clear explanation of this procedure and the forms you'll need, go to the Self-Help section of the California Courts Judicial Branch website at www.courts.ca.gov/10440.htm. You can also find your local superior court on the California Courts Judicial Branch website (see www.courts. ca.gov/find-my-court.htm).

During the probate proceeding, the executor must notify all known creditors and publish a notice in a local newspaper to give any other (unknown) creditors the chance to come forward and make a claim against the estate. Before the estate can be closed, the executor must also prepare and submit an inventory listing the value of all of the estate's assets. Once that's been done and the executor has paid all outstanding debts and taxes, the probate can be closed and the executor can transfer what's left to the beneficiaries named in the will or who would inherit under California intestacy law.

 RESOURCE

Want to learn more about California probate procedures, paperwork, and forms? You'll find extensive information on the probate court section of your local (county) superior court website. To find yours, see the California Courts Judicial Branch website at www.courts.ca.gov/find-my-court.htm. Also, check out *How to Probate an Estate in California*, by Julia Nissley (Nolo). This 400-page book will definitely help you understand why people prefer avoiding probate.

How Long Does Probate Take and What Does It Cost?

Probate has to last at least four months (to give creditors time to make claims), but, in my experience, it usually takes nine months to a year for an executor to complete the process and receive a court order to distribute the assets in California. If you own property in more than one state, your estate will have to conduct probate proceedings in each of those states as well. Some states have streamlined and simplified the probate process, but California isn't one of them.

In California, the cost of probate is based on the value of the assets in your estate (see "Costs of Going Through Probate in California," below). My clients often think of this as a tax because the probate fee is determined by a percentage of the value of the estate, but it isn't a tax: The statutory fees go to the attorney representing the estate and to the executor appointed by the court.

Here's how it works: At the end of the probate process, the executor asks the court to issue an order that distributes the estate's assets to the beneficiaries. As part of the petition, the executor also requests fees for the attorney and for the executor, based on the size of the probate estate. These fees are the maximum fees allowed under state laws for the work of settling the estate, but it's okay to request less or to waive the fees. Most attorneys (as you'd expect) will request the full statutory fee but many executors waive the fee, if they're also inheriting assets in the estate. Still, to calculate how much probate would cost an estate, double the statutory probate fees (which assume that the attorney and the executor each take the allowable fee).

The value of assets in your estate is the fair market value (FMV) of those assets—what they'd be worth if you sold them at the date of death. For many California homeowners, this makes probate expensive. A few examples:

- If you leave your house to your children in a will, and your house could be sold for $500,000, but you owe $450,000 on the mortgage, the probate court will count the $500,000 figure as the home's value, not the $50,000 of equity that's actually yours. In this case, your estate would pay $13,000 in statutory fees. Here's the math on this example, where you start with $500,000: $4,000 (for the first $100,00) + $3,000 (second $100,000) + $6,000 (for the remaining $300,000) = $13,000 in probate fees.

- Probating an estate worth $200,000 would result in $7,000 in statutory fees; an estate worth $1 million would result in $23,000 in statutory fees.
- An estate worth $10 million would result in $113,000 in statutory fees.

Cost of Going Through Probate in California		
Estate*	Statutory Probate Fee	Cost of Probate
First $100,000	4%	$4,000
Next $100,000	3%	$3,000
Up to next $800,000	2%	$2,000
Up to next $9 million	1%	$1,000 per $100,000

* Your estate includes only assets that are subject to probate, such as cash; stocks, bonds, and brokerage accounts; personal property, such as jewelry; and property that is not in a trust, a payable-on-death (POD) account (such as a bank account), or a transfer-on-death deed (such as for your house).

What Property and Assets Must Go Through Probate

There's some good news here. Not all of your assets are subject to probate. Probate exists to prevent fraud after someone dies. The idea is that the court steps in to make sure that the decedent's wishes are respected and that their assets are identified and distributed to the proper people.

Assets that are held in a trust, or have a beneficiary designation, or that pass to a surviving joint tenant don't go through probate. And this makes sense, because in these cases we already know who gets the asset (the surviving joint tenant or the named beneficiary). Those assets are going to those people because there's *already* a binding legal contract that says it goes to them—we don't need a court order to make sure that happens.

Assets Outside of Probate

The first thing that I do at an initial estate planning appointment is to draw a line down the middle of a piece of paper. On one side, I write "Probate" and on the other side I write "Not Probate." Most of my clients don't make that distinction. But it is important for estate planning. Judges don't need to supervise the distribution of the Not Probate side of the diagram. And wills and trusts don't distribute them. For those assets you'll need to make sure you've designated the right beneficiaries. Your will or a trust is what you'll need to distribute the assets for on the Probate side.

Two Kinds of Assets	
Not Probate	Probate
Retirement assets	House
Life insurance/annuities	Investment accounts
Joint tenancy property	Bank accounts
Payable-on-death accounts	Tangible personal items
Transfer-on-death accounts	Partnerships, sole proprietorships
Transfer-on-death deeds	

The most common examples of assets that *won't* be subject to probate include:

- **Assets in a living trust.** The main reason you create a living trust is to avoid probate for your assets on the Probate side of the list. In fact, the reason that I draw that line down the middle of the paper is to help my clients understand why they need a trust for the assets on the Probate side—these are the assets that would cost them time and money to send through probate without a trust. (See Chapter 3 for details.)

- **IRAs, 401(k)s, and similar retirement accounts.** These accounts all have beneficiaries you've named on record with a plan administrator or investment manager. Those beneficiaries will receive any money left in those plans when you die; normally, retirement assets are not distributed to your will or trust. (For details, see Chapter 10.)

- **Life insurance policies.** The proceeds from a life insurance policy are often the major source of immediate cash for a surviving spouse or young children. (See Chapter 10 for details.)

- **Annuities.** Annuities are similar to life insurance policies (discussed in Chapter 10). You sign a contract with a company in which you agree to deposit a certain amount of money, and the company agrees to pay that money back to you over a certain period. Sometimes the policies pay a benefit to survivors, and sometimes not.

- **Payable-on-death bank or transfer-on-death brokerage accounts.** You can fill out a form with the company that holds the accounts to make them "payable on death" (POD) accounts, or "transfer on death" (TOD) accounts, which means that they will pass to the person you designated, just like the retirement accounts with designated beneficiaries. (See Chapter 10.)

- **Real estate with a transfer-on-death deed.** As of 2016, Californians can leave real property to designated beneficiaries by using a transfer-on-death deed, as opposed to establishing a living trust. (See "Transfer-on-Death Deeds: How to Keep Your House Out of Probate," below, for more information on these deeds.)

- **Property that passes automatically to a surviving owner.** Any property you own with someone else and for which someone has a right of survivorship (which would typically be the case of a house you co-own with your spouse) won't be subject to probate. The right of survivorship means that when one co-owner dies, the survivor owns the property automatically, without probate. So property you own with your spouse (or someone else) as joint tenants or community property with right of survivorship, won't go through probate when the first owner dies. (In Chapter 7, I will discuss both of these forms of property ownership and how to tell if you hold property in one of these ways.)

Assets That Go Through Probate

When you take away any assets that will pass without probate (because you've designated a beneficiary or they will pass to a co-owner automatically), whatever's left must go through probate. For most people, that means assets such as:

- cash in the bank
- investments, such as stocks or mutual funds
- household property, including furniture, furnishings, jewelry, art, your car, your clothes, and anything else that you own, and
- real estate that is not held in either joint tenancy or community property with right of survivorship or that is not subject to a transfer-on-death deed.

EXAMPLE: Violet owns a house in Sacramento and two checking accounts with her husband, Jesse, as a joint tenant. She also inherited a cabin in the mountains near Truckee from her mother, which she owns as her separate property. Violet wrote a will, leaving the cabin to her niece Stella. At Violet's death, the cabin must go through probate so it can be transferred to Stella. The home and bank accounts, however, pass to Jesse automatically because he's the surviving joint tenant.

TIP

Probate has nothing to do with estate tax. When you die, everything you own, whether it goes through probate or not, is tallied up for federal estate tax purposes. But only the very wealthy are subject to the estate tax. Currently (in 2017), you can leave up to $5.49 million of property, plus an unlimited amount to your spouse (as long as your spouse is a U.S. citizen), without tax. (See Chapter 9 for details on the estate tax.)

Why Avoid Probate?

Most people will want to avoid probate for these reasons:

- Your heirs gain nothing by probate. The court process and fees take thousands of dollars out of the estate—money that otherwise would go to your loved ones.
- Most families don't need a court to supervise the distribution of assets, assuming no one is fighting about the estate and there are no messy creditor problems to resolve. Waiting months or a year to distribute the assets to your children, for example, is just a waste of time.
- Probate is a public process, so everything you file with the court (including your will) is a public document, open to all who care to inspect them. So if you want to keep the terms of your estate private, you'd want to create a living trust, which does not need to be filed with the court. (Your heirs and beneficiaries will still be entitled to a copy of the trust when you die, but it won't be a public record at your local superior court.)

When Does Probate Make Sense?

Probate court can be a useful place to sort out complicated creditor issues or other weird family dynamics. If your estate is complex and you think having a public forum would help resolve problems, probate might be the right choice for you.

How to Avoid Probate

If your probate estate is under $150,000, your estate already avoids probate and can be distributed to your heirs without a probate proceeding or a court order. You simply need to do the simple affidavit procedure (See "Simple California Court Procedure for Small Estates," above.)

If your probate estate exceeds $150,000, then you have some planning to do. Many people create living trusts to avoid probate, which provides the most flexibility and works best if you want to benefit multiple beneficiaries or distribute complicated property. But trusts are not the only way to avoid probate. People with simple estates, who just want to benefit one or two people, can make use of beneficiary account designations, joint tenancy, community property with right of survivorship, and transfer-on-death deeds to avoid probate and pass their assets to their loved ones simply.

Each of these methods lets you move an asset from the Probate column of my Two Kinds of Assets diagram to the Not Probate side. For example:

- You can fill out a form at a bank or an investment company to designate a specific account as a payable-on-death account. At your death, the assets in that account will go directly to the named beneficiaries.
- You can record a deed with the county assessor and add a person as a joint tenant, name a transfer-on-death beneficiary, or change a community property deed to a community property with right of survivorship deed. When you die, the surviving joint tenant/owner/beneficiary will own the property and no probate will be necessary. (But there may be tax implications, so please don't do any of these things without consulting an accountant or attorney.)

I love these techniques, and they have their place in many people's plans, but they usually aren't a substitute for an estate plan—beneficiary designations can't, for example, help your loved ones care for you if you are incapacitated, help manage property for minor beneficiaries, forgive debts or loans you've made during life, or transfer assets to another beneficiary if the first one dies before you do.

RESOURCE

If you want to learn more about ways to avoid probate, read
8 Ways to Avoid Probate, by Mary Randolph (Nolo). This book offers practical
tips and techniques that you can use to convert bank and investment
accounts into payable-on-death or transfer-on-death accounts, to own
property as joint tenants or use a transfer-on-death deed, and use the
small estates affidavit process to avoid probate.

The Workhorses: Wills and Trusts

For your estate plan to address all of the issues it needs to—
transferring property, planning to manage property for children,
addressing incapacity, and planning to minimize taxes—you need
more than just a beneficiary designation or a survivorship deed.
Wills and trusts are the documents that you need to make your plan
comprehensive. They can be simple or complicated, that's up to you.
But no estate plan is really a plan for what happens after you die
without one of these documents.

Wills

A will's most important functions are to leave property to beneficiaries
and to nominate guardians for minor children. Each person creates
their own will, though married couples usually create wills that are
coordinated and, if they have minor children, nominate the same
guardians for those children.

At a minimum, to create a will you will need to decide who to
nominate as your executor (the person who will be in charge of
settling your estate) and how to distribute your property. If you have
minor children, you will also need to nominate guardians to care
for those children to age 18 and establish a trust to manage their
property until they are old enough to manage that property for
themselves.

A will can accomplish all the critical estate planning tasks and is easy and inexpensive to create. If you decide a will makes the most sense, see Chapter 2.

But now you also know that Californians have to take probate into account before deciding on using a will as their main estate planning document. Sadly, in California, probate is a slow, not consumer-friendly, and expensive process. Many states have streamlined their probate procedures and reduced probate costs. In those states, avoiding probate is not important. But we don't live there. In California, avoiding probate can save your loved ones both time and money after you die, which is where a living trust comes in.

Who Should Do a Will

Given that probate is slow and expensive in California, and that the high cost of real estate means most of us would be subject to it at death, why do some people still use wills instead of living trusts? There are five main reasons why a will can be the right choice:

- You don't own a house.
- You have minor children and your main, immediate goal is to nominate guardians.
- You can't afford to create a living trust or just don't want to.
- You don't care about probate costs.
- You have complicated creditor problems and would appreciate a court's sorting these out.

A will is easy and inexpensive to create. In Chapter 2, I will walk you through the basics of doing just that. For young families just starting out, a will is an excellent choice for a first estate plan because it accomplishes their main goal: making sure that they have nominated guardians for minor children. Later, when a couple buys a house or acquires more assets, they can always revisit their plan and create a living trust.

For people with a small estate, or who simply don't care that probate will cost their heirs some money and time, a will is a perfectly effective estate plan.

And, of course, there's just financial reality. It is expensive to live in California, and we can't always afford to do things perfectly. A living trust is usually more expensive to create than a will. Not being able to afford a living trust isn't a good excuse for doing nothing at all. A will is a perfectly serviceable document to put in place now. When you can afford to do a trust, you can always upgrade.

Living Trusts

A living trust is a legal document that serves one main purpose: avoiding probate. By creating a living trust and transferring your largest assets (such as your house or small business) to it, your estate won't be subject to probate upon your death. Here's why: All of the assets owned by the trust aren't considered "yours" at your death—these assets are owned by your trust, and not by you.

If you fund your trust properly, you will die owning only a few small assets in your own name, such as an everyday checking account, your car, and your furniture and furnishings. To the California probate system, you will look like someone who has a small estate, owning less than $150,000 (the cutoff to be considered a "small estate" in California and outside of the probate process). Your executor won't need to get a court order to distribute your assets to your loved ones. Instead, your trustee will be able to settle your estate without court supervision or delay and for far less money than the statutory fees dictated by the state probate code.

If you decide a living trust is the right way to go, see Chapter 3. If you are in a blended family, see Chapter 7 to learn about ways that you can use trusts to take care of your current spouse or partner and children from previous marriages. Keep in mind that even if you decide to do a living trust, you'll still need to create a simple will that works with it, but that will is different from a will that stands alone.

Who Should Do a Living Trust

Living trusts have several benefits:

- Unlike a will, a trust does not need to be filed with the court and is not a public document.
- Establishing a trust and transferring your biggest assets to it also makes it easier for people to manage these assets for your benefit if you become incapacitated later on—your successor trustee (the person you name to manage your trust after you die) can step in to manage these assets for your benefit at that point.
- Finally, a trust can be highly customized to your needs: managing property for children with special needs; creating complex multigenerational trusts that are designed to minimize estate taxes; or setting up trusts to skillfully manage the competing demands of blended families.

While a will can be drafted to create complex trusts after your death, if you want to do that kind of sophisticated planning a trust is the vehicle to do it; if your estate is big enough for that kind of planning, probate would be expensive.

If you own a house in California, or expect to soon, or own assets worth more than $150,000 that do not have a beneficiary designation, and can otherwise afford it, a living trust is a good investment. In each case, avoiding probate will save your loved ones time and money in the end. If you anticipate being wealthy, with an estate worth $5 million or more, a trust with tax planning is a good idea. If you are in a second marriage, own complicated assets (like a privately held company), or have children with special needs, a trust also makes sense.

Living Trusts vs. Wills		
	Living Trust	**Will**
Privacy	Your trust is not a public record, and your trustee transfers assets without court supervision.	Your will is filed in the probate court and is a public record, and a judge supervises the settling of your estate.
Cost to set up	A bit more work than making a will; if you work with an attorney, costs more than making a will.	Simpler to set up; easily done without an attorney.
Hassle to set up	You have to actually transfer certain property to the trust. This requires filing deeds and filling out forms. It isn't extremely difficult, but it is work.	No extra forms need to be filled out, and no property must be transferred.
What you can do with it	Leave property. Name someone to manage trust assets if someday you can't.	Leave property. Name a guardian for your children.
Process after a death	Most trusts can be settled quickly, getting assets to the beneficiaries sooner than if there were a will.	Probate is usually necessary; costs more and takes longer than wrapping up a trust.

Preparing a Personal Inventory and a List of Beneficiaries

Once you've got the basic strategy in mind for your plan, the next step is to understand what you own. The best way to do this is prepare an inventory of your assets and property. Making an inventory will prompt you to gather all the information you'll need to make your estate plan. You might even be surprised at what you find. For many of my clients, this is the first time that they've actually sat down and made a list of all of their myriad accounts. Alternatively, if you are one of those people who already has this information in a nice, neat spreadsheet, you're already done!

Why Do an Inventory?

Knowing what your assets are will help make sure your estate plan properly deals with them. It might help you decide the will versus trust question, too. For example, if you don't own any real estate, you might decide to designate your investment account and bank account as payable-on-death accounts (which avoids probate) and stick with a simple will. Or you might see that since you own a home, a vacation cabin, and an investment account, a trust is a good investment. Once you've completed the Personal Inventory, you can fill in the Net Worth Calculation Worksheet to see your assets all in one place.

A sample Personal Inventory and a Net Worth Calculation Worksheet you can use as templates in preparing your own are shown below.

 FORM

Personal Inventory and Net Worth Calculation Worksheet.
The Nolo website includes downloadable copies of the Personal Inventory (for you to use to create your own inventory), and a Net Worth Calculation Worksheet (to create a list of your key assets in one place). See the appendix for the link to these and other forms in this book.

Personal Inventory

Use this form to prepare an inventory of your assets and property.

What Is It?	Where Is It?	Who Owns It?	How Much Is It Worth?	Electronic Access?
Cash				
Checking Accounts				
Checking Account #1234-6789	Bank of America; Duane Street	John and Mary	$12,000	PIN # = 4321 PW = Family ID = 1234-789
Savings Accounts				
Savings Account #1234-6789-123	First State Bank	John	$1,000	No
Certificates of Deposit (CDs)				
Certificate of Deposit #123-567-890002 3-year term; matures 2009	Citibank	Mary	$25,000	No
Safe Deposit Boxes				
Box 1162	Bank of America Duane St.	John and Mary		
College Savings Plans and Custodial Accounts				
Custodial Accounts				
Charles Schwab, CUTMA Account, No. 34-999 For benefit of Jane	Account statements in financial binder, left bookcase	John is custodian	$10,000	Yes: PIN #: 567-888JKL
529 Investment Plans				
Scholars Choice College Savings Plan Billy's: Account No. 12-56, Jane's: Account No. 13-56	Colorado plan; statements in file cabinet of desk	Mary is custodian; John is backup custodian for both	Billy's: $8,500 Jane's: $3,500	Yes: User ID = DoeFamily Password = elvisrocks
Education Savings Accounts				
Edward Jones, Coverdell Education Savings Account, No. 23-888 For benefit of Billy	Account statements in financial binder, left bookcase	Mary is owner	$4,000	No

			How Much	Electronic
Personal Inventory (continued)				
What Is It?	**Where Is It?**	**Who Owns It?**	**Is It Worth?**	**Access?**
		Real Estate		
House				
House	1234 Redbud Lane, Center City, CA	John and Mary, husband and wife, as joint tenants	$675,000 mkt. value; $600,000 equity	No
Condo	1126 Union Court, #23 City, CA	John, Mary, and Jane, as tenants in common	$355,000 mkt. value; $255,000 equity	mortgage account can be accessed: PW = mollycat ID = 1234-90
		Other Investments		
Brokerage Accounts				
Charles Schwab One Account, No. 23-456	Schwab	John	$23,000	User ID = HWong PW = sailboat
Mutual Funds				
Franklin-Templeton Investments, Tax-Free Bond Fund, Acct. No. 123-999	Franklin-Templeton	John and Mary, JTWROS	$10,000	None
Partnerships				
Stock Options				
		Retirement Investments		
Roth IRA, Number 123-456	Vanguard	Mary	$45,000	PIN = 23-45
401(k)	TIAA-CREF	John	$62,000	PW = parkingspace2
		Automobiles		
2015 minivan	home	Mary & John	$10,000	No
2014 Camry	home	John	$4,500	No

			How Much	Electronic
What Is It?	**Where Is It?**	**Who Owns It?**	**Is It Worth?**	**Access?**

Personal Inventory (continued)

Personal Property				
Jewelry				
wedding ring	home	mary	$3,000	No
Furniture				
miscellaneous	home	mary & John	$8,000	No
Other Collectibles				
Art				
Life Insurance, Pensions, and Annuities				
West-Coast Insurance Co., 20-year term life policy (expires 2020)	File cabinet of desk	mary, Policy Number 123-4567; beneficiaries: John, primary; children, secondary	$500,000	No
West-Coast Insurance Co., 20-year term life policy (expires 2020)	File cabinet of desk	John, Policy No. 123-4559; beneficiaries: mary, primary; children, secondary	$500,000	No
Planters Beneficial Life, Universal Life Insurance	Safe deposit box at Bank of the North	mary, Policy ABX-009-YHHT; beneficiaries: John, primary; children, secondary	$500,000	No
Large Company, Group Life Policy	Check with H.R. department at work	John, Group Certificate No. 234-56	$900,000	No
State Employee Pension Plan	Information is available at the state website	mary, No survivor benefits; Employee ID No. 345-56-7889	Depends on when mary retires	Yes: User ID = mDoe Password = sail
Planters Beneficial Life	Policy is in safe deposit box at Bank of the North	John, Beneficiary: mary Doe Fixed Annuity Contract, No. 2307777	$25,000	No

Net Worth Calculation Worksheet

List your assets and liabilities on this worksheet.

Assets	Value	Liabilities	Net Value
Your house	$675,000	$75,000 mortgage	$600,000
Condo	$355,000	$100,000 mortgage	$255,000
Cash (savings, checking, CDs)	$38,000	$5,000 credit card debt	$33,000
Nonretirement investments (brokerage accounts, mutual funds, etc.)	$33,000		$33,000
Retirement accounts	$107,000		$107,000
Life insurance policies (what they would pay out if you died)	$2.425 million		$2,425,000
Personal property (cars, jewelry, etc.)	$25,500		$25,500
Annuities	none		none
Business assets (what you think they could be sold for)	none		none
		Total Net Worth	$3,478,500

Without some organizing up front, it can take your spouse, partner, or loved ones months, or even years to figure out where your safe deposit box is or where your bank accounts and life insurance policies are. An inventory will make it a lot easier to settle your affairs and transfer assets to the right people. Worse, you wouldn't want your loved ones to miss inheriting assets just because no one knew they existed.

If you don't own many assets (for example, if you rent an apartment, have a small checking account, and a 401(k)), doing an inventory should be fairly simple.

But if finding and organizing all of this information sounds daunting, remember that you can do it in small pieces. Keep in mind that much of this information isn't likely to change often. After the initial inventory, you'll just need to update when you open a new account, close an old one, or buy a new home. Or you can just take an annual look at the list to see what, if anything, has changed. I recommend that my clients do this in January, when they get 1099 forms in the mail for their tax returns.

As you start identifying and valuing your assets, don't be overly concerned with exact financial figures. The inventory isn't meant to substitute for a financial plan. The reason you want to try to place a value on your assets is so that you can determine, in a general way, how much would be left behind for your family and loved ones should you die unexpectedly.

How Assets Pass to Their New Owners

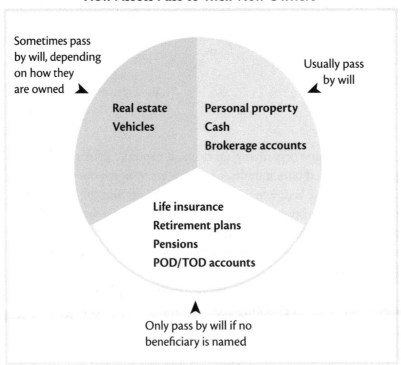

Sometimes pass by will, depending on how they are owned ▲

Real estate
Vehicles

Usually pass by will ◢

Personal property
Cash
Brokerage accounts

Life insurance
Retirement plans
Pensions
POD/TOD accounts

▲
Only pass by will if no beneficiary is named

You also need to know what kinds of things you own so that you can be sure your estate plan properly deals with them all. You need to make a complete inventory and make sure that you deal with everything on the list. That's what the rest of this book is for—but to get the best use of it, you need to do some homework first. I've also included a Current Beneficiaries List in this book (see sample in Chapter 10) that you can use to list the current beneficiaries of your retirement, life insurance, and other beneficiary-designated plans.

How to Complete an Inventory

Your inventory is really just a list of:

- **What you own.** This includes your house and other real estate; all financial accounts (checking, savings, etc.); custodial accounts for children (discussed in Chapter 5); retirement plans and life insurance policies (discussed in Chapter 10); automobiles and vehicles; jewelry and other personal property; life insurance, pensions and annuities.

- **Where each asset is.** This will help your executor find them after you die—it's a list of where your accounts are held, or where your assets are stored.

- **How you own the asset** (for example, whose name(s) are on the accounts).

- **How much the asset is worth.** Don't be overly concerned with exact financial figures. You basically want to place a value on your assets so you can determine, in a general way, how much you would be leaving behind should you die unexpectedly (especially important if you have children).

- **How to access an asset electronically.** Many of us store lots of important information and assets online. Make sure that your loved ones know where you've stored these assets and how to access them.

Your Safe Deposit Box

If you have a safe deposit box, be sure to write down (on your Personal Inventory) where it is and (very important!) where the key is. If you are going to store your important estate planning documents in the box, know that in California it can take several weeks after someone dies for the executor or trustee to gain access to the box. (Chapter 12 discusses storing your estate plan in more accessible ways.)

RESOURCE

Want to be even more organized? For a terrific book on how to organize all of your personal and family's records, see *Get It Together: Organize Your Records So Your Family Won't Have to*, by Melanie Cullen with Shae Irving (Nolo).

Special Estate Planning Issues When You Own Real Estate

If you own a home, you need to understand how you own it—legally, the way you hold title to it. This is important because if you own your home with others or create a deed that transfers ownership to another person at your death, the form of title affects who would own it upon your death.

If you don't know how you own your house, you are not alone. Most people don't remember what they put on the forms when they were signing that six-inch stack of papers to get their home loan. To find out, look for the grant deed that transferred legal ownership of your house from the former owner to you.

If you can't find your grant deed, don't panic—just read the tips below. If you have something called a deed of trust in that file folder that you have from when you bought the house, that's not what you're looking for. That's what gives your lender the legal right to repossess your property if you don't pay off the loan, but it isn't the piece of paper that states that you own the house in the first place.

How to Order a Copy of Your Deed

If you have a copy of your deed or know how it's owned (form of title), you can skip this section. Otherwise, read on.

Call your county's recorder's office or visit their website (it's easy to find by doing an online search) to find out how to order a copy of your deed. Most counties allow you to order a copy in person, by mail, or by telephone. You'll need to provide the following information: your name, the name of the party that sold you the home, and your parcel or tax identification number, which is on your property tax bill. You may need to search the county recorder's online index to find out some of this information.

Forms of Property Ownership

Once you've found your deed, take a look and see what it says about how you own the property. Here are examples of what you might find:

- John, as his sole and separate property (SP)
- John and Mary as joint tenants (JTWROS)
- John and Mary, husband and wife, as community property (CP)
- John and Mary, husband and wife, as community property with right of survivorship (CPWROS), or
- John, Mary, and Jane, as tenants in common (TIC).

Each way of owning property describes how the people on the deed share ownership and affects what happens when one of them dies.

Separate Property

Owning property as separate property usually means that the property is yours to give away at death to whomever you want. I say "usually," though, because in California, which is a community property state, a spouse may own a share of such property, even though only the other spouse's name is on the deed itself, if wages earned during the marriage were used to pay off the mortgage or make improvements on the property. (See Chapter 7 for a more in-depth discussion on how spouses can own property and leave it to each other.)

Joint Tenancy

The most common way for couples to own property is as joint tenants. This means that they each own an equal share in the property and that when one owner dies, the survivor owns the entire property by what lawyers call "right of survivorship." The surviving joint tenant gets the property automatically; property owned in this way can't be left to others by a will or a trust. The reason that this form of property ownership is so common is that it allows the surviving joint tenants to avoid the probate process altogether. Joint tenancy is usually spelled out on a deed, but sometimes it is abbreviated as "JT."

Community Property

Married couples (and registered domestic partners as well) can own property as community property. That means that they each own a half interest in the property. Unlike joint tenants, owners can pass their halves by a will or trust upon their death. Community property is usually spelled out on a deed, but sometimes it is abbreviated as "CP."

Community Property with Right of Survivorship

California also allows married couples (and registered domestic partners) to own property as community property with right of survivorship. When couples own property this way, when one of them dies, the survivor automatically owns the entire property by right of survivorship, without a probate proceeding. Community property with right of survivorship is usually spelled out on a deed, but sometimes it is abbreviated as "CPWROS."

Tenancy in Common

You might also see a deed in which multiple owners are listed as tenants in common, especially in cities where apartments are being sold to multiple owners in the hope of eventually converting each unit into a separate condominium. Tenants in common can divide their interests in unequal ways (one person can own 80% and another 20%, for example), and each owner can pass his or her interest by a will or trust at death. Tenancy in common is usually spelled out on a deed, but sometimes it is abbreviated as "TIC."

To see how you can organize property information in your Personal Inventory, take a look at the real estate section of the sample form included in this chapter.

Transfer-on-Death Deeds: How to Keep Your House Out of Probate

Transfer-on-death deeds are an inexpensive way to transfer real property without having to go through the time and expense of probate or establishing a revocable living trust.

As of January, 2016, and lasting until January, 2021 (unless extended by the Legislature), revocable transfer-on-death deeds are now legal in California. (Revocable means you can change the deed any time before you die—for example, by naming a new beneficiary or selling your property.) Just as you can designate a bank account or brokerage account as a payable-on-death (POD) account, a revocable transfer-on-death deed lets you name beneficiaries for real property, such as your house. Upon your death, your beneficiaries become the property owners by filing specific legal forms, including an affidavit, a death certificate, and a notice of change of ownership. That's it. No probate and no trust administration necessary.

The revocable transfer-on-death deed must be substantially similar to the statutory form in Section 5642 of the California Probate Code, which includes the name of the grantor, the full names of the beneficiaries and their relationship to the grantor, the property description, and a statement saying that the grantor hereby transfers all of their ownership in the described property to the named beneficiaries upon death.

Transfer-on-death deeds must be notarized and recorded within 60 days of signing to be effective and can be revoked at any time during the grantor's life. If a beneficiary dies before the grantor does, their gift lapses and goes to the surviving beneficiaries, if any. If no beneficiary survives, the transfer doesn't happen.

Transfer-on-death deeds can only be used for residential properties of up to four units (such as a single-family house), a condo, or a single tract of agricultural land that is 40 acres or less that is improved with a single-family residence.

To use a transfer-on-death deed, an owner of real property must have legal capacity to sign a contract (this is a higher standard than that required to sign a will), and must (obviously) be the owner of the property being transferred. Any such property transferred will still be subject to any liens or encumbrances that are attached to the real property, but it will not be subject to an estate recovery claim for Medi-Cal reimbursement because a transfer-on-death deed passes outside of probate. (If you are transferring your house to a family member, see Chapter 8, to learn about how to do that while maintaining your low property tax rate.)

RESOURCE

To learn more about what property is exempt from Medi-Cal Recovery Laws, download "The New Medi-Cal Recovery Laws" booklet from the California Advocates for Nursing Home Reform (CANHR, at www.canhr.org/publications/PDFs/Medi-Cal_Recovery.pdf).

While convenient and inexpensive, transfer-on-death deeds are not going to solve other estate planning issues. A transfer-on-death deed isn't the best way to transfer real property, and won't be a substitute for a living trust or will and durable powers of attorney if you want to do the following:

- leave your house in a trust, for example, for the lifetime benefit of one person (like your partner) but for the ultimate benefit of someone else (like your daughter)
- plan to reduce estate taxes, or
- make sure that a trusted person can maintain or sell the property if you become incapacitated.

That being said, transfer-on-death deeds are a great tool for people to do simple estate planning and a good alternative to probate.

RESOURCE

Where to find California transfer-on-death deeds. For sample language and details on the state's transfer-on-death deed form, see the California State Board of Equalization website at www.boe.ca.gov/lawguides/property/current/ptlg/other/5642.html. Also, California transfer-on-death deeds are available for sale from Nolo (search the store at www.nolo.com for this form).

Other Real Estate Issues Related to Estate Planning

Of course there are many more real estate issues you may want to research. A common one is how to transfer property ownership to your children or other family members in order to quality for Medi-Cal nursing home coverage. This topic is beyond the scope of this book. See an experienced estate planner or elder law attorney for advice on the subject.

RESOURCE

More about property. For more information on property ownership (and just about every other estate planning topic), see *Plan Your Estate*, by Denis Clifford (Nolo). And for more information on domestic partners' property rights, see *A Legal Guide for Lesbian & Gay Couples*, by Denis Clifford, Frederick Hertz, and Emily Doskow (Nolo).

Wills

Making It Legal 44

A Will Is Just One Part of Your Estate Plan 45

Right of Survivorship: Property You Own With Others 47

Choosing an Executor 49

    What to Look for in an Executor 50

    Who to Choose as Executor 51

    Naming an Alternate Executor 54

    Talking to Your Choice for Executors 54

Choosing Guardians and Managing Money For Children 55

Planning for Pets 55

    Leaving Money to a Pet-Loving Friend 56

    Creating a Pet Trust 56

    Leaving Money to a Pet Rescue Organization 57

Preparing a Will Worksheet 58

Making a Will: A DIY Project or Not? 60

    Preparing a Simple Will 60

    When to Get Help Preparing a Will 61

Once You've Done Your Will 62

What Happens If You Don't Make a Will? 63

    Who Gets Your Assets 63

    Who Will Be the Guardian for Your Children (If Any) 64

Read this chapter if:

- You think you should use a will, not a trust, to structure your estate plan.

- You want to learn more about wills.

- You want to choose an executor.

- You want to fill out a Will Worksheet to organize and collect the information you'll need to prepare a will.

I f, after reading Chapter 1, you've decided that a will makes the most sense for you, this chapter will guide you through the basic decisions you'll need to make a simple one:

- **What do you own and how do you want to give it away?** The first step in creating any estate plan is determining what you've got to give away. The Personal Inventory included in this book (and discussed in Chapter 1) will help you sort that out. Your next step is to use that information to fill out the Will Worksheet included here and put a plan in place to distribute those assets. You'll need to think about all of your assets, not just the ones that your will controls after you die.

- **Who do you want to settle your estate?** Choosing someone to serve as your executor, also called your personal representative, to settle your estate is key. This is the person who will put your plan into action.

- **Who do you want to take care of your kids?** If you have minor children, choosing guardians for those kids is often the hardest part of making your will. Chapter 4 of this book covers naming guardians for minor children and offers a few ways of getting past being stuck if you can't figure out who to name. You'll want to read Chapter 4 before filling out the Will Worksheet in this chapter.

- **How do you want to leave money to children?** If you want to leave money to children, yours or those of others, you'll need to think about how to make sure that the money is managed for those children until they're old enough to manage it for themselves. Chapter 5 of this book discusses how to manage money for children by using custodial accounts or trusts. You'll want to read Chapter 5 before filling out the Will Worksheet in this chapter.

You might need to skip ahead to read chapters about certain matters that either confuse you or that are relevant to your life, such as property tax (Chapter 8); owning international assets, making gifts to noncitizens, or naming noncitizens as trustees or guardians (Chapter 6); planning for blended families (Chapter 7); or understanding estate or income taxes (Chapter 9) before you can fill out the Will Worksheet in this chapter. That's just fine. Welcome to estate planning, where everything is connected and it can be hard to know where to start.

What a Simple Will Can Do

A simple will can accomplish a lot of your estate planning goals. For example it can:

- leave all property to someone—often your spouse or partner (or if you're single, to your children or to relatives, friends, or charities)
- say what to do if that person dies first or at the same time as you do
- nominate your executor and an alternate
- nominate a personal guardian and a property guardian (and an alternate) for children
- set up a trust or custodial accounts for children, in case they inherit money from you while still young, and/or
- leave money for the care of a pet and name a caretaker for that pet.

TIP

Consider a trust, too. If, after reading Chapter 1, you decide that it makes more sense to create a living trust, that's just fine. You can, if you want to, go ahead and fill out the Will Worksheet below, but then use it to help you fill in the Trust Worksheet that comes with Chapter 3. Almost all of the decisions you're making for the Will Worksheet apply to trusts as well: You still need to know what you own, and whom you want to distribute those assets to and choose a person to make your plan happen. The major difference is that this person is called the trustee, not the executor.

Making It Legal

There are just a few formal requirements for a will to be legal in California:

- You must be at least 18 years old and mentally competent.
- Your will should be typed or printed from a computer. A handwritten will (called a "holographic will") is legal in California, but it is much better to type a will so people can't add things to it later.
- You must sign and date your will in front of two witnesses who don't inherit anything under the document. The witnesses must also sign the will.
- It's not a legal requirement in California to make a will valid, but it makes it easier to submit the will to a probate court after you die, if you also have your witnesses sign what's called a "self-proving" affidavit—a statement made under penalty of perjury stating that the witnesses saw you sign the document of your own free will and that you appeared to know what you were doing and why.

A Will Is Just One Part of Your Estate Plan

You've decided to make a will. But is it all you need? The truth is that even though a will is the key legal document in your estate plan, it is only part of it. You probably own significant assets—perhaps the most valuable things you own—that aren't governed by your will at all. You need to take them into account, too. You'll also need to create a durable power of attorney and an advance health care directive so that your loved ones can take care of you if you are incapacitated. (See Chapter 11 for advice on preparing those documents.)

Houses, retirement accounts, proceeds from life insurance policies, and even some brokerage and bank accounts aren't usually subject to what your will says. If that surprises you, you're not alone. Many people have no idea that their wills don't control what happens to some of their most important assets.

In Chapter 1, I listed the assets that don't go through probate—remember the Two Kinds of Assets diagram with the Probate/Not Probate line down the middle? Assets that don't go through probate include assets with beneficiary designations, such as retirement assets, life insurance proceeds, and assets that you own with others with a right of survivorship, like joint tenancy and community property with right of survivorship, and assets held in living trusts. Guess what? These are the very same assets that are not subject to your will. And this makes sense: Probate governs *only* assets that pass by will or intestacy (California's laws about who inherits when there is no will).

When you open up a retirement account, purchase a life insurance policy, or own a house with a right of survivorship, you name a beneficiary or a joint owner. That creates a legally binding contract—the named beneficiary gets that account, or owns that property regardless of what your will says.

For your estate plan to work the way you want it to, you have to coordinate your will with assets that pass outside of that will. Here's how I explain it to my clients: Your nonprobate assets are one train track, carrying assets to the named beneficiaries or surviving owners, and your probate assets are on another train track, carrying assets to the named beneficiaries of your will or trust. If you don't coordinate the two tracks, you can have a train wreck on your hands.

EXAMPLE 1: In your will, you leave everything to your partner. But years ago, you named your sister as the beneficiary for your retirement plan and forgot to change it when you got involved in your current relationship. When you die, your sister, not your partner, will get the money from the insurance policy.

EXAMPLE 2: In your will, you leave everything in equal shares to your three children. But your life insurance policy, which you bought when you had your first child, only names him as the beneficiary. You never got around to updating the beneficiaries of the policy. When you die, your three children split the assets held in your bank accounts and investment accounts and the proceeds from the sale of your home, but only your first child gets the $1 million life insurance proceeds.

EXAMPLE 3: In your will, you leave your estate to your favorite charity. You own your home as a joint tenant with your brother. When you die, your brother gets the house. The charity inherits your checking account, your savings account, and the furniture and furnishings inside of the house.

In Chapter 10, I'll go into detail on how to integrate your retirement accounts, life insurance policies, and other beneficiary-designated accounts into your estate plan. One of the things you'll do then is to make sure you've named the right people as beneficiaries on those plans. Sometimes this is as simple as remembering who you've already named—and making sure that these beneficiaries still reflect your current wishes. The Current Beneficiaries List that you (hopefully) filled out in Chapter 1 can help: If you don't remember who you've named, you need to contact the company directly and ask them for a current beneficiary list.

Right of Survivorship: Property You Own With Others

Your will doesn't affect certain property that you own with others, because that property will automatically go to the surviving property owners when you die. For example, if the deed to your house shows that you and your spouse or partner own it "as joint tenants with right of survivorship," then when one of you dies, the survivor will automatically own the whole house.

The legal term for this automatic inheritance is a "right of survivorship," and property owned this way is often called "survivorship property." Joint tenancy is the most common form of property ownership with the right of survivorship, but California also allows married couples to own property as community property with right of survivorship. See "Forms of Property Ownership" in Chapter 1 for an explanation of the ways you can own real property in California.

You need to know how you own property when doing your estate plan. If you don't, your plan might not accomplish your goals. And, of course, if the way you own property doesn't reflect your wishes for it, you should change it. Now.

EXAMPLE: Aileen owns her home in joint tenancy with her partner, Simon. Aileen's will leaves her estate to her daughter, Janet. When Aileen dies, Simon owns the home and Janet inherits Aileen's investment account and bank accounts. Aileen wanted to give her one-half interest in the home to Janet, so that Simon would have to buy Janet out in order to own the whole home, but she never got around to changing the ownership in the home from joint tenancy with Simon.

Houses are commonly owned in joint tenancy, but brokerage accounts, bank accounts, and vehicles can also be owned that way. Unmarried partners also use joint tenancy to own property and money together in this way, as do older parents and caretaking children.

Couples often own many kinds of property as joint tenants, but if they are married, it's better to change from joint tenancy to community property with right of survivorship. Here's why: In California, the surviving spouse gets a big tax advantage from owning property that way. To understand why, you have to know that when you buy something for a low price (called the "basis") and sell it for a higher price later, you have to pay capital gains taxes on the difference between the basis and the sales price. Read Chapter 7 (see the section "Community Property and Taxes") for a more detailed explanation of how this works, but here's a preview to get you interested.

Because California is a community property state, if property is held as community property and one spouse dies, the survivor gets all of the community property revalued as of the date of that death. This is called a "step-up" in basis and it means that the survivor will not have to pay capital gains taxes on that appreciated property, unless they don't sell it for a long time and the property continues to go up in value. If that same property is held as joint tenancy, the survivor only gets one-half of the property revalued.

EXAMPLE: Pauline and Isaac purchased their home in Orange County in 1963 for $50,000. Pauline died in 2017. The house was appraised for $3.45 million. If Pauline and Isaac owned the house as community property with right of survivorship, Isaac would get a step-up in basis for the entire house. His new basis would be $3.45 million. If Isaac then sells the house for that amount, he'd owe no capital gains taxes.

If Pauline and Isaac had owned the house as joint tenants, though, Isaac would only get a step-up in basis for Pauline's one-half of the property when she died. The half he owns still has a basis of $25,000 (one-half of the original $50,000 that they paid for the house.) If Isaac then sells the house for $3.45 million three years after Pauline's death, he would owe capital gains taxes of approximately $478,000! Here's how this number was calculated: Isaac received $1.7 million of gain from the sale. Isaac can reduce that by using his homeowner's exclusion of $250,000, so he owes capital gains taxes on $1,450,000 x 33% = $478,000. (If Isaac had sold the house within two years of Pauline's death, he could have excluded $500,000 of that $1.7 million of capital gain.)

You can't override the right of survivorship in your will. If, for example, in your will you leave "everything to my spouse" but you own an apartment building in joint tenancy with your sister, she, not your spouse, would own the building after your death.

EXAMPLE: Andrea and her sister, Caitlin, inherited a home in Santa Barbara when their mother died. They used it as a vacation rental. Andrea's will left her estate to her spouse, Alan. When Andrea died, Caitlin became the sole owner of the Santa Barbara house. Alan inherited Andrea's remaining assets, but had counted on a share of the rental income from the Santa Barbara property to fund his retirement.

Choosing an Executor

A key task in preparing your will is to pick someone who will serve as the executor of your estate. The executor's job is to gather all the deceased person's property, pay debts, expenses, and taxes, and distribute what's left to the right people (your beneficiaries). To do all of this, the executor follows both California law and the instructions left in the will. And although technically it's not the executor's job, many also make sure that beneficiaries receive all life insurance and retirement plan benefits that they're entitled to.

If your estate plan consists of just a will, your executor will probably need to take the estate through a probate court proceeding (described in Chapter 1) or hire an attorney to help do it. If your estate plan includes a living trust (see Chapter 3), and the trust holds the majority of your assets, your estate won't go through probate, and your executor won't have that part of the job. But your executor will still have some important things to do: They'll have to step in and, essentially, represent you personally. As your executor it is their job to deal with all the things you've left behind as an individual, such as cancel your credit cards and subscriptions, return your cable television switch box, clean out your house, and file your last tax returns.

What to Look for in an Executor

So, who do you pick for the job? My advice is to pick the person you trust most to do a thorough and fair job of settling your affairs. The most well-thought-out estate plan means nothing if the person you've chosen to execute that plan doesn't do a good job of it or manages to make everyone who benefits from it suspicious, irritated, or downright hostile.

Ready, Able, and Willing

Your executor doesn't have to be a financial genius. Just pick someone who is organized, trustworthy, and willing to get the job done. Executors can hire experts—lawyers or tax preparers, for example— to help them and can use estate funds to pay these experts.

Good Communicator and Affable

It also helps to choose an executor who generally gets along with everyone who inherits under your plan. Settling an estate doesn't always bring out the best in people. Often, in fact, it brings out the worst in them, as otherwise mature people find themselves in heated fights over who should get grandmother's teacup collection or cuckoo clock. A good executor will be a good mediator—someone who can listen well, crack a joke when humor can help, and stand firm when the will clearly requires it.

Lives in California

An executor who lives outside of California, such as on the East Coast, might not be the right choice. It might be too expensive or complicated for someone who lives far away to administer an estate, and it will almost certainly require that they spend some time where you lived to put things in order. If you know a responsible person who lives closer, consider naming that person for the job of executor.

Although California law does not prohibit out-of-state executors from serving, most California judges place restrictions on out-of-state executors. Each county's superior court issues its own local rules on such things. Out-of-state executors will usually be required to post a bond in order to be appointed by the court—a kind of insurance policy to protect the will's beneficiaries—based on the size of the probate estate. Executors who live abroad can be nominated in a will to serve, but will also have to post a bond, and, since part of being an executor is signing lots of documents that must be filed with the court, it can be difficult to work with someone who lives abroad.

Who to Choose as Executor

You, as the "testator," a fancy legal word for the person who is creating a will, get to *nominate* an executor. If your estate ends up going through probate, the judge will actually *appoint* that executor to serve after the executor petitions the court to be appointed. Once appointed, the court will issue what are called "Letters Testamentary" which is sort of like a driver's license. The document gives your executor the power to manage the estate's property and pay the estate's creditors.

Spouses: The Usual Choice for Married Couples

As a rule for married couples, spouses get picked first for the job of executor because they are the ones most familiar with all of the assets and because most of the time, they'll be transferring the assets to themselves. Transferring assets after the death of one spouse is generally a straightforward process, as long as the executor knows where all of the assets are.

You don't, of course, have to name your spouse as your executor. If your spouse would have a difficult time dealing with the details following your death, or if your family has complicated politics, naming a third party, such as a trusted family friend or a bank's trust officer, might be the right thing for you.

Close Friends and Family Members

If you are single or divorced, or if your children wouldn't be the right choice for this job, you might consider naming close friends or other family members, such as siblings or nieces or nephews to serve. Some of my clients worry that they'd be burdening their friends by asking them to serve as executor. But, in my experience, most people are willing to do this when asked—they often feel honored to be asked and happy to help. You can also consider naming a professional fiduciary or a bank to do this job.

More Than One Executor

Parents of adult children often choose their children to serve as their second and third choice executors. This, of course, raises all sorts of family questions: Will your daughter Kerry be offended if you pick her brother Ryan to serve as executor, and not her? Will Kerry and Ryan stop speaking to each other if Ryan makes a decision as executor that Kerry doesn't agree with or thinks is unfair?

Some parents skirt the issue entirely by naming all of their children as coexecutors. But be warned that this means that all of them must agree on every action taken on behalf of the estate and sign off on all of the paperwork, unless the will gives the children the authority to act independently.

If your children get along harmoniously, this can work. If they don't get along, or if they live far away from each other, serving as coexecutors can be a logistical nightmare no matter what the will says. But trust yourself here—you know your children better than anybody. In some families, coexecutors make perfect sense. If, for example, one sibling is efficient and organized, but abrasive, and another is easy-going and genial, but a procrastinator, together they may get the job done better than either one could alone.

Professional Executors

If you anticipate leaving a large estate, or if you have fractious relatives, complicated debt issues, or unusual assets, you may want to consider naming a professional executor, such as a bank trust company, or professional fiduciary. The professional can serve either as the only executor or as a coexecutor with a family member. By doing so, you'll have the advantage of a neutral third party, with experience in taking care of an executor's duties and financial expertise that may serve your family well.

Professional fiduciaries are individuals (often retired bank trust officers or estate planning attorneys) who, for a fee, will serve as an executor, trustee, and (sometimes) agent under a durable power of attorney. They can manage money for incapacitated adults, or settle estates and trusts for beneficiaries. For people without children, or with children not well suited to serving as trustee or executor, a professional fiduciary may be a good fit.

If you are considering naming a bank or professional, you should check with them before you complete a will to see what their services cost and whether they have a minimum-size estate that they'll take on.

A professional executor's fee is usually a percentage of the total estate going through probate, and many professionals handle estates only if they're worth at least a certain amount. An executor's fee for an estate that goes through probate is set in California by state law (see Chapter 1) and must be approved by the court before it's paid. Family members, though they're entitled to fees for the services they provide, don't always choose to take these fees. (Why? Well, the fees are subject to income tax, but the inheritance they'll get once the estate is settled is not. For most people, waiting to inherit is a better tax move.)

RESOURCE

Where to find professional fiduciaries. Check out the Professional Fiduciaries Bureau (www.fiduciary.ca.gov), a state agency (part of the California Department of Consumer Affairs) that licenses and regulates professional fiduciaries in California, and the Professional Fiduciary Association of California (www.pfac-pro.org), a good place to find a professional near you.

Where to Find California Rules on Executors

To find out your local court's probate rules on out-of-state executors and other matters, start with your local superior court website. Find yours at www.courts.ca.gov/find-my-court.htm.

Naming an Alternate Executor

After you settle on your first choice for executor, you should also come up with one—or even better, two—names of alternate executors, in case your first choice is unable to serve. Just as when you made your first choice, you should pick someone who is good on logistics and details and who could spend the necessary time identifying assets, notifying creditors, dealing with tax returns, and keeping good records. Most importantly, you should pick someone you trust. Your executor will be carrying out your last wishes, and it's not always an easy task.

Talking to Your Choice for Executors

No matter who you pick to be your executor (and alternate), it's important to discuss the matter with them before you write your will. It's not fair to surprise someone with such a big responsibility. Someone who doesn't want to serve could always decline to serve when the time comes—and if that's going to happen, it's better to clear it up now.

Discussing this with your choice for executor now makes sense for them, too. Your future executor will probably have questions about how you want things handled and where your assets are. Though it can be an awkward discussion to begin, you both might find it a useful one to have.

RESOURCE

Resource on executors. For a well-written and comprehensive guide to serving as an executor, you can't do better than to read *The Executor's Guide: Settling a Loved One's Estate or Trust*, by Mary Randolph (Nolo).

Choosing Guardians and Managing Money For Children

If you have to choose guardians for minor children and set up a system to manage their money, you will need to read through Chapters 3 and 4 before continuing with the Will Worksheet included in this chapter. I apologize for asking you to skip ahead and work through Chapters 3 and 4, but each topic requires a separate chapter to even begin to do it justice.

Here's what you'll need to decide to fill in the Will Worksheet:

- who to nominate as the custodial guardian of your children until they reach age 18
- who to nominate as the property guardian of your children to manage money left to those children outside of a custodial account or trust, and
- how to manage assets left to children until they are old enough to properly manage it themselves.

Planning for Pets

If you want to leave money for a beloved pet, you can absolutely do that in your will. Pets, of course, can't inherit assets directly. And, if you don't make any particular plans for them, they are considered to be your "property" so would pass to whomever inherits your estate otherwise: If you leave a will, that would be your beneficiaries and if you don't leave a will, that would be the person who would inherit your estate under state law. Luckily for pet owners, there are several ways to leave money for their pets' care. Here are three ways that my clients have used most often to give pet care responsibilities.

Leaving Money to a Pet-Loving Friend

You may leave money to a trusted friend for the care of your pet by making a gift to that person in your will. You are trusting your friend to take good care of your pet, but that's what friends are for. This is informal, but it often works just fine.

EXAMPLE: Lisa's will leaves $5,000 to her friend, Kathy, for the lifetime care of Lisa's cat, Solar Sam. Lisa's will says that if there's any money left after Solar Sam's death, she requests (but does not legally require) that Kathy donate that money to the SPCA in her town. (Legally, this gift is to Kathy with no strings attached, so, if Kathy doesn't use it to care for Solar Sam, no one can sue her.)

Creating a Pet Trust

California law allows you to create a pet trust to hold money for the benefit of your pet. If the trustee of the pet trust doesn't use the money to care for your pet, they can be sued. This is more formal than the gift to a friend, but unlike the gift method, it is legally binding.

To create a pet trust, you need to do the following things:

1. Name the pets that are covered. They have to be alive when you create the trust; you can't create a trust for future pets.
2. Name a person who will take care of the pets.
3. Leave a set amount of money for the care of the pets.
4. Describe how you'd like your pet to be taken care of.
5. Name a person who can go to court to enforce the terms of the trust.
6. Say what should happen to any money left over after the last pet named in the trust dies.

EXAMPLE: Frederick's will creates a pet trust for the lifetime benefit of his English bulldog, Sarge. He names his friend, Cal, as the trustee and his sister, Cora, as Sarge's caretaker. Frederick names his brother, Hector, as the person with the right to go to court to enforce the trust's terms, if he thinks that they aren't being followed. The trust specifies that the money in the trust is to be used for medical care, food, and adequate housing for Sarge. If there's money left when Sarge dies, Cal is directed to donate it to an English bulldog rescue group of his choosing. (Legally, if the money in the trust isn't used for Sarge, Hector could go to court to enforce the terms of the trust.)

RESOURCE

To learn more about pet trusts. The American Society for the Prevention of Cruelty to Animals has an informative website at www.aspca.org/pet-care/pet-planning/pet-trust-primer.

Leaving Money to a Pet Rescue Organization

You might explore leaving money to a pet rescue organization, often called no-kill sanctuaries, for the lifetime care of your pet. Many of my clients have used this method to both benefit an organization and their pets.

EXAMPLE: Mavis's will left $5,000 for the lifetime care of her beloved canary, Tweetie, to the BirdHouse, an organization that Mavis knew about that provides care for canaries. Her will also stated that if Tweetie died and there was still money available from that gift, it should be used for Bird-House's other birds.

Preparing a Will Worksheet

Now it's time to organize the information you'll need to cover in your will. I include a Will Worksheet here you can use for this purpose. If you find yourself writing down the same two or three people over and over again, that's completely normal, most of us have a limited number of trusted friends and family members. The worksheet includes:

- **Information on yourself and your family.** If you are single, just fill out what's relevant for you.
- **How you want to dispose of your property, including gifts to charities, to guardians, to friends or family members, or for the care of your pets.** You don't list what property you own in a will, you just say who should get it. First, you list any specific gifts you want to make. Then, you say who should receive the "residue," which means everything else. If you are leaving your money to minor children, you need to figure out when that trust will end and whether you want to make any interim distributions to the children before that time. Finally, you should decide who should receive your estate if no one you've named survives you. I call this the "god-forbid" provision.
- **Your choice of executor (and alternate) of your estate.** This is the person who will settle your estate. You can name family members, friends, or professionals here.
- **Who you will nominate as personal guardian for any minor children:** (covered in Chapters 4 and 5). The guardian does the custodial work of raising a child—getting them to school, to the doctor, and making sure they have a safe home.
- **Who you will nominate to manage money for your children.** There are two categories: a trustee, who will manage any trusts that your will creates for your children, and a property guardian (usually the same person).

See the sample Will Worksheet below as a model in preparing your own.

Will Worksheet

Use this worksheet to organize the information you'll cover in your will.

1. Family Information

Your name: __Mary Ruth Doe__

Spouse's/Partner's name: __John Richard Doe__

Children's names and birthdates: __Stephanie Ann Doe, April 11, 2000__
__Charles John Doe, December 2, 2003__

2. Disposition of Property

Specific gifts: __$10,000 to Marie Gonzales, my dear friend__

　　Charities: __$1,000 to Camp Kessem__

　　Family/Friends: __N/A__

　　Gift to guardian: __$20,000__

　　Gifts for care of pet (in trust or to person or organization): __$5,000 for the__
__care of "Sasha," my Siberian Husky, and to be given to Jennifer Rose Smith__

Rest of estate goes to: __John Richard Doe, my husband__

If spouse/partner doesn't survive me, to: __Stephanie & Charles, my children__

If to children, in trust until age of: __27__

　　Interim Distributions: __10__ % at age __23__　　__20__ % at age __25__

　　　　　　　　　　　　_____ % at age _____　　_____ % at age _____

If spouse and children don't survive me, to: __Jennifer Rose Smith, my sister__

3. Executor (*Choices after spouse*)

First choice: __Jennifer Rose Smith, my sister__

Second choice: __Joseph Arthur Doe, my husband's brother__

Third choice: __Sam Thornton, my dear friend__

4. Personal Guardians for Children

First choice: __Joseph Arthur Doe, my husband's brother__

Second choice: __Marilyn L. Johnson, my dear friend__

Third choice: __Jennifer Rose Smith, my sister__

5. Trustees for Children's Trust

First choice: __Jennifer Rose Smith, my sister__

Second choice: __Joseph Arthur Doe, my husband's brother__

Third choice: __Sam Thornton, my dear friend__

6. Property Guardians for Children

First choice: __Same as trustees__

Second choice: __Same as trustees__

Third choice: __Same as trustees__

FORM

Will Worksheet. The Nolo website includes a downloadable copy of the Will Worksheet. See the appendix for the link to this worksheet and the other forms in this book.

Making a Will: A DIY Project or Not?

Wills don't have to be (and shouldn't be, really) complicated. Like recipes, they are written in a certain ritualized way and designed to do a specific thing. As long as you get the basic information in your will and have it properly signed and witnessed, it will do what it is supposed to: Set out your last wishes clearly and in a legally binding way.

Preparing a Simple Will

Even better, you are fully competent to make a simple will yourself. The law's on your side—it wants to make it easy for people to make their last wishes binding. Your best bet is to use a do-it-yourself online tool or software that will guide you through the decision-making process and provide the legal language that will make it easy for your heirs to settle your estate.

My two favorite options are Nolo's Online Will and *Quicken WillMaker* (Nolo). The online version allows you to fill in a simple questionnaire at Nolo.com and then print out a will. *WillMaker* is software that you install on your computer. It guides you through a series of questions (providing lots of help along the way), compiles your answers, and prints out your will.

When to Get Help Preparing a Will

DIY wills aren't for everyone. Here are a few situations when it makes more sense to work with an attorney rather go completely on your own:

- You are in a second marriage or nontraditional relationship, or have children and want to disinherit one of them, or treat certain children differently than others (read Chapter 7, too).
- You are expecting trouble from a member of the family or expect someone to challenge your mental competence.
- You own assets that are hard to split up, like a family business or a vacation home.
- You own assets in another country, or have family members in another country that you would like to nominate as executors or guardians (read Chapter 6, too).

In more complex families, or for those with complicated assets, working with an attorney makes it possible for you to get your wishes down in writing properly and to insulate yourself, as much as it's possible to do so, from challenges that may arise from disappointed family members. Even though you are asking for professional help, working through the Will Worksheet and reading the chapters in this book that are relevant to your situation will make your work with a lawyer more efficient and more satisfying. The better prepared my clients are, or even the more perplexed they are, the richer the conversations can be.

If you work with an attorney, a will is usually prepared as part of an estate plan that also includes a durable power of attorney for finance and an advance health care directive (covered in Chapter 11). Generally, the cost of doing a will is less than half the cost of preparing a living trust because a will takes less of the lawyer's time to draft.

See Chapter 13 for advice on finding and choosing an attorney.

Disinheriting Children

If you have a child that you specifically want to disinherit, you should say so explicitly in your will. If you don't do that, and you just neglect to mention that child or leave that child anything, you risk having the child make a claim against your estate as what the law calls an "omitted heir." This law primarily protects children born or adopted after the execution of a will, but even children who were born before a will was executed (and were not mentioned in the will) may have a claim against the estate if they can prove that the person making the will was unaware of their existence or thought that they were dead. An omitted heir is entitled to what they would inherit if the person died without a will at all, so an omitted child could inherit a significant share of a person's estate.

EXAMPLE 1: Eli made a will in 1983 leaving his estate equally to his two children, Levi and Alex. Eli had another child, Evie, after he executed that will and never updated his documents. When Eli died, Evie made a claim against his estate as an omitted heir. She inherited one-third of Eli's estate.

EXAMPLE 2: Marlena had four children. Her oldest son, Ramsey, joined a cult that Marlena did not approve of. In her will, Marlena stated that, "I leave nothing to my son Ramsey for reasons known to him." When Marlena died, her other three children inherited her estate. Ramsey had no claim as an omitted heir.

Once You've Done Your Will

After you execute your will, make sure to keep the original in a safe place. You could keep in your safe deposit box (if you have one), or a fireproof box or a safe at home. Make sure that your nominated executor will know where to find it. You don't have to give anybody a copy of it if you want to keep its contents secret. If you want to write a letter to your guardian or executor explaining the choices you've made, you could keep that letter with your will, with instructions for that envelope to be opened only in the event of your death.

See Chapter 12 for advice on updating your will.

What Happens If You Don't Make a Will?

People often ask me what would happen if they don't make a will. I hope knowing the answer will motivate you to get it done.

Who Gets Your Assets

If you don't make a will or any other provisions for distributing your property, your spouse (or registered domestic partner) and your children would inherit your assets. If you don't have a spouse or children, parents and siblings are next in line. Exactly how much they each would get is governed by the California Probate Code. The laws for who gets what are called the rules of "intestacy" or "intestate succession."

California law distributes your property based on who in your family survives you. Community property is distributed differently than separate property. Only spouses (and partners in registered domestic partnerships) and blood relatives inherit under California law. If you have a surviving spouse, they will get the largest share. For example, your spouse will inherit all of your community property and either one-half or one-third of your separate property, depending on how many children you have. If you are married, but have no children, but you have siblings (but no surviving parents), the surviving spouse gets all the community property and one-half of your separate property (your siblings get the other half of your separate property).

Bottom line: California has specific rules for who would inherit your property. But wouldn't you rather make up your own?

Without a will, your unmarried (and unregistered) partner, close friends, charities, and anyone else you want to take care of upon your death will not receive a penny from you under state law.

RESOURCE

For more information on the distribution of community property, see the Nolo article "Intestate Succession in California," at www.nolo.com/legal-encyclopedia/intestate-succession-california.html.

No Will: No Luck

I know of one committed couple who had lived together for many years. Neither had wanted to marry because they'd both been through several marriages. Sadly, one partner died unexpectedly, leaving behind no will. The survivor inherited nothing and had no protection under California law. The artist known as Prince died without a will in Minnesota, leaving behind an estate valued at $150 million. Despite being generous to charities during his lifetime, none of Prince's estate will go to charity—Minnesota state law distributes property, like California, only to his surviving heirs.

Who Will Be the Guardian for Your Children (If Any)

Not making a will affects more than property. Without a will, a judge would appoint, without any guidance from you, a personal guardian to raise your children and a property guardian to manage their inheritance. Judges try hard to pick the right people for these jobs, but obviously it's better to leave a list to work from. When you make a will, you state your choice for guardian—a wish a judge would almost certainly honor. Finally, the only way to ensure that your children won't inherit everything you've left them at 18 is to make a will or trust, providing for an alternative to a court-ordered property guardianship.

Living Trusts

What Is a Living Trust? 67

    Living Trusts Are Revocable 68

    Living Trusts Include a Will... 68

    Trusts Are Like Plays With Three Acts.. 68

Creating a Living Trust: The Settlor's Job 72

Casting the Play: Selecting Trustees and Beneficiaries............................. 74

    Trustees.. 74

    Beneficiaries.. 76

Preparing a Trust Worksheet 78

Creating a Living Trust: DIY Project or Not?... 80

    Preparing a Living Trust Yourself.. 81

    When to Work With a Lawyer.. 81

Transferring Assets Into the Trust 84

    What Goes Into a Trust.. 85

    Transferring Property Into a Trust... 85

Pour-Over Wills 87

    How a Pour-Over Will Gets Property Into the Trust................................... 87

    Nominating Guardians in a Pour-Over Will.. 89

    Nominating Executors in a Pour-Over Will 89

    Who Creates the Pour-Over Will 89

Read this chapter if:

- You think you should use a trust, not a will, to structure your estate plan.

- You want to learn more about trusts.

- You want to choose a trustee.

- You want to fill out a Trust Worksheet to organize and collect the information that you'll need to create a living trust.

I f you read Chapter 1 and concluded that a living trust makes sense for you, read on. As I wrote there, a will is not always the least expensive or quickest way to transfer property at your death. That's because, with a will, your estate will probably be subject to a probate court proceeding after your death. To spare your loved ones the expense and delay of a probate proceeding, you can leave your property to your loved ones by using a living trust instead of a will as your main estate planning document.

As I hope I made clear in Chapter 1, avoiding probate by using a trust instead of a will is a good thing for Californians to at least consider. The real question is whether it is worth it to you to do the planning required to avoid probate now, or wait until later. If you just want to get the basics done at this point and postpone anything more until your children (if any) are older or until you acquire more assets, you may, with perfect serenity, skip this chapter. But if you'd like to learn more, read on.

What Is a Living Trust?

A trust is a legal agreement where one person (the trustee) agrees to hold property owned by another person (the settlor) for the benefit of someone (the beneficiary). Trusts were invented in the Middle Ages, when knights rode off to the crusades and wanted to leave their land in the care of someone else, but without giving up ownership, just in case they made it back in one piece.

Trusts aren't separate legal entities like corporations or partnerships, but they function a lot like them in some ways. The trustee has a fiduciary duty to the beneficiaries, sort of like a corporate officer has to stockholders, to manage the trusts' assets according to the trust's specific terms, such as how money can be used (the California probate code sets out many rules for what trustees can and can't do). A trustee, for example, is held to high standards of honesty, must keep excellent records, and must never act to benefit him- or herself at the expense of the beneficiaries. The settlors, who establish the trust, retain certain rights, too: Usually they are the only people who can amend or revoke the trust, and if the trust is revoked, they get their property back.

Trusts can be used to manage all sorts of property for all sorts of reasons. You may have heard of or met wealthy "trust fund babies," who are the beneficiaries of trusts that their parents created. There is an entire industry of trust companies and advisors that help the mega-wealthy preserve family wealth for generations. You may have heard of land trusts, which hold property for the benefit of certain families or the public.

A living trust, my focus here, is just another kind of trust agreement. It is "living" because it is created by a settlor, while that person is alive, and is held for their benefit during their lifetime.

Living Trusts Are Revocable

Living trusts are also often called "revocable trusts." The terms are used interchangeably. A living trust is a revocable trust during the lifetime of the person or persons who created it because a settlor can revoke or amend the trust at any time while he or she is alive.

Living trusts are used only for estate planning. You can't use a living trust, for example, to protect your assets from creditors, to limit your liability for a rental property, or to give away your property during your lifetime to your children (or to anyone else) permanently. Actually, living trusts serve only one purpose: They allow you (the settlor) to transfer your trust assets after death without the court supervision of a probate proceeding.

Living Trusts Include a Will

A living trust is also called a "will substitute" because, like a will, the trust determines who will inherit your assets after you die. But that's a bit misleading: Even estate plans that use living trusts still include wills. When you have a trust, though, your will is quite short and does much less than a will that does all of the estate planning work, which I call a "stand alone will" (the focus of Chapter 2). The kind of will you create when you use a living trust is called a "pour-over will" because it says that any assets that you own at your death that weren't in the trust should be transferred to (poured over into) the trust and it names guardians for your minor children, if you have any. (See "Pour-Over Wills" at the end of this chapter for more information.)

Trusts Are Like Plays With Three Acts

I tell my clients to think of a trust like a play. All trusts have three different roles for people to play:
- settlor or grantor, the owner of the property that will be placed in the trust, such as real property and investment accounts
- trustee, the one who is going to manage that property while it is in the trust, both during the settlor's life and afterwards, and

- beneficiaries, those who get to use the property that's in the trust or will and eventually own it after the trust terminates.

The trust document is like the script for the play. It states who will play each role (and names their understudies). It tells the actors what to do so that the play can be performed. It states what property will be held in the trust, who can use it, how it will be invested and spent during that time, and when the trust will end. And for the grand finale, it says who will get the trust property when the trust ends.

The Trust's Cast of Characters	
Settlor or Grantor	The person who contributes property to the trust
Trustee	The person who manages the trust assets
Beneficiary	The person or organization, such as a charity, that benefits from the trust assets and also the person or organization that receives property when the trust ends; they can be different people and/or organizations.

EXAMPLE 1: Irving and Rebecca (the settlors or grantors) set up a trust for the benefit of their three children (the beneficiaries). They appoint William, Rebecca's brother, to serve as the trustee. The trust document (the script) requires William to distribute $10,000 to each child on that child's 18th birthday and to give each child an equal one-third of the estate when the youngest child turns 21.

EXAMPLE 2: Marjorie (the settlor or grantor) establishes a trust for her nieces and nephews (the beneficiaries). Her brother Christopher is to serve as trustee. The trust funds may be used only for the nieces' and nephews' education and medical expenses not covered by health insurance. When the youngest beneficiary finishes college or turns 23, whichever happens first, the trust (the script) says that Christopher must distribute any trust funds that are left to the nonprofit organization the Seva Foundation.

EXAMPLE 3: Amy and Nila (the settlors) create a living trust. They transfer their residence, their investment accounts, and their rainy day savings account to that trust. When both Amy and Nila die, their successor trustee, Jamie, will be able to distribute the couple's assets to their children, Wallace and Henrietta, without having to go through probate because the assets outside of the trust total less than $150,000. It will take Jamie about six months to settle the estate and cost the trust about $5,000 in fees for accountants and lawyers—far less time and money than it would have taken to go through probate.

In our living trust drama, one actor starts out playing all three roles. If you create a trust for your property (that means you are the settlor or grantor), you are usually also the trustee, the person who manages that property during your lifetime. You are also the beneficiary of the trust during your lifetime—the assets are to be used for whatever you need. The trust will state who gets the property after your death—if you have children, it's usually them (they become the beneficiaries then). If you don't have children, your beneficiaries are likely to be other family members, friends, or charities.

You don't give up any rights to the property that you transfer to a living trust. Of course, it depends on how a particular trust is written (that's the script). But a well-drafted living trust allows you to do everything with your property after it's been placed in trust that you could do before—including buying, selling, borrowing against, or giving away assets. You can also change any of the trust's terms or revoke it entirely if you want to. You start out as both settlor and trustee of the trust, but if you ever need help, others can step in and manage the trust assets for you—you don't have to play both roles forever.

People create living trusts because property in a trust is not subject to probate when the settlor dies. Instead, the trustee takes care of the transfer of trust assets without probate court supervision. This means the assets can often be transferred much more quickly. A simple trust can be settled within a few months of the settlor's death. Probate, in contrast, takes four months to a year (or more) in California, and much of that time is spent waiting for certain court-required deadlines.

There are usually some fees and expenses associated with settling a trust, which is called trust administration, but they are almost always less than those of a probate proceeding. Most trustees hire an attorney to help them figure out what to do and are charged on an hourly basis for this legal advice. But most of what needs to be done can be relatively simple, such as having real property appraised, paying taxes and bills, and dividing up the assets in the trust and distributing them equally to the trust beneficiaries.

EXAMPLE 1: Jackson and his wife, Claudia, decide to create a living trust as part of their estate plan. They are the settlors of the trust and contribute their property to it. During their lifetimes, they will serve as trustees and manage the trust assets for their own benefit. After one spouse dies, the surviving spouse will serve as trustee alone. At the death of the second spouse, Jackson and Claudia's four children will inherit the trust property in equal shares. There will be no probate necessary for the transfer of property in the trust.

EXAMPLE 2: Aaron created a living trust to hold his house and his Charles Schwab account. He named his two daughters, Carol and Ruth, to serve as cotrustees. After Aaron died, Carol and Ruth worked with an attorney to administer the trust. The sisters sold the house, paid Aaron's last taxes, and distributed the house sale proceeds and the Schwab account to themselves in equal shares. They spent $3,000 on lawyer fees; $600 to have Aaron's tax return prepared; $400 to have the house appraised; $1,000 to ready the house for sale, and paid their real estate broker a commission on the sale of the house.

RESOURCE

More on trusts and trust administration. For a great overview of living trusts and how you might use them in your estate plan, see *Plan Your Estate*, by Denis Clifford. To learn more about trust administration, see *The Trustee's Legal Companion*, by Carol Elias Zolla and Liza Hanks. Both books are published by Nolo.

Creating a Living Trust: The Settlor's Job

To create a living trust, you need to make a few decisions. Whether you draft a trust yourself or hire a lawyer to help, you'll need to select the cast and set the stage. I hope this chapter can help you do just that. This chapter includes a Trust Worksheet so that you can write down your decisions, such as who you want to name as trustee, who you want to leave your trust's asset to at death, and how you want to leave such assets—outright or in some kind of trust.

Whether you decide to create a trust yourself, or seek a lawyer's help, the more homework you do upfront, the easier the process is going to be. As with the process of filling in the Will Worksheet in Chapter 2, you might have to skip ahead and read certain chapters that discuss issues relevant to your decisions, such as property tax (Chapter 8); owning international assets, making gifts to noncitizens, or naming noncitizens as trustees (Chapter 6); planning for blended families (Chapter 7); or understanding estate or income taxes (Chapter 9). That's perfectly normal—creating a trust requires thinking through many distinct issues, one at a time.

Here are the main decisions you'll need to make:

- **What is the purpose of the trust?** Your living trust is designed to avoid probate, but what else do you want it to do? Do you want to leave assets for the benefit of children or other people? To charity? To friends? To pets?

- **Who will you choose as a trustee, or cotrustee, of the trust?** Your trustee is the person who is going to administer the trust after you can't. Naming the right person or people or institution to do this is really important.

- **Who will be the beneficiaries of the trust and how will you structure their inheritance?** Managing money for children requires putting a system in place to make sure that a responsible person is in charge. Managing money for other beneficiaries, such as partners (or pets) also requires some careful attention.

- **How many trusts are you going to create?** Single people, or unmarried couples, will usually create separate trusts because they own property separately. In California, married couples usually create just one joint trust. If you are in a blended marriage, or one partner owns separate property, such as assets they've inherited from a parent, or property they've brought to the marriage, you might want to keep that property separate, and create a trust to hold that property separately. (See Chapter 7 for strategies that blended families use for planning.) Some couples create one trust for their community property and one, or two, separate property trusts for separate property.

Here are variations of trusts for five couples, all of whom have been married for 20 years.

EXAMPLE 1: Ivan and his wife, Ludmilla, decide to create a living trust as part of their estate plan. They are the settlors of the trust and contribute their property to it. They have been married for 20 years, they have two mutual children, and all of their property is community property. They will create one living trust to hold their assets.

EXAMPLE 2: Jason and his partner, Claude, have been together for 20 years also, but they were married in 2016, and each brought separate property to the marriage that they each intend to keep as separate property. Before Jason and Claude married, they signed a premarital agreement stating that all of their property will be kept as separate property. They will create two trusts, each will hold one person's separate property.

EXAMPLE 3: Kristy and her spouse, Barry, have also been together for 20 years. But Kristy has recently inherited property from her father and she wants to keep that inheritance separate from their community property. Kristy will create one trust to hold her inheritance and Kristy and Barry will create one trust to hold their community property. Both trusts will distribute all of the property to their two adult sons when the second spouse dies.

EXAMPLE 4: Russell and Shirley have also been married for 20 years. Both have children from their prior marriages. Each owns some separate property that they brought to the marriage and they also own some community property assets that they acquired during their marriage. They create one trust, but, at the first partner's death, that person's assets are held in trust for the surviving spouse and will then be distributed to that person's children (not to their spouse's children).

EXAMPLE 5: Kate had been married for 20 years, but is now divorced and living with Gordon. She has three daughters from her first marriage. Gordon has no children. Kate creates a trust to hold her property and leaves it in trust for Gordon, for his lifetime, and then it will be distributed to her daughters. Gordon creates a trust to hold his assets. His trust holds his assets in trust for Kate, for her lifetime, and then leaves what is left to Guide Dogs for the Blind.

Casting the Play: Selecting Trustees and Beneficiaries

Once you determine how many trusts you are going to create, your next step is to decide who will manage the trust and who will benefit from it.

Trustees

As explained above, the first role (the settlor) creates the trust. The second role (the trustee) is the star of the show. Without a strong trustee the whole production may never be a success. Your trustee is the person who will manage the assets once they're in the trust. During your lifetime, you (the settlor) will usually also serve as the trustee. Most people create living trusts to make the transfer of their assets easy after they've died, after all, and don't want anyone else to manage those assets while they are alive.

But you also need to name a successor trustee, who will take over as trustee at your death, and transfer trust property to the beneficiaries you named in the trust. If you become ill and can no longer manage the trust assets, the successor trustee will also manage the trust property for your benefit.

TIP

If you become incapacitated and your successor trustee starts managing trust assets for your benefit, you still need an agent under a valid durable power of attorney to manage your assets outside of the trust, such as your retirement accounts and life insurance policies. Your agent will also need to manage your personal bills, such as credit cards, and service providers, such as gardeners, house cleaners, or babysitters. (See Chapter 11 for more information on durable powers of attorney.)

A good trustee is someone you can trust to do a good job of settling your estate. A trustee needs to be organized, responsible and a good communicator. If you have minor children, your trustee must also be someone who could do a good, long-term job of managing your children's inheritance. Your trustee does not have to be a financial wizard, just a responsible, careful person who is smart enough to get help when he or she needs it.

Chapter 5 includes a discussion of what trustees do because many people select their successor trustees for the purpose of managing money for their children. (It also includes a discussion of professional trustees, if that subject interests you.) If you have minor children, please read Chapter 5, too. But here's a summary of the key things you need to know about trustees:

- Trustees must manage trust assets carefully, competently, and honestly. If the trust has more than one beneficiary, the trustee must be impartial and can't favor one beneficiary over another.
- The trustee's job is to administer the trust solely in the interest of the beneficiaries. Trustees are not allowed to use trust assets to benefit themselves or for any nontrust purpose.
- Trustees don't need to be stellar money managers, just prudent and diligent ones.

- Trustees are allowed to hire people to help them make good decisions and get good advice. For example, it's common for a trustee to consult a lawyer at the beginning of the process and to get an investment adviser to help figure out how to invest the trust funds properly. Trustees may use trust assets to pay these experts reasonable fees.
- The trustee must file annual trust tax returns with both the State of California's Franchise Tax Board and the IRS, reporting the income and expenses of the trust in each tax year.
- The trustee must also provide periodic accountings to the beneficiaries, detailing how the money has been invested and spent, at least annually. (If you are the settlor and also the trustee, you are not required to provide an accounting to yourself, but you should still keep good records.)

Beneficiaries

The beneficiaries are the third actors in the play. During your lifetime, you, as the settlor, are also the beneficiary of the trust. You have complete control over the assets and can use them for whatever you want. Your trust states what happens after you die. If you are married, your spouse is often the beneficiary of the trust, then your children after that. If you are single, you might name a partner, a friend, a parent, or a charity as the beneficiary.

If you die with young children, or want to leave money to young children, the assets can be distributed to a children's trust or held in a custodial account to age 25 for their benefit. If you want to leave money in trust for a partner, a parent, or a friend, your trust can leave money to them outright, or in a trust for a certain period of time, or for their lifetimes. Your successor trustee can manage any of these trusts, or distribute the property outright.

 TIP
If you want to leave money for the care of a pet, please read "Planning for Pets" in Chapter 2.

EXAMPLE 1: Renaldo and Joan have two young boys. They decide that for them, a living trust makes sense. They create a living trust and fund it with their home in Merced, their Fidelity investment account, and their credit union account. They name Leslie, Joan's sister, as the successor trustee. The name their children as the beneficiaries after they both die.

During Renaldo and Joan's life, they have full control over their trust assets. If one of both of their children is over 30 when both of their parents die, that child will get his share outright and can invest and spend it as he wishes. If a child is under 30, his share will be placed in trust for him until he turns 30. Leslie will manage trust funds for the boys until they both turn 30. If they are both over 30 when their parents die, Leslie will pay the debts and taxes owed by Renaldo and Joan and distribute what's left, in equal shares, to the boys.

EXAMPLE 2: Susan is a single woman without children. She creates a living trust and transfers her home in Los Angeles and investment account to the trust. She names her friend Deborah as successor trustee. She names her mother, Joanne, as her beneficiary, and her assets are to be held in a lifetime trust. At Joanne's death, any assets left in the trust are to be distributed to the Alzheimer's Foundation.

When Susan dies, Deborah sets up a trust for Joanne and manages the assets for her benefit. Three years later, Joanne dies. Deborah pays the last expenses and taxes for the trust, then distributes what is left in the trust to the Alzheimer's Foundation.

EXAMPLE 3: Keith is a divorced man with three adult children. He creates a living trust and funds it with his home in San Diego, his bank account, and his Vanguard mutual funds. Keith names his daughter Donna as his successor trustee. At his death, Donna is to distribute his assets equally between her siblings, outright and free of trust.

When Keith dies, Donna appraises the property, values the mutual funds, and pays Keith's last bills and taxes. Then she distributes the trust's assets in equal shares to herself and to her two brothers. They decide to keep Keith's San Diego home as a rental property, and each own an equal one-third of the property as tenants in common.

Preparing a Trust Worksheet

Now it's time to organize the information you'll need to cover in your trust. I include a Trust Worksheet here you can use for this purpose. If you've already filled out the Will Worksheet, this will look familiar. The decisions you're making are essentially the same. As with the Will Worksheet, if you find yourself writing down the same two or three people over and over again, that's completely normal, most of us have a limited number of trusted friends and family members. The worksheet includes:

- **Information on yourself and your family:** If you are single, just fill out what's relevant for you.
- **How you want to dispose of the trust's property, including gifts to charities, to the guardian of your children, to family members, or for the care of pets:** First, you list any specific gifts you want to make. Then, you say who should receive the "residue," which means everything else. If you are leaving your money to minor children, you need to figure out when that trust will end and whether you want to make any interim distributions to them before that time. Finally, you should decide who should receive your estate if no one you've named survives you. I call this the "god-forbid" provision.
- **Your choice of trustee (and alternate) of your trust:** This is the person who will gather, value, and ultimately distribute the trust's assets. You can name family members, friends, or professionals here.

See the sample Trust Worksheet shown below as a model in preparing your own.

Trust Worksheet

Use this worksheet to organize the information you'll cover in your trust.

I. Family Information

Your name: Mary Ruth Doe

Spouse's/Partner's name: John Richard Doe

Children's names and birthdates: Stephanie Ann Doe, April 11, 2000
Charles John Doe, December 2, 2003

II. Disposition of Property

Specific gifts to guardian: $20,000

Specific gifts to family: N/A

Specific gifts to friends: $10,000 to Maria Gonzales, my dear friend

Specific gifts to charities: $1,000 to Camp Kesseul

Gifts for care of pets (in trust or to person or organization): $5,000 for the care of "Sasha," my Siberian Husky, to be given to Jennifer Rose Smith

Rest of estate goes to: John Richard Doe

To spouse or partner? Yes

Trust for someone like a parent or partner? No

If to children, in trust until age of: 27

    Interim distributions: __10__ % at age __23__

    Interim distributions: __20__ % at age __25__

    Interim distributions: __N/A__ % at age _____

If spouse/partner/children/other beneficiary doesn't survive me, to:
Jennifer Rose Smith, my sister

III. Trustee
(Choices after Spouse)

First choice: Jennifer Rose Smith, my sister

Second choice: Joseph Arthur Doe, my husband's brother

Third choice: Sam Thornton, my dear friend

FORM

Trust Worksheet. The Nolo website includes a downloadable copy of the Trust Worksheet. See the appendix for the link to this worksheet and the other forms in this book.

Creating a Living Trust: DIY Project or Not?

To set up a living trust, you have to create a trust agreement by signing and executing it properly. Then you have to transfer your assets to the trust (fund the trust) by changing the legal owner of each asset. And once you've done that, you will have to make sure that over time the trust continues to hold your biggest assets so that you can avoid probate. A trust with nothing in it when you die does you absolutely no good.

Of course, that's a little like saying that all you have to do to buy a house is sell the one you own now, find one you like better, make an offer, have the offer accepted, get a loan, and move in. The devil is in the details.

Once you've decided that a trust makes sense, you have to decide whether to draft the trust yourself or seek a lawyer's help.

RESOURCE

Two great ways to draft your own living trust. On Nolo.com, you can go through a simple question-and-answer process (using Nolo's Online Living Trust) to create a living trust; on the basis of your answers, you'll get a living trust designed to meet your wishes. If you'd prefer a book, check out *Make Your Own Living Trust*, by Denis Clifford (Nolo); it comes with all the forms you'll need to create a living trust that's right for you, and has helpful information on how to transfer assets into a trust and manage trust assets over time.

Preparing a Living Trust Yourself

If you like to do things yourself, you're in luck. A person with a few straightforward assets can put together a living trust that will avoid probate and properly manage assets for their kids. It's not that hard. You'll need to work with well-drafted forms, gather the important information, and figure out answers to nuts-and-bolts questions.

When to Work With a Lawyer

In my opinion, you should talk to a lawyer if you fit into one or more of these categories:

- You own assets (including life insurance, retirement assets, equity in your home, and cash in the bank) worth more than $5 million now, or they're likely to be worth that much in the near future.
- You are married to someone who's not a U.S. citizen.
- You have children or separate property from a prior marriage.
- You own your own business.
- You own complicated assets, such as private company stock or an interest in partnerships.
- You have a child with special needs who will likely need lifelong financial support.
- You want your estate plan to take care of aged parents as well as your children.

If any of these apply to you, a well-trained lawyer ought to be worth the fee. A good lawyer's judgment and experience will add value to your estate plan. The lawyer will ask you to think about issues that you haven't thought about and will draft a trust agreement that addresses them.

Watch Out for Trust Scams

Sooner or later, you'll find a flyer on your doorstep or car advertising a "Low-Cost Living Trust Seminar." Watch out. While some may be legitimate, others are only a pretext for a hard sell.

To get you to attend, an unscrupulous company will offer a living trust for a fraction of what an attorney would charge. Often called "trust mills," these companies usually offer a one-size-fits-all trust that's churned out with minimal, if any, supervision by an attorney. To entice you, they often use wildly inaccurate stories about the horrors of probate and oversell the advantages of living trusts, implying that once you die, your heirs will have little or nothing left to do to settle the estate (also not true).

The quality of these trusts is generally quite low. Clients have shown me trusts that don't have complete sentences or that just don't make sense. Some have come to me with trusts that don't have any assets in them, or the wrong ones. (An empty trust does nothing to avoid probate.)

Worse, some trust mills use seminars as a way to pry personal financial information out of you. They forward this information to insurance agents, who may contact and pressure you to try to buy inappropriate annuities and other insurance products that you don't need. (There's nothing wrong with an annuity, but many have big penalties for early withdrawals, offer high commissions to sales agents, and are inappropriate for seniors, who are often the target of these tactics.)

If you're approached by a low-cost trust operation, the California State Department of Justice, Attorney General, has helpful consumer information at https://oag.ca.gov/consumers/general/living_trust_mills and offers a form for reporting complaints here: https://oag.ca.gov/contact/consumer-complaint-against-business-or-company. The California State Department of Justice also recommends that you file complaints with the Consumer Fraud Section of your local district attorney. Here's how to find yours: www.cdaa.org/district-attorney-roster. They also recommend you file a complaint with the California Department of Insurance, www.insurance.ca.gov/01-consumers/101-help.

When working with a lawyer, here's what you'll be paying for:

- **Professional focus.** You'll have to get yourself organized because you're paying (a lot) for someone to sit down with you and think things through.
- **Project management.** A good lawyer will help you complete the estate planning process by setting deadlines and seeing that you meet them.
- **Guidance.** A lot of times, people aren't sure of the best way to structure things in a trust. For example, clients often ask me what an appropriate gift to a guardian might be or when a children's trust should end. Someone who has done hundreds of trusts can give you guidance on what might work best for your family.
- **Funding the trust.** Lawyers can help you with the transfer of assets into a trust (an extra step that isn't necessary when you just do a will). This is straightforward for most people, but figuring out which forms to get and how to fill them out makes some of us nuts.

How much does it cost to get a living trust drafted by an attorney? Costs vary widely across California, of course. But I've found that as a general rule, a trust will take about ten hours of a lawyer's time. So a lawyer who charges $300 an hour will prepare a trust for about $3,000. Someone who charges $400 an hour might charge you about $4,000 for a trust. Trusts that cost significantly less than this may be drafted by paralegals under only nominal supervision by attorneys. Trusts that cost a lot more are usually drafted by law firms that offer fancy tax expertise (and often, fabulous offices) that is useful for the very wealthy, but probably not for you.

See Chapter 13 for advice on finding and choosing an estate planning lawyer.

TIP

Shop around. When you're looking for an estate planner, make sure to ask whether the fee for a living trust includes the cost of preparing a will and durable powers of attorney for finance and health care (see Chapter 11 for more about those documents). These documents should all be created at the same time, so that your estate plan is comprehensive. Also ask whether the transfer of your house to the trust is included in the fee. If the attorney wants to charge on an hourly basis, ask them why they do that. Many planners work for a flat fee, which is more predictable and makes it easier for you to feel comfortable asking lots of questions (which you absolutely should).

Transferring Assets Into the Trust

After you've created a living trust, there's one more step: You've got to transfer certain assets into it. This is called funding the trust. This is different from what happens after you create a will. (Nothing actually happens after you create a will; you just store it somewhere really safe. When you die, the executor figures out what you owned, and the fun begins.) But a trust doesn't do you any good at all unless you transfer assets into it during your lifetime. If those assets are outside of the trust when you die, a probate proceeding will be necessary for them. Having an empty trust is a complete waste of time and money, but lots of people end up with one. It's the most common thing that people do wrong.

EXAMPLE: Fifteen years ago, Bertha set up a living trust and she named her sister, Meg, as the successor trustee (Bertha wanted to avoid making her three children go through the hassle of a probate proceeding). Bertha owned a house, a Fidelity investment account, savings and checking accounts, and an IRA. Bertha didn't much like her estate planning attorney, who made her feel stupid when she asked questions. She signed all the papers and promptly forgot about the whole thing.

When Bertha died, Meg went to a different estate planner to find out what she was supposed to do. After reviewing the title on the house and the statements for Bertha's accounts, the lawyer told Meg that Bertha hadn't transferred the house, the Fidelity account, or the bank accounts to the trust. Before any property could be transferred, Meg had to take the whole estate through probate.

What Goes Into a Trust

Transferring assets into a trust is a minor hassle, but it's not impossible. The first step is figuring out what goes into the trust. Not everything you own goes into a trust. Only your big-ticket items should be transferred to the trust, and not even all of those.

You only need to transfer the assets that you own that do not have a beneficiary designation or that are not held with some form of right of survivorship. That means that you are not going to have to transfer your retirement accounts, your life insurance policies, or any payable-on-death or transfer-on-death accounts. You are also not going to transfer your everyday checking accounts, because that's just a hassle and it won't trigger a probate if the balance is small. (You can transfer up to $150,000 outside of your trust without triggering a probate. Most everyday checking accounts hold $10,000 or less.) You are going to transfer what's left to the trust: your large bank accounts; your real property, such as your house; your investment accounts; your partnership interests; your stocks and bonds; and any other valuable asset that does not have a beneficiary designation. You should have these listed on your Net Worth Calculation Worksheet included in Chapter 1.

Transferring Property Into a Trust

If you want to transfer financial accounts to your trust, you have to notify the financial institutions that hold your money that you want to own the accounts as a trustee. They'll send you the proper forms to fill out. Banks will usually make you fill out their own forms. Generally, all of the forms require you to fill in the name of your trust, the date it was signed, the names of the trustees, and the Social Security number of one of the trustees (this is used as a tax ID number). You won't have to file separate tax returns for your living trust, but all financial institutions want a tax ID number, anyway.

To transfer a house into a trust, you have to file a deed that transfers ownership to yourself(ves) as trustee(s). If you work with an estate planner they'll usually file the deed for you. Some planners also transfer accounts for you, though often for an extra fee. Don't pay it; you can do it yourself.

EXAMPLE: Eduardo and Maria signed their living trust. Then they transferred their house in San Francisco into the trust by filing a deed with the county recorder in San Francisco County. Now the deed identifies the owners as "Eduardo Gonzales and Maria Sanchez Gonzales, as trustees of the Gonzales Family Trust, dated November 28, 20xx." They also transferred their Fidelity brokerage account to the trust by filling out a trust account application that they downloaded from the Fidelity website. Now their statements are sent to "Eduardo and Maria Gonzales, TTE" (that stands for trustee).

Finally, Eduardo and Maria transferred their large savings account at the credit union to themselves as trustees by filling out a form at the credit union. Those statements also come to "Eduardo and Maria Gonzales, TTE." They don't bother to transfer their everyday checking account, which rarely holds more than $5,000.

You can't transfer any assets into the trust until you've signed and notarized the trust agreement. That makes sense, since a bank or other financial institution wouldn't let you transfer an account to something that doesn't yet exist. When you're creating a trust, just gather the forms you'll need. That way, you can sign the trust and fill out the forms at the same time, while you're thinking about it. People make more of the hassle factor than necessary. If you have enough assets to require a trust, you're smart enough to fund and maintain one.

Pour-Over Wills

If you decide to create a living trust, do you still need a will? Yes. But it will be a slightly different from the one in Chapter 2. That will, called a "standalone will," is designed to be your main estate planning document. It instructs the executor to do the big jobs—divide up your assets properly and manage them for your children until they mature.

If you create a trust, though, you'll create a will, called a "pour-over" will, that is coordinated with the trust. The two legal documents have to be consistent—otherwise, your loved ones will have a mess on their hands. You don't want the trust leaving property to one person and the will leaving the same property to someone else. If you have a will already, don't worry; it's easy to create a new one. Any will states right at the beginning that you are revoking your previous will. (But also destroy the old one. That way there won't be any confusion about which one's valid.)

When you use a living trust to transfer property to your loved ones, suddenly the will has a lot less work to do. One way to think of the relationship between the two documents is to think of the trust as a cup, holding your biggest assets to avoid probate, and the will as a saucer. It simply catches any property that doesn't make it into the trust and instructs the executor to pour it into the trust upon your death. This kind of will is called a pour-over will.

A pour-over will has three main jobs: getting property into the trust, nominating guardians (if necessary), and nominating an executor.

How a Pour-Over Will Gets Property Into the Trust

The will's first big job is to get property into the trust. A pour-over will directs the executor to transfer all the property that you own that's outside the trust into the trust after you die. That way, just one document (the trust) says who gets what. As long as the property that's outside of the trust isn't large enough to require a probate proceeding, transferring these assets is an easy task. If you forgot to put a big asset into the trust, though, the executor might have to go through probate to transfer that asset to the trust. And that, of course, wipes out the benefits you were hoping to get by using a living trust in the first place.

If the total value of the assets outside of the trust (not counting retirement and other assets that will transfer by beneficiary designation) is less than $150,000, your successor trustee can transfer them with what's called a small estate's affidavit. But if the value of the property outside of the trust is worth more than $150,000, they'll have to probate those assets.

EXAMPLE 1: Parker created a living trust before he died. He transferred his house and his investment account to the trust but he forgot to transfer in one account that he held at a local bank. After his death, his trustee, Nick, had to bring the bank a small estates affidavit that said that Parker's assets were not going through probate and that he was the successor trustee of Parker's trust. Because the bank account held less than $150,000, Nick did not have to go through probate to transfer that one account.

EXAMPLE 2: Bertha, the settlor who died with an empty trust (mentioned earlier in this chapter), left her trustee and executor, Meg, with a bit of a mess on her hands. Meg has to hire an attorney to probate Bertha's house, Fidelity account, and checking and savings accounts because the total value of those three assets was $990,000. At the end of the probate, these assets are transferred to Bertha's trust, and then Meg can distribute them in equal shares to her nieces and nephews. This process might take a year and will cost Bertha's beneficiaries thousands of dollars in fees. Most of the time and money could have been saved had Bertha properly funded her trust.

Nominating Guardians in a Pour-Over Will

The will's second big job is to nominate guardians for your minor children. That's the job most parents are most worried about. You can't do this in a living trust; it takes a will.

Nominating Executors in a Pour-Over Will

The will's third big job is to nominate executors. Your pour-over will names an executor and at least one backup executor. If you have a trust and fund it properly, your executor is not going to have to take your estate through probate. But the executor must still file an income tax return, pay debts and expenses, and take care of the logistics that are necessary after any death. Most people name the same person as executor and trustee, but they don't have to be the same person.

Who Creates the Pour-Over Will

If you hire a lawyer to draft a living trust, make sure that you also receive a pour-over will with it. If you decide to do it yourself, make sure that you also create a backup will, to leave any property outside of the trust to those you designate.

A backup will does a lot of what a pour-over will does. It names guardians and executors and deals with any property that you have outside of a trust. Instead of pouring into the trust, though, it just leaves the property to those you name in the will directly. One set of rules governs the trust assets and the will says who gets everything else. That also works. As long as your will doesn't conflict with your trust, it gets your property to the right people, and that's the most important thing.

Estate Planning for Minor Children: Choosing a Guardian

Get It Done 93

What Guardians Are (and Are Not) Responsible For.................................... 94

Court Approval and Oversight of Guardians... 96

Picking the Right Guardian 97

    The Ideal Guardian... 98

    Making Your List of Potential Guardians 102

    Narrowing Down Your Choices 103

Common Problems and Some Solutions 106

    Your First Choice Is Older Than You Are... 106

    Your First Choice Is Not a Good Money Manager 107

    You Don't Like Your First Choice's Spouse..107

    Your First Choice Lives Far Away...108

    You Have Children From Previous Marriages....................................109

    You Don't Want Your Ex-Spouse or Partner to Get Custody 110

    Your Family Doesn't Like Your Choices 111

    You Worry That Your Children Won't Like Your Choices..................... 113

After You've Chosen a Guardian: Talking It Over.. 113

Giving Guardians Some Written Guidance 115

Congratulate Yourself on Choosing a Guardian! 117

Read this chapter if:

• You have minor children.

• You don't know whom to name as a guardian.

• You aren't sure that you've named the right person as guardian.

• You want to know more about what guardians do, and how courts are involved in California.

• You want to make sure your guardian has important information about your kids.

Picking trusted adults who will take care of your children if you can't is the most important (and often the most difficult) estate planning task for parents of minor children. You'll do this as part of writing your will (the focus of Chapter 2).

This chapter covers some strategies that might help you choose the right guardian for your children and explains how guardians are appointed in California, so that you understand the process. If you are nervous about picking anyone, or just plain *hate* the idea of having to make a decision about who would raise your children to adulthood, that's pretty normal. It's horrible to imagine dying before your children grow up. And it's not easy picking someone to do your job as parent.

But here's the thing that I tell my clients: No one is in a better position than you are to make these tough decisions. You gain nothing by procrastinating or avoiding this task altogether. Instead, if you don't choose a guardian, and the choice ever needs to be made, you simply lose control over a decision that could have a huge influence on your children's lives. If you don't nominate someone, a judge will make that choice, and the judge doesn't know your brother (or his wife) like you do. And it's not like whatever you decide is written in stone—you can change your mind and nominate a new guardian at any time by changing your will.

Single-Parent Households in California

If you are a single parent, you are not alone. In California, 34% of children are being raised in single-parent households, the majority of which are headed by single moms.

Get It Done

For many of my estate planning clients with young children, the difficulty of picking a guardian is the single biggest reason for not getting their will and other estate planning done. It's just too hard to think about the unlikely scenario of dying while your kids are young—and emotionally too wrenching to imagine needing a guardian, let alone naming one (plus a backup or two).

Hopefully, you'll discover, as many of my clients have, that making an estate plan and choosing a guardian for your children actually reduces your anxiety about dying when your children are young. There's something about making a contingency plan that can be comforting. You still can't control untimely fate, but you can be secure in knowing that you've done everything you can to make sure that your children would be safe and well cared for if the unexpected did happen.

So think hard about estate planning for a while, and once you're done putting some key decisions in writing, move on to other, more rewarding plans, like your next vacation or how to redo the living room.

TIP

Californians plan ahead. While choosing a guardian is not quite the same as having fire or flood insurance or keeping an earthquake preparedness kit in the back shed, the idea is similar: Be prepared. And remember that making plans doesn't make it more likely that disaster will actually happen. If you're prone to anxiety and catastrophizing, now's a good time to take a deep breath and remind yourself that planning ahead is the best (and only) way to ensure that your wishes will be known and that, to the greatest extent possible, you will have some control over the process of naming guardians for your minor children.

What Guardians Are (and Are Not) Responsible For

If a child has two parents, and one dies, the survivor carries on as the sole parent if he or she is willing and able to do so. But if both parents die together, or if a single parent dies or can't raise a child, someone must be legally responsible for the child. That person is known as the "guardian of the person." When I use the term personal guardian, or just guardian, in this book, I am referring to the guardian of the person—the person with custodial responsibility for a minor child.

There's also a guardian that can be appointed to manage your child's money (or the money of any child who's a beneficiary of your estate) to age 18, called the "guardian of the estate" or property guardian. Often, the same person is appointed to both jobs: guardian of the person and guardian of the estate. This chapter focuses on personal guardians, while Chapter 5 covers property guardians.

A guardian of the person has the legal authority and responsibility to care for a child, just as a parent does. The guardian's job is to provide a child's food, shelter, education, and medical care and to ensure the child's safety, security, and comfort until the child turns 18. And guardians of the person, like parents, are legally responsible if children under their control hurt another person or damage their property because they weren't supervised properly.

EXAMPLE: Shae is the guardian of her 10-year-old niece, Shelby. Shelby had to move from her home in Long Beach to Shae's home in Glendale after her parents passed away. Shae is responsible for making sure that Shelby gets to school every day and is well fed and well taken care of. If Shelby is having difficulty adjusting to her new school, it is Shae's job to call the principal, discuss matters with Shelby's teachers, and take any other action that would be appropriate for a parent to take in the same situation.

Legal responsibilities aside, guardians of the person, like parents, also end up having a lot of influence over a child's many day-to-day experiences. If your children are ever cared for by a guardian, the guardian will be the one to decide which movies your children watch, which activities they engage in (including how much screen time they have), what food they eat (and don't), and whom they spend time with. Guardians (like parents) would also influence the big decisions your children will make, such as where to go to college, what kind of jobs to take, and whom to marry.

Although guardians are responsible for the general safety and well-being of the minor children in their care, usually called wards, guardians are not legally responsible for their wards' financial support. What that means is that guardians don't have to spend their own money to take care of their wards and can apply for public assistance programs on behalf of them.

Hopefully, your children won't ever be in that situation, though, because you are doing important financial planning for them right now—for example by setting up a trust or custodial account for your children (as explained in Chapter 5). In fact, a guardian of the estate only needs to be appointed to manage your children's money to age 18 if you haven't put a trust in place to manage their money for them in your will or trust, and only if the children inherit more than $5,000 directly (an amount set by California law). One of the main benefits of putting together an estate plan is that you can use trusts to manage money for children until they are old enough to manage that money for themselves, which, for most kids, is long past age 18, the age when a guardianship has to end in California.

Court Approval and Oversight of Guardians

It's a judge's job (in a probate court proceeding) to give the people you've chosen the legal authority to serve as guardians, if it's ever necessary. Guardianship proceedings happen in the probate division of the superior court in the relevant county. Judges give the people you name in your will priority over anyone else. A court would still, however, need to make sure that your nominated guardians would do a good job. In California, that means that there would be a court-ordered investigation of the prospective guardian's background and home before the judge made the formal appointment. These investigations will include a background check and a home visit. The court investigator would then file a report with the judge about the suitability of the nominated guardian.

California law requires the judge to act in the best interest of the minor and to take into account the ability of the guardian to manage and preserve the minor's estate and the guardian's concern for and interest in the welfare of the minor. This is all quite vague, but the court-ordered investigation would include items like these:

- the love and affection between the child and the proposed guardian
- the capacity of the proposed guardian to provide a loving, stable home
- the mental and physical health of the proposed guardian
- the guardian's moral fitness, and
- the child's preference.

By and large, once a personal guardian has been appointed and approved by a judge, the court steps out of the picture and does not supervise the situation closely. Generally, a guardian must file annual status reports with the courts in California, reviewing how well the children are doing and where they're living and alerting the court to any changes that have occurred since the guardian was appointed—for example, moving to another county.

California state law determines the rules, but there are a few things that usually require the guardian to get the court's approval. For example, a guardian would need to get court permission before moving a child out of state. And a family member who felt that a guardian wasn't taking adequate care of a child could ask the court to terminate the guardianship and appoint someone else.

RESOURCE
For helpful information on the guardianship process in California, see www.courts.ca.gov/selfhelp-guardianship.htm, the "Guardianship" section of the California Courts Judicial Branch website. This offers an overview of the process of becoming a guardian, a guardian's rights and duties, and helpful links to the necessary forms to get the process started.

Picking the Right Guardian

You know that there is no one on the face of the earth capable of fully replacing you as a parent. Still, you've got to do the best you can. This means picking two, and preferably three, people to nominate as guardians. These are people who you believe will be able to give your children a loving home, share your values, and get the kids to school, to the doctor, and anywhere else they need to be, until they are legal adults. You should choose more than one person because you want to make sure that you have a backup or two, just in case your first choice isn't available if the need ever arises.

What About Godparents?

Godparents are important people in many children's religious lives. But they have no special legal standing. If you want to nominate your children's godparent as a guardian, you must do so in your will.

The Ideal Guardian

The first step in choosing a guardian for your children is to sit down and write out all the qualities that you'd like to find in your ideal guardian, such as their financial situation, religious affiliation, and where they live. Then rank each of these qualities on a scale of 1 to 10. (You can assign the same rank to more than one quality.) Although you aren't likely to find all those qualities in any one person—possibly not even in yourself—your list will help you see which qualities you are willing to compromise on and which ones are not negotiable.

If you are raising your child with the other parent, it's a good idea for you to make separate lists. That way, each of you will be able to think about what matters most to you as an individual. After you've come up with your lists, you can compare them and see whether you can agree on at least the most important guardianship qualities and values. Your first lists may look very different—but don't see the divorce lawyer yet. It may take some time and effort, but you'll almost certainly be able to agree on a few important qualities, if not all.

Even though you and your child's other parent will each make your own separate will, it's important to pick the same guardians, so that there's no confusion about what you both want for your children. Even divorced parents, if they can communicate amicably, should try and pick the same guardians for their children.

The best reason to do this is that many children want to know who they would go to should the unthinkable happen and you and your child's other parent die at the same time; it gives children a feeling of security. And it's nice for them to know that both parents agree on these choices. It also prevents confusion over whom to name as a guardian if parents name different people in their wills and then die at the same time.

If you feel that it is appropriate for your children, you might broach this subject by telling them that you are making a plan, just in case someone else would need to take care of them. You might ask your children how they would feel if Uncle Bob was that person, or how they would feel about moving to another state or attending another school if you were not able to take care of them. Listen to what your children have to say about this—you might find out that your kids have different ideas of what might work for them than you do. Obviously, the older your children are, the more likely they are to want to stay in their schools, with their friends. You might name guardians that work now, and revisit your choices as your children mature.

If parents don't die at the same time, the surviving parent's will controls where the children would go next—so the last parent surviving is the one who really has control over guardianship. But naming the same guardians avoids the possibility of an ugly challenge to a guardianship appointment at the second parent's death by the people named in the first parent's will.

I've included an example here of how Judy, a single mom with three children, ages six to 12, ranked what was important to her in terms of an ideal guardian. For purposes of this example, assume that the children's father is deceased. If Judy was still married, she and her husband would each fill out the Ideal Guardian section of the Planning for Minor Children Worksheet included in this book.

Planning for Minor Children

Use this worksheet to record your choice for guardian and trustee for any money you wish to leave to children.

I. Ideal Guardian

Quality	Why It's Important to Me	Rank (10=essential; 1=no big deal)
Patience	A parenting skill required on a daily basis	10
Sense of humor	An even MORE important parenting skill	10
Enough money	To take care of my children's needs	8
Spiritual outlook/religious affiliation like mine	To give my children perspective	6
Has children	To give my children companions	3
Doesn't have children	To give my children adequate attention	3
Member of my family	So that they stay close to grandparents and other relatives	1
Lives close by	So that my children don't have to move far from their friends	6
Loved by my children	Because my children need to be happy	10
Values education	So that my children complete college	7
Lives a healthy lifestyle	So that my children learn to eat and exercise properly	7
Is politically aware and active	Because I am, and it is important to me that my children learn to be activists	3
Loves sports	Because I love sports and they have been important in my life	6
Reads all the time	Because I do	7
Is already a parent	Because I want someone who has already proven that they can deal with the ups and downs of parenting	7

II. Potential Guardians		
Person	**Best Quality/Value**	**Major Drawbacks**
Sister Anna	Very patient; kids love her	Lives across the country
Friend Carl	Spiritually like me; funny	Single, not living in one place long; doesn't live a healthy lifestyle
Brother Joe and sister-in-law Alicia	Live nearby; kids love them; big dog to play with; she coaches soccer and volleyball	Small house; struggling financially; will have their own children soon
My parents	Financially well-off; patient; close to the children	In late 70s; no other children nearby; don't like their politics
Sister Cristina	Financially well-off; funny; patient; shares my religion	Husband not someone that I want my children to live with
Brother-in-law Charles and sister-in-law Lois	Have two kids close in age to mine; both patient and kind	Live in another country
Friend Madeline	Is loved by my kids; has three children and many cats and dogs; funny and patient; values education highly	Bad at managing money

III. Guardians for My Children

First choice: __Madeline__

Second choice: __Brother Joe (will make gift)__

Third choice: __Sister Anna__

FORM

Planning for Minor Children Worksheet. The Nolo website includes a downloadable copy of the Planning for Minor Children Worksheet for you to list and rank the qualities that are important to you in choosing a guardian, as well as the names of potential guardians who meet your criteria. See the appendix for the link to this worksheet and other forms in this book.

Making Your List of Potential Guardians

After you've listed the qualities and values that matter the most to you, your next job is to try to identify people who possess some of them and could serve as guardians. Again, if there are two parents, each parent should make a list and then compare it with the other's. For now, just brainstorm all the likely possibilities without analyzing or eliminating, even though all of your candidates will probably fall short in one important way or another. (If you can't think of anyone, take a look at "Common Problems and Some Solutions," below, for help.)

When you make your list of potential guardians, think of individuals, not couples. If you want to name a couple to serve as guardians together, you can do that. But if a couple was ever to split up after being appointed as guardians, one of them would have to resign as guardian or they'd have to negotiate what would happen to your children as part of their divorce settlement. In the worst case, your children could be the subject of a custody fight. To avoid that, you can name just one person who would remain the guardian even if there were a divorce.

An example of the list of potential guardians that Judy came up with (and the pros and cons of each person) is shown above. (See the Potential Guardians section of the Planning for Minor Children Worksheet (see sample above) included in this book.)

Special Concerns for Same-Sex Couples

If you are raising children with a gay partner, the best estate planning strategy is to make sure that you are both the legal parents of your children. Marrying and then adopting any children born prior to the marriage is the easiest way to do this. That way, if one of you died, the surviving partner would be the remaining legal parent, and there would be no need for a court to get involved or name a guardian. In California, stepparent adoption is simpler and less expensive than regular adoptions—the spouse of a custodial parent can petition to adopt the minor children of their spouse.

If the second parent can't adopt or just hasn't done it yet, the legal parent should name the second parent as the guardian. Otherwise, if the legal parent dies, the survivor might not get legal custody.

RESOURCE
For more information on gay and lesbian parents and guardianship, see *A Legal Guide for Lesbian & Gay Couples*, by Denis Clifford, Frederick Hertz, and Emily Doskow (Nolo).

For useful resources and information on gay families, check out the websites of the National Center for Lesbian Rights (www.nclrights.org/our-work/family-relationships/family-relationships-resources) and Rainbow Babies (www.therainbowbabies.com/Links.html).

Narrowing Down Your Choices

Once you've identified the values that matter most to you and made a list of potential guardians, it is time to narrow your choices. First, eliminate anyone whose drawbacks are just too big.

EXAMPLE: Because Judy would not want her children to live with her sister Cristina's husband, she crosses Cristina off her potential guardian's list. She also crosses off her parents. Much as Judy loves them, and much as her children love their grandparents, she doesn't feel that two people in their late 70s should, or could, raise three active children. Judy has mixed feelings about her sister Anna, who lives across the country—Judy's oldest child is just beginning middle school, and moving so far away from his friends seems like too much of a burden to put on him.

Now you're probably getting down to the final few people on your list of potential guardians. If, at this point, you feel like giving up completely, hang in there. Remember, no one can replace you as a parent (even if there are times when your kids think that pretty much anyone else on earth would do). Choosing a guardian is always a second-best choice, but it is still one that you can make better than anyone else. Take a look back at your list of qualities and values and focus on the qualities that you ranked as a 9 or 10.

Now, try to choose two or three people from the names remaining on the list who bring at least one, if not more, of your most important qualities to the job. It's easy to get bogged down by all of the things that these people are not. Most important, of course, they're not you. But their names wouldn't be on your lists if they weren't also special to you and your family in some important ways.

If no one left on the list of potential guardians is the obvious choice, pick the person you feel most loves your children and that your children most love. Don't judge the answers you get; just listen to what your heart tells you to do.

EXAMPLE: One couple I know (I'll call them Sofia and Lucas) spent years trying to decide which of their sisters to choose as guardians. All of the couple's sisters were lovely, but all of them had some drawbacks. One lived too far away. One had three kids already. One had children already grown and out of the house. One was struggling financially. So Sofia and Lucas did nothing and had no estate plan at all.

One day, as the couple was about to go to the hospital for the birth of their third child, Sofia's best friend, whom she'd known since high school, arrived to take their other two children to stay at her house. The children hugged their parents goodbye and clambered into her car. As the friend backed out of the driveway, with the children waving away and grinning tearfully, Sofia and Lucas both knew suddenly that the friend, not one of their sisters, was the right person to name as guardian. After that, writing their wills was easy. (They had the baby first, though.)

Your Choice Is Not Set in Stone

Making a choice that works for the next three to five years is much better than doing nothing at all. Depending on your children's ages, you can—and should—reevaluate your decisions in five years, anyway. As your children grow and your relationships with family and friends change, your guardianship choices may very well change, too.

And if you still feel less than certain about your decision, remember that you can always amend your will (see Chapter 12 for advice) to change these names as your children get older, as your friends' and family's lives change, or for any other reason.

After you make your choices, write them down. There's a place, called Guardians for My Children, to record the names of your first, second, and third choices at the end of the Planning for Minor Children Worksheet, see the sample above. But before you get too excited, be sure your choices are willing to take on this responsibility in the unlikely event they need to do so (see "After You've Chosen a Guardian: Talking It Over," below, for advice on the subject).

But if you've gotten this far and still can't figure out who to pick, read "Common Problems and Some Solutions," below, to see whether any of those ideas can help break the logjam. If none of them do, here's my advice: Pick someone anyway. Make yourself choose at least one guardian and get your will done, and resolve to revisit your decision in a year. If the decision is this hard for you, you don't want to place it in the hands of a judge. And remember: This is not a permanent decision. See "Your Choice Is Not Set in Stone," above.

Common Problems and Some Solutions

If, despite your best efforts, you find yourself really stuck on whom to name as guardian, it might be because you've run into one of the problems listed below. These go beyond the "nobody's perfect" problem. If you've hit one of these, you're probably not being persnickety. Your problem is that, for one reason or another, *nobody* on the list is a likely candidate. Solving your problem will take some creativity, determination, and flexibility. Read on for some tips that may help.

Your First Choice Is Older Than You Are

Solution: Forget about what could happen in ten years; just pick someone now and reevaluate in five years.

Many parents find it easier to come up with potential guardians if they focus on who could take care of their young children in the next three to five years, knowing that they can change their guardian choices as their children, and the nominated guardians, grow older. When children are young, grandparents and other family members are often the best choice. But as children grow up, they become increasingly connected to their own friends and community and don't want to move away from their homes. And grandparents aren't usually the guardians of choice for teenagers. Remember, right now you're choosing someone for the next few years only. When some time has passed, you can reevaluate and make changes.

EXAMPLE: Phillip and Clara have two young sons, aged one and four. They live in Los Angeles. Clara's parents, who are in their mid-60s, are in good health and live in Raleigh, North Carolina, where Clara grew up. Phillip and Clara think that for now, Clara's parents would be the best possible guardians for their boys. They agree to name them as guardians now and to revisit that choice in no longer than ten years, when the boys will be 11 and 14.

Your First Choice Is Not a Good Money Manager

Solution: Name someone else to handle the finances.

Sometimes parents hesitate because the person they like best for personal guardian is not a good money manager. That problem is easily fixed. You can name someone else to manage your children's money and leave the guardian with only the job of making sure your child grows up well cared for and as happy as possible. (Naming a guardian of the estate is covered in Chapter 5.)

EXAMPLE: Bernard's sister, Hailey, has a terrific relationship with his two daughters, aged six and eight. Hailey would make a wonderful guardian—except that Bernard is concerned that Hailey wouldn't do a good job managing the money he'd be leaving for the girls (Hailey would spend it all on treats and fancy toys and clothes). So Bernard names Hailey as the personal guardian for his girls but he puts his sister-in-law, Jasmine, in charge of their money. Jasmine's job would be to manage the money, letting Hailey focus on providing a loving home for the girls.

You Don't Like Your First Choice's Spouse

Solution: Name the individual, not the couple.

What if only one person in a couple is your choice for guardian? Just name the person you want—not both of them—as guardians. That way, if the couple divorced, your kids would stay with the person you feel closest to.

EXAMPLE: Jon wants to nominate his sister Suzanne as the guardian of his three children but would not want Suzanne's husband, David, to ever have legal responsibility over them. The solution to this is to name only Shirley, not David, as a guardian. As long as Suzanne and David are married, the children would live with both of them, but if Suzanne and David were to divorce (as Jon secretly hopes that they will), the children would stay with Suzanne.

Of course, if you are certain that you wouldn't want your child to live with the spouse you don't like, then you'll have to name someone else entirely. If you object to the person that strongly, it's going to be a deal-breaker.

Your First Choice Lives Far Away

Solution: Name a temporary guardian in addition to a permanent guardian.

With today's scattered families, it's common to want to name a guardian who lives in a different state than California or even another country. There's no requirement that a guardian live where you live, but as part of the court proceeding in which a judge appoints a child's guardian, a nonresident may have to post a bond (a sum of money or an insurance policy) as insurance that they will faithfully perform their duties as a guardian. In addition, an out-of-state guardian would have to ask the court in the county where the probate proceeding is occurring to move the guardianship proceeding to the state where he or she lives. This means more hassle (and more lawyer's fees), but it is something that courts will approve if it makes sense for the child.

For international guardianship (covered in Chapter 6), the guardians living in another country will have to ask the court here (that is, in California) to name them as temporary guardians, and then travel back to their home country and ask a court there to appoint them as permanent guardians. Once that's in place, the guardian would notify the court in California and terminate that initial, temporary guardianship.

If you want to name someone far away as a guardian, it also makes sense to nominate someone local who could serve as a temporary guardian. This person could take care of your children until your permanent guardian could get to them. You can do this by stating in your will that you want the named person to serve as a temporary guardian, if that's ever necessary.

EXAMPLE: Veronica lives in Eureka. She has three minor daughters. She has nominated her sister, Ariana, who lives in Italy, as guardian. Veronica nominates her neighbor and good friend, Timothy, to serve as a temporary guardian to take care of the girls until Ariana can travel to Eureka.

You Have Children From Previous Marriages

Solution: Focus on the needs of your children. You may end up naming different guardians for different children.

Blended families are common these days, making guardianship choices even more complicated. Some parents name different guardians for the children of different marriages. Others make a plan that would keep all the children together. The only rule of thumb is to do what's right for the children. Remember that guardianship doesn't come into play at all if a child has a surviving parent, and that's more likely when their parents are not living or traveling together.

EXAMPLE: Lynda and Harold both have children from previous marriages. Lynda has a teenage daughter, Isabel, who lives with her and sees her father in the summer. Harold has a teenage son, Justin, who lives part time with his mother and part time at Harold's house. Lynda and Harold also have two young children, Richard and Will, together.

In her will, Lynda nominates her best friend, Daisy, as guardian for Isabel, in case Isabel's father couldn't, or wouldn't, take custody of her. Lynda also nominates her sister-in-law, Alyssa, as the guardian for her little ones, Richard and Will, in case she and Harold die before the boys grow up. Lynda doesn't name a guardian for Justin, who is her stepson.

In his will, Harold nominates his brother, Henry, as a back-up guardian for Justin. He also nominates his sister, Alyssa, as the guardian of Richard and Will. Harold does not name a guardian for Isabel, who is his stepdaughter.

You Don't Want Your Ex-Spouse or Partner to Get Custody

Solution: Name a guardian and state in your will why your ex shouldn't get custody.

If you're divorced, you may be unhappy with the idea that should you die first, your ex-spouse would get custody of your children. If you never married, you might be equally unhappy with your former partner having custody of your child. That's the reality, though, with just a few exceptions. A court could deny custody to a parent who has abandoned or abused children. Or a parent could agree that another person, such as a stepfather, could serve as the child's guardian. But such situations are rare.

If you really don't want your ex-spouse or partner to take custody of your children, you can explain why in your will. Wills, however, are public documents after someone dies, so you might not want to put such personal information in yours. One alternative is to write a letter stating your reasons for not wanting your former spouse or partner to get custody. Include court records, police reports, or any other evidence of your ex's unsuitability as a custodial parent. Give that letter to your first choice for a guardian, to be used in the case of a court proceeding as evidence of your wishes.

EXAMPLE: Connor is a divorced father of a five-year-old son, Ethan. He has sole custody of Ethan and is not on good terms with Martina, his ex-wife, whom he believes has a drug abuse problem. In his will, Connor nominates his sister, Amelia, and his brother-in-law, Brent, as guardians for Ethan. Connor states in his will that it is his wish that Martina not be granted custody of Ethan. He also writes a letter stating his reasons. In it, Connor details his experience with Martina's drug abuse. He gives the letter to Amelia and Brent and tells them to use it (in court) if Martina tries to get custody of Ethan.

Your Family Doesn't Like Your Choices

Solution: Explain your wishes in writing.

You may want to make a guardian choice that you're pretty sure your family wouldn't support. Whether it is because you've adopted a different religion or moved to California, or because you are gay and your family doesn't approve of your partner or friends, this can be a painful part of estate planning.

Your first loyalty is to your children, and you should always make the choices that you think will serve them best. You should also know that a court challenge to your choice of guardian is very unlikely in California—and very unlikely to succeed. A family member who wanted to overturn your choice of guardian would have to go to probate court and prove to the judge that there was a very good reason—say, a child abuse conviction—to set your choice aside.

Still, for the sake of your children, it's best to prevent conflict and preserve family relations as much as you can. One way to address possible family dissent is to simply discuss the issue with those family members you most fear will oppose your choice of guardian. You might be favorably surprised at their reaction.

Whether or not your fears turn out to be well-grounded, it's good to leave a written explanation of your choices for guardian. It can calm tension later, when family members have different recollections of what you told them. And if necessary (again, this is very unlikely), your written explanation could be used in court. After all, if there ever is an argument, you won't be around to defend your choices.

Of course, deciding what to do is a personal choice, which depends on your family members and your relationship with them. Doing nothing is a common choice—the prospect of a family fight over guardianship can be paralyzing. But making some effort now may save a lot of heartache later.

Here are a few different techniques to consider.

Write a letter to family members. In the letter, explain why you feel that your choices are best for your children and ask your family to respect your wishes. Make sure to label the letter so that it's clear it's to be opened only in the event of your death. Keep it with your estate planning documents.

Write a letter to the person you've chosen to be the guardian. Explain in detail all the reasons why you don't want certain people in your family to be granted guardianship and give this letter to your guardian, to be used as evidence in a court proceeding in the future, if necessary.

Put your reasons in the will itself. You can go into as much detail as you want, but keep in mind that your will is going to be a public document upon your death.

EXAMPLE: Matthew and his husband, Gary, who live in Oakland, have a three-year-old daughter, Chandler. They have both adopted her. Matthew and Gary feel that if it were ever necessary, Chandler should be raised by Gary's sister Kyra and her husband, who also live in the East Bay. But Matthew believes that his mother, Victoria, would fight his wishes in court if she didn't get custody of Chandler, whom she adores. Matthew feels that Victoria would only be hurt by any discussion of this issue now (and, of course, he expects to live long past Chandler's 18th birthday). So Matthew decides to write a letter to his mother, to be opened only if he and Gary die before Chandler is an adult, explaining that he and Gary love Victoria very much but want Chandler to grow up in a household on the West Coast, with other children, in a community that is more supportive of gay parents than the one that Victoria lives in (in Texas).

SEE AN EXPERT

Get help now if you fear a challenge later. If you think that there is a serious possibility that someone in your family would contest your guardianship nominations, you should see an estate planning attorney, who can help you design an estate plan to withstand such a challenge.

You Worry That Your Children Won't Like Your Choices

Solution: Talk it over with them.

If you are worried that your children won't like your nominations for guardians, you might want to discuss it with them, especially if your children are already in their teens. Even younger children, though, often have opinions about this and sometimes are comforted in knowing who would take care of them if parents couldn't. Also, in California, children 14 or older may ask the court for a different guardian from the one nominated by their parents. The judge will take their wishes into account along with other factors.

After You've Chosen a Guardian: Talking It Over

After you've narrowed your list down to two (or even better, three) people, you need to ask them whether they'd be willing to serve as your children's guardians. (You don't, of course, need to tell your other friends and family that you haven't chosen them, unless you feel that will help them accept your choices. Boundless candor is not always the best policy.) But if you are worried that people won't understand the choices you've made, you might consider leaving a letter behind, to be opened only in the event of your death, in which you explain why you choose the guardians that you did, and to express your wish that your family respect your choices.

It's really important to have this conversation with the people you've chosen—*before* you list them as guardians in your will. You might find out that they've already agreed to serve as guardians for other friends or family and feel uncomfortable taking on another potential obligation. You might learn that your ideal guardian is going to need more financial assistance to make a blended family work than you thought. Hopefully you're going to provide money for your children's needs, but if the guardian needs a bigger house or a car, you'll need to do some planning to make sure that you can provide that for them also.

How should you bring this up? Try being direct. Find a quiet moment and mention that you are doing estate planning. Say that you would like to know if your relative or friend would be willing to be named as a guardian in your will. Let them know that you thought long and hard about it and made the choice because you love them, or that your children do, and let them know why you chose them. Was it because of their values? Where they live? Your history together? It can be one of many factors, but it is helpful to share your decision-making process with your guardian choices so that they better understand why you want them for the job.

But also make it clear that you understand that this is a big responsibility, even though the odds of their being needed to take on the job of guardian are, thankfully, low. Make it clear that "no" is an acceptable answer, and find out whether there's anything that you can do to make the prospect of being your children's guardian easier. Maybe you could take out more life insurance or arrange things so that if your relative or friend became guardian, they could live in your house until your children are mature. Assuming that you've also created a will or a trust, your guardian's just going to have the custodial job, not the job of also managing your child's inheritance.

You may find out that your choices for guardian haven't done any estate planning themselves (many people haven't). You might find out that they've been meaning to ask you to be the guardian of their children. Or you might find out that there are reasons why you shouldn't choose them as guardians, reasons that you would never have known if you hadn't had the conversation. Truthfully, there's no downside to this chat. You really have to have it if you're going to feel comfortable with the decision you've made. And, of course, you want to make sure that your guardian is more than willing to take on this responsibility. Honestly, if you're not comfortable with the conversation, maybe you need to reconsider your choice.

TIP

Hit the road. Before you finalize your choice of guardian, think about taking a short vacation with your first-choice candidates, even if it's just a quick trip to the beach or mountains. I can't tell you how many times clients have chosen guardians during our initial interview, then called the next week and changed their minds after a disastrous weekend together. Sometimes, when you're really trying to visualize someone else as your child's guardian, you'll see things about their parenting style that you just didn't notice before.

Giving Guardians Some Written Guidance

Now that you've chosen your guardians and discussed this with them, you might also want to write a letter to your potential guardians, explaining why you chose them and what you hope they will be able to do for your children. Or you might record a video in which you can say why you chose them for the job. This letter or video is to be opened or viewed only in the event that someday they're appointed (which means that you're not there to discuss things). Sometimes the very thought of this letter/video to potential guardians brings parents to tears. If you feel that way, don't write it. (And please don't beat yourself up about not doing this. Feel good that you've managed to pick a guardian at all.) But if writing down your thoughts and feelings will make you feel good and provide some guidance to the guardians, now's an ideal time to do it.

Below are the kinds of things you might want to include in a letter or video.

Your reasons for choosing the person as your child's guardian. If you have chosen a friend, not a family member, explain why. This section is important if you think that your family might contest your choice. But it's always a good thing to let your family know that you thought long and hard about this and to explain why you decided as you did.

What you want them to know about your kids. Here's where you can write down any special instructions on how you want your children raised, such as lessons in violin, karate, or surfing, travel to certain places, and important family rituals or connections.

Your feelings about education. If you have strong feelings about how your children should be educated, let the guardians know. Some parents want their children to go to certain high schools or colleges; others have strong feelings about graduate schools or other professional programs. Still others want their children to travel a lot and not over-obsess about going to college right out of high school.

Your feelings about religious education or faith. If it is important to you that your children maintain their ties to a particular church or congregation, rabbi, or minister, let the guardian know. If you want your children to celebrate certain life events, like a confirmation, bar mitzvah, or quinceanera, that's important to share.

Your wishes concerning your children's relationships with extended family. If you want your children to visit Costa Rica to see their grandparents every year, let the guardian know. If there are certain family members that you do not want your children to spend time with, let them know that, too.

Your wishes concerning ethical values. If you want your children to learn certain ethical values or to continue your family's commitment to certain social goals, such, as environmental activism or contributing to charities, write that down, too. You might also want to write a letter to your children about these values, so they know what was important to you and why. There are lots of useful resources online, including the Celebrations of Life website (https://celebrationsoflife.net/ethicalwills).

Congratulate Yourself on Choosing a Guardian!

Whew! You've just done the hardest part of estate planning for parents of young children. You should feel extra good right now. After working through guardianship, the rest is just details and logistics. There's nothing so emotionally charged left for you to do. But don't stop, either. You still need to make some important choices about how your children's inheritance will be managed for them. And until you put your choices down in a legally witnessed will or properly executed trust, they don't count in a court of law.

What If You Don't Nominate a Guardian?

If you don't nominate a guardian in your will, or if you die without a will at all, then it would be the judge's job to select and appoint someone. Typically, a family member comes forward in this situation and requests to be named as guardian. If the judge determines the person who has come forward would take good care of the child, the judge will go ahead with the appointment.

But if no family member has come forward or you haven't put your wishes in writing, the judge will have to choose a guardian without any idea of whom you wanted to raise your children. That may well be someone you would never choose to raise your children. That's why it's so important you name a guardian.

Leaving Money to Children

Money and Kids: The Basics 121

    Know What You've Got 121

    Pick a Good Manager 122

    Pick the Right Structure 124

Custodial Accounts 125

    Setting Up a Custodial Account 126

    What Custodians Do 127

    Naming a Custodian 128

    When Custodial Accounts Make Sense 129

Children's Trusts 131

    Setting up a Trust 132

    What Trustees Do 133

    Naming a Trustee 136

    One Trust or Many? 143

    How Long Should Your Trust Last? 145

    Giving Out Money Before the Trust Ends 146

    How Much Should You Control a Trust From Beyond the Grave? 148

Your Backup Plan: Appoint a Property Guardian 149

Pull Your Plan Together 151

Life Insurance Primer 153

    What Is Life Insurance? 153

    Do You Need Life Insurance? 155

    What Kind of Life Insurance Is Best for You? 155

    How Much Life Insurance Is Enough? 159

Read this chapter if:

- You want to leave money to children and don't know how.
- You want to learn about custodial accounts.
- You want to learn how to use a trust to manage property for children.
- You want to learn more about life insurance and what kind or how much to buy.

I f you have children, along with choosing a guardian, you must choose someone who would be responsible for safeguarding, investing, and spending any money your children inherited from you while they were still young. And, of course, that's also true if you want to leave money to children who aren't your own, such as a niece or grandchild.

Parents have a tough job choosing guardians, whose job it will be to actually raise their children if they can't. Fortunately, picking someone to manage the money and property that a child might inherit shouldn't be nearly as challenging. The job of this person (called a guardian of the estate or property guardian) is to make good investment decisions and spend that money for a child's benefit. And that's not a decision exclusive to parents. Anyone who wants to leave money to children needs to be thoughtful about how that's done.

Until a child is 18 years old, they can't receive more than $5,000 of property directly. (Under California law, if a gift is more than $5,000, the child needs adult supervision for it.) And even after age 18, when a child is legally capable of owning a gift, you might want that money to be managed for several more years by someone older and more experienced. You don't need to find the next Warren Buffett. You just need to choose someone who is diligent, responsible, honest, and thoughtful about money management.

This chapter will help you get an overview of your options if you do want to leave money to children, yours or anyone else's. Here's the sneak preview:

- Don't leave children under 18 a gift of more than $5,000 without adult supervision.
- If you want your gift to be used for certain purposes (or not used for others), make sure that you leave that gift in a way that allows you to place limits on its use.
- Finally, if you leave money to older children, think about how old you want those children to be before they have full access to it.

Money and Kids: The Basics

Leaving money to children requires some strategic planning. How and when a child has access to money, who should manage it until that time, and what that money can and should be used for are all things that you should address in your estate plan.

Know What You've Got

It's possible that you don't have much to leave to children. If that's the case, the basic rules for leaving money to minors still matter for what you do have to give. Life insurance is often a way that a person can provide immediate cash to children. But many of my clients are surprised at just how much their kids or other young beneficiaries would inherit at their death. When they add up the value of their life insurance, home equity, and retirement, my clients realize that, even though they feel cash-strapped now, they have more to leave behind than they thought.

And it's important to know what you might be leaving behind. It matters. You might be happy to have a 25-year-old inherit $50,000 outright, but it would be a completely different situation if the amount were $500,000 or $1 million. The more money children stand to inherit when you die, the older you're likely to want them to be before it falls into their hands.

You can use the Net Worth Calculation Worksheet (see the sample in Chapter 1 and included on this book's companion page) to fill in the big-ticket numbers so that you can get an estimate. All you need is an approximation, so round things off to the nearest $10,000 or so.

Pick a Good Manager

To figure out who to name as someone who can manage money for children (a money manager) start by jotting down the people who first come to mind. You can make your final decision when you've picked a method for managing the money children might inherit.

For parents with minor children, the personal guardian and the money manager are often going to be the same person. That's a great choice for many families. After all, most parents do both jobs—get the kids ready for school *and* manage the family's money to make sure that there's enough to take care of their needs.

But if the person that you want to name as your children's guardian isn't good with money—you fear he or she would squander your children's money on electronic gear or be overwhelmed by the task of responsibly investing and spending their money—you can pick someone else. If you are a divorced parent you might not want your ex-spouse or partner to be in charge of your child's money, so you'd name someone else, too.

Whomever you choose, you should pick someone who will invest the child's money even more carefully than they would invest their own. You should trust this person to exercise judgment about how that money should be spent and be fair to all beneficiaries. And if you pick someone other than the guardian (for minor children) to manage the money, you'll need to make sure that the two of them will be able to work together and communicate well.

If you are leaving money to other people's children, it's important that you are leaving them money thoughtfully. An outright gift of

$25,000, for example, to a ten-year old niece is going to require that her parents go to court and get a property guardian appointed, which limits how the money can be invested and requires court oversight. This is because a direct gift to a minor child over $5,000 in California requires a court-appointed guardian of the estate.

Grandparents sometimes want to leave their IRAs to their grandchildren. The grandchildren would then have Inherited IRAs, and could withdraw these assets slowly over time. (Read Chapter 10 to learn more about retirement plans and estate planning.) Leaving retirement assets to grandchildren can be a great idea, but not if the grandchildren are minors and are named directly, since that requires a property guardian be appointed before these accounts can be created. To avoid that outcome, you shouldn't leave money to minor children directly. Instead, you should name a custodian for the gift—often a parent, but not always. Read on.

EXAMPLE: Marion, a divorced woman in her 70s, had an IRA worth $200,000. She named her two grandchildren, aged 9 and 11, as the beneficiaries of the IRA. After Marion died, Kelly, her daughter, contacted the plan administrator to transfer the IRA into Inherited IRAs for each of her children. The plan administrator told Kelly that they couldn't distribute the money without a court order appointing a property guardian for each child. Kelly had to go to the superior court in her county and begin the process of having herself appointed as property guardian for her children. After Kelly submitted the required forms, there'd still be a court hearing and an interview with a court investigator. Kelly was not happy about the amount of background information she was required to submit to the court, including whether or not she'd had a restraining order filed against her, and whether or not she'd been arrested for a felony or misdemeanor. If Marion had named her daughter Kelly as a custodian for each grandchild under the California Uniform Transfer to Minors Act on her beneficiary forms for the IRA, Kelly would not have had to be appointed as property guardian at all.

Pick the Right Structure

In addition to picking the right people to manage children's money, you'll need to pick the right way for them to manage that money. You have two good choices in California, both of which are discussed in detail below:

- **Custodial account.** With a custodial account, you select someone to serve as custodian to manage assets for children in a custodial account. This type of account allows someone you've named to manage a child's money and property until that child turns 25 (the age limit under California law).

- **Trust.** With a trust, you select someone as a trustee to manage money and other property for whatever purposes you specify, until a child turns whatever age you choose. You can create trusts for each minor beneficiary or one "pot trust" for all of them, if appropriate. You can set up a trust in your will or your living trust.

Each method, custodial account and trust, makes sense for some people and some situations. In many ways, they're similar. Each method provides a way to manage children's property until they're adults; each allows the money manager to take reasonable compensation for the work of taking care of children's money.

But custodial accounts and trusts differ significantly in several key respects, including:

- how long management lasts, and
- how much flexibility they offer.

To know whether a custodial account or a trust is better for your situation, you need to understand how each one works. It's a little like shopping for the latest smart phone or tablet. You might not need all the bells and whistles that the most expensive model offers. Sometimes, a simpler, lower-cost option has everything you need. The important thing is to understand which features are essential and which ones you can live without, based on the size of your estate and other factors.

Children With Special Needs

If you want to help a child who may never be able to manage and invest funds without help, you face a special challenge, and the estate planning techniques discussed in the rest of this chapter will not accomplish your goals. If that child relies on government benefits for essential services and support, inheriting money could jeopardize eligibility for those services, at least until the funds are spent. For most families, the key fear is losing Medicaid coverage, because their special needs child may never have a job that provides health insurance.

Medicaid and some other programs are available only to those who can't pay for such care themselves. This means that leaving a disabled child money directly can cause a result opposite to that intended by a well-meaning adult.

To leave a special needs child money to live a meaningful and comfortable life, without losing the support of government programs, you will probably want to create (or make a gift to) a "special needs trust," also called a "supplemental needs trust." This type of trust can be structured so that a trustee manages a child's property for that child's entire lifetime. Because legally the child does not own or control the trust assets, those assets won't cause that child to be disqualified from receiving essential government benefits.

For lots of helpful information on this topic, including how trusts work and how to use them as part of your estate plan, read *Special Needs Trusts: Protect Your Child's Financial Future*, by Kevin Urbatsch and Michelle Fuller-Urbatsch (Nolo).

Custodial Accounts

A custodial account is usually a bank or brokerage account that is opened in the name of a minor child. You can open an account like this at any time. If it is part of your estate plan, it would be opened after your death by the person you named as your executor in your will. The person in charge of the account is called its custodian.

If you don't mind the idea of children getting complete control over their inheritance at a relatively young age—18 to 25—then you may want to use a custodianship. It's definitely the simplest method and can work well for the right gift. If you are leaving more money than you'd comfortably leave to a 25-year old, or you want to restrict the use of the money for specific things, like for the purchase of a house, or for education only, however, a custodial account won't work.

Setting Up a Custodial Account

Setting up a custodial account is easy. All you need to do is to state in your will or trust that any money a child inherits from you should go into a custodial account and name a custodian to manage that account. If there are other kinds of assets—real estate, for example—the custodian can manage them, too.

There must be a separate custodianship for each child; you can't pool your assets for the benefit of them all. Each child's account can be used to benefit that child only. If one child had extraordinary medical expenses, for example, the custodian couldn't dip into a brother's or sister's custodial account to pay those bills. This can be a significant drawback to using custodianships.

State law (the California Uniform Transfers to Minors Act, or CUTMA) determines how the account must be managed, and when the account must end. Under state law, the custodianship ends when a child reaches the age of 25. Funds in a custodial account may be used for the minor's benefit, but you can't restrict such an account to certain, specific purposes.

A custodial account is really a simple trust created for a child's benefit, with standard terms, that you can use and everyone else understands. For example, banks and other financial institutions in California know exactly when the property in a custodial account must be distributed to a child and what the money can and can't be used for. And opening a custodial account at most banks and other financial institutions is free.

Using Custodial Accounts for Your Children's Assets	
Pros	**Cons**
Easy to set up	You can't restrict the use of the money for any specific purpose, such as education.
Low or no cost	
One size fits all	An account can't be set up to benefit multiple children.
Familiar to all financial institutions and easy for a custodian to manage	An account must end at age 25 in California. After a custodial account ends, the money must be turned over to the child with no strings attached.

What Custodians Do

Once money or property is placed into a custodial account, the assets belong to the minor child but are controlled by the custodian. The custodian is required to manage the money prudently—no investments in risky start-ups or penny stocks would be legal. The custodian may spend the money for the use and benefit of the child. For example, money in a custodial account could be used to pay for housing, food, education, a computer that a child would use for school, summer camp, extracurricular activities, a car, or a trip to Bali.

Custodians must keep good records on how they spend the funds in custodial accounts, and they have to file tax returns on behalf of the minors who benefit from them. (Income from a custodial account must be reported on the child's tax return and is taxed under the "Kiddie Tax" rule, which uses the parent's tax rate after the first $2,100 of unearned income.

What's the Kiddie Tax?

The Kiddie Tax is designed to discourage parents from shifting income-earning assets to their children as a way to reduce the tax on those earnings. There's a federal and a California Kiddie Tax on investment income. Before it existed, parents would sometimes transfer income-earning accounts to their children's names to reduce taxes.

There is no court supervision of custodians, and there are no specific restrictions on how a custodian must manage the assets, other than carefully and for the benefit of the child. The custodian has a legal duty to be scrupulously honest, keep custodial funds separate from personal funds, and act in the child's best interest. But no one is looking over the custodian's shoulder to make sure that this happens.

Naming a Custodian

Picking a custodian for a child's custodial account is often simple. You're looking for the person you know who is the most trustworthy and the best able to manage money. This will vary depending on the situation:

- If you have minor children and the custodian is the same person you've already chosen to serve as your child's guardian, that's fine. But it's also fine to name a different person for the money job—if the two get along.
- If you are leaving money to other people's children, you can name a child's parent, or a friend or another relative to serve as custodian.
- If you are divorced, you can name a friend or a relative, but they'll still have to deal with your ex, since your child will most likely be living with that person.
- It also makes sense to name an alternate custodian, just in case your first choice is unable or unwilling to serve as custodian later.

When Custodial Accounts Make Sense

Easy to understand and set up, inexpensive or even free, custodial accounts can be great in certain circumstances. A custodial account's main virtue, simplicity, is also its main vice. Custodial accounts are terrific for people leaving small gifts to nephews and nieces but are not usually a great choice for most parents. There are two main reasons.

First, most parents don't want their children to inherit everything at age 25. But that's the longest that you can keep assets in a custodial account in California.

Second, most parents would like to provide for more flexibility in how their children's money should be managed. They might want to provide more money for one child than another, to require a money manager to give money for certain life events such as graduation or marriage, or to allow money to be used for certain things but not for others (for college, but not for motorcycles). For this kind of control and flexibility, it is best to use a trust. You can set up accounts for children with different amounts, or leave instructions for the custodian on how you'd like the money spent (please don't spend money for video games), but it's probably simpler to create a trust where you can spell out the division of assets between children and make your restrictions on how the money is to be spent legally binding.

EXAMPLE: Bert left 2,000 shares of Apple stock to his nephew, Ben (10), and his niece, Mindy (13), in a custodial account. Bert had purchased the stock in 1980, for $2.75/share and he just hadn't paid much attention to that stock as he grew older. When Bert died in 2015, the stock was worth $125/share. Ben and Mindy's parents did not want their children to inherit $125,000 each at age 25. They asked their estate planning attorney what to do: she suggested that they use the money in the custodial accounts to pay for school, camps, computers, and anything else Ben and Mindy might need so that there wouldn't be so much left to them at age 25.

However, if you are leaving behind a modest estate, or making a modest gift, a custodial account might be a terrific option. It's hard to define "modest"—but for most people, it's an amount that a custodian could reasonably be expected to spend before a child turns 25. For example, if college costs $25,000 per year, leaving $100,000 in a custodial account might be just the ticket. That way, after four years of college, the money would be spent, so you wouldn't have to worry about a child's ability (or inability) to manage it at 25.

Custodial accounts cost nothing to set up, although some financial institutions require a minimum investment. If your will leaves money to children and states that it should be held in a CUTMA custodian-ship, then your executor, working with the named custodian, would open custodial accounts for the children after your death. Banks and financial institutions would help them fill out the proper forms. Once the accounts were opened, the children's money would be managed by the trusted adult you chose and could be spent on anything those children needed.

A custodian is legally entitled to compensation for managing an account, but in most families, custodians choose not to take any pay for the job.

EXAMPLE: Emory, who is eight years old, inherited $500,000 when her parents passed away. In their wills, they had named Emory's Aunt Agatha as the custodian of an account, to be established for the benefit of Emory, that would hold their entire estate. Her parents had also requested that a custodial account for Emory be created to hold the proceeds from their $250,000 life insurance policy. Until Emory is 25, her aunt can use that money to provide for Emory's health, education, and welfare. Agatha put most of the money into a custodial brokerage account, where it is invested in a balanced portfolio. The rest is in a custodial bank account that she uses to pay for Emory's daily needs.

When Emory turns 25, whatever money is left in both accounts will be entirely hers to invest and spend as she chooses. This worries her Aunt Agatha, who feels that Emory (who took a few gap years after high school) should finish college and make a start in life before taking over the management and investment of her inheritance. But there's nothing Agatha can really do when Emory turns 25, except to offer to keep managing the money for Emory and hope she takes her up on the offer.

Children's Trusts

A trust is a legal entity that holds assets (money and other property) for the benefit of certain people, called the beneficiaries—children, in this case. Trust assets are managed by a trustee you choose, who follows the rules you've laid out in the trust. For example, you might leave your nieces and nephews money for college or graduate school, or for medical expenses not covered by insurance. I've written trusts that hold money for children to use for the purchase of a home, or to pay for a wedding, or to travel or to volunteer for a nonprofit organization.

If you want to leave a significant amount of money to children, pick someone to manage it until the children are older than 25, and you want to be able to give the person in charge both clear instructions and flexibility, then a trust is the way to go.

When you use a trust, you identify which assets should go into the trust, pick the trustees you want to manage these assets, and decide how old the beneficiaries should be before they inherit the assets outright.

As an estate planning tool, trusts are flexible. For example, you could specify that children not get control over all the money you've left them until they're 35. Or, if you want to ensure that the money will be used only for certain things (a down payment on a house, but not a sailboat trip around the world), you could impose restrictions on the use of the money. You can make one trust for all your beneficiaries (a pot or a pooled trust) or a separate trust for each one, with the same or different amounts of money.

Setting up a Trust

You can set up a trust for children by making certain decisions about all these issues and writing them down in your will (see Chapter 2) or in your living trust (see Chapter 3). Either way, the trust created for children will function in exactly the same way.

It's important to remember that the children's trusts you may create as part of your estate plan won't exist unless you die, and only then if your beneficiaries are younger than the age you've chosen for ending the trust. (The example below of Lee and Marnie should make this clear.) Until then, you are in charge of the money and can use it for whatever you want to.

Think of a trust as the constitution for a small country: It lays out how the money will be used during your lifetime, possibly during your spouse's or partner's lifetime, and then who will inherit it after that. If your will or your trust creates a trust for minor beneficiaries after your death, your successor trustee will set that trust up after your death by getting a tax identification number for the trust and opening up a trust account according to the trust's terms.

EXAMPLE 1: Lee and Marnie, a couple with four young children, create wills leaving their estate to their children in trust until the youngest child turns 30. Their will says that if they die after their youngest turns 30, the children each receive an equal share, outright. Lee dies first. When Marnie dies, the youngest child is 42. All of the children receive 25% of the estate left by their parents. A trust is never established at all.

EXAMPLE 2: Anthony, a single man with no children, wants to leave his estate to his five nieces and nephews in equal shares. Anthony's living trust leaves everything to the nieces and nephews, in trust for any child under the age of 25. When Anthony dies, three nieces are over 25, so they each receive their inheritance outright. The successor trustee sets up a trust account for the nephews, ages 17 and 20.

Things to Decide When You Create a Trust

You need to make a few decisions to create a trust for children.
Here are the big ones:

- whom to name as trustee, the person who will manage the property
- whether to establish a separate trust for each child (perhaps in different amounts) or to pool the money for the benefit of all of them, or to do both—a pot trust until the youngest child turns 18, then separate trusts after that so college comes out of each child's share
- what the trustee can and can't use the money for, and
- when the trust will end, giving the beneficiaries money outright.

What Trustees Do

Before you choose a trustee, it's good to get an idea of what trustees do and what they should be good at. For once, a legal term is very descriptive—you should pick someone you trust completely. Your trustee will be in charge of managing a child's money. Unless someone challenges the trustee's performance and goes to court, the trustee will be doing it without court supervision, possibly for many years.

Trustees must manage trust assets carefully, competently, and honestly. If the trust has more than one beneficiary, the trustee must be impartial. Treating beneficiaries impartially doesn't mean treating them all equally. If you created a pooled trust for three children, for example, it wouldn't be proper or legal for the trustee to send one of them to Pomona because she liked that child best, but to tell the other three that there was no money left for their college expenses at all. But if one child needed an expensive medical procedure, and one of the trust's purposes is to provide funds for the beneficiaries' medical care, it would be proper for a trustee to use trust assets to take care of that child, even though it would leave less money for the other children.

The trustee's job is to administer the trust solely in the interest of the beneficiaries. That means that trustees are not allowed to use trust assets to benefit themselves or for any nontrust purpose. It wouldn't be okay, for instance, for a trustee to purchase trust assets (such as a house) for personal use; spend trust money to buy personal things (such as a new car); or invest trust funds in his or her own company. It would also be improper for a trustee to live rent free in a house owned by the trust while serving as trustee, unless the trust said that was okay. A well-written trust might, for example, explicitly say that a child's guardian may live in your house rent free until the guardianship terminates, and that would be fine, even if that person was also the trustee.

Trustees don't need to be stellar money managers, just prudent and diligent ones. The California Uniform Prudent Investor Act requires that trustees must, unless a trust says otherwise, invest and manage trust funds by looking at the portfolio as a whole, rather than at each investment in isolation. They must also balance risk against return given a particular trust's purpose and beneficiaries. That means that a trustee of a children's trust could invest money in a stock that is growing quickly but not paying dividends yet, as long as other investments provided more long-term stability. Unlike California, some states haven't adopted this law, and place more restrictions on investments. For example, trustees in Louisiana are limited to certain kinds of conservative investments, such as bonds, instead of growth stocks.

Getting Expert Help With a Trust

To help sort out which investments to make and how to comply with state and federal law, trustees are allowed to hire people to help them make good decisions and get good advice. For example, it's common for a trustee to consult a lawyer at the beginning of the process and to get an investment adviser to help figure out how to invest the trust funds properly. Trustees may use trust assets to pay these experts reasonable fees.

Filing Tax Returns

The trustee must file annual trust tax returns with both the state of California's Franchise Tax Board and the federal government (the IRS), reporting the income and expenses of the trust in each tax year. Trust taxation has slightly different rules from those for personal income taxes, mostly around the issues of how to tax capital gains earned by the trust. That's why many trustees hire accountants with expertise in trust accounting, called fiduciary accounting, to prepare these returns.

Reporting to Beneficiaries

The trustee must also provide periodic (at least annual) accountings to the beneficiaries, detailing how the money has been invested and spent. Depending on the terms of the trust itself, these reports can be informal (such as a copy of the annual tax return or a simple spreadsheet showing income, expenses, gains, and losses) or formal, prepared by an accountant following the standard rules of fiduciary accounting. In either case, a trustee who understands what is required should be able to do the reports or to hire an accountant for the job.

Getting Compensated

Trustees are entitled to reasonable compensation for the work that they do to manage trust assets. It can be a big job to manage a trust if there are complex assets to manage or if the trust lasts for many years. In many families, however, trustees, like custodians, often choose not to be paid. In most cases, the trustee gets to decide what's "reasonable" compensation, given the work that they've had to do. But, since trust beneficiaries are entitled to an accounting, the trustee needs to be able to explain why their fee is reasonable. Trustees, for example, might pick an hourly rate in their area for bookkeeping or accounting and use that rate for the hours that they've spent. Alternatively, a trustee may charge a percentage of the assets they've managed, usually not more than 1% as a fee, which is close to what many professional trustees will charge.

CAUTION

Unreasonable trustee's fees can trigger demands by the beneficiaries for an accounting of all the trustee's actions, and even, litigation. I advise my trustee clients to be conservative with their fees, to keep very good records, and to be able to document the fees for comparable work in their area.

RESOURCE

To learn more about the trustee's job, how to manage an ongoing trust, how to deal with taxes, and how to invest trust assets and deal with beneficiaries, read *The Trustee's Legal Companion*, by Carol Elias Zolla and Liza Weiman Hanks (Nolo).

Naming a Trustee

Picking a trustee for a children's trust, like picking a custodian, is usually pretty straightforward. Pick the person you know who is the most trustworthy and the best able to manage money. Again, if you have minor children and that's the same person you've already chosen to serve as the children's personal guardian, that's fine if the person can do both jobs well. (You do both jobs, after all.)

Some families, however, select different people to serve as personal guardian and trustee because one person is better at managing money or because they want to keep both sides of the family involved with the ongoing care of the children. Divorced parents almost always choose someone other than their ex-spouse or partner to manage their children's money. It's fine to name a different person for the money job, as long as the guardian and the trustee can work together and communicate well.

EXAMPLE: Diego and his wife, Carmen, nominated Grace, Carmen's sister, as guardian of their two children. They named Valeria, Diego's sister, as trustee. They did this because Valeria is a certified public accountant and because they wanted both families to be involved in their children's lives if a guardianship were ever necessary. Valeria and Grace get along well and both live in the San Jose area.

If Diego and Carmen die, Grace, the guardian, will have to request that Valeria transfer trust funds to her on a periodic basis to cover everyday living expenses for the children. If Valeria doesn't agree with Grace's wish to spend trust funds on a certain private school or a new computer system, she'll have the final word because she has the power of the purse. Unless Grace, or someone else concerned about the welfare of the children, is willing to bring a lawsuit against Valeria for violating the terms of the trust or her duties as trustee, there won't be much Grace can do about it.

If the children you want to benefit are over age 18 (in which case, there's no requirement for a legal guardian of their property), leaving them money with adult supervision may still be a good idea. After all, it takes a long time for many children to grow into the job of managing money. A custodial account works to age 25, but if you want to wait until a child is older than 25, a trust is the way to go. Trusts can last for as long as you want them to last, even for a child's entire life.

EXAMPLE: Millie wants to leave a gift of $25,000 to each of her partner's children, who are 19 and 21. Both children are still in college, and neither one has had much experience with managing money. Millie leaves each of them a gift in her will, but leaves each gift in trust to age 30, to be used only for medical expenses not covered by insurance or for graduate school, as long as the trust lasts.

More Than One Trustee

You can name two people to serve together as trustees. This is called serving as cotrustees. Sometimes, families who do this are trying to make sure that both sides of a family stay involved with the children, or they want siblings to work together. There's no legal barrier to naming cotrustees, but there are some personal and logistical factors to consider before you do so.

Because cotrustees share the legal responsibility for the trust decisions they make, such as how to invest and spend funds, the general rule is that any power shared by cotrustees is shared equally—they must both agree on all actions.

If cotrustees can't agree, important trust decisions might not get made quickly—or at all. At the least, you could be looking at all sorts of bad feelings. At the worst, if cotrustees just can't work it out, and there are no provisions in the trust to resolve conflicts, one cotrustee would have to go to court to settle the dispute. Because one of the main reasons families create trusts is to avoid court meddling in family affairs—and because lawsuits eat up huge amounts of money and escalate family fights—nobody wants this to happen.

On the logistical side, even if both cotrustees agree, getting their signatures on all documents can be a hassle if they don't live in the same place. You can give cotrustees the power to delegate certain actions to each other, but if a trust says nothing about this issue, the general rule (all cotrustees must authorize everything) applies. One client of mine resigned as a cotrustee so that her brother, the other trustee, could take care of trust business without needing her to cosign documents.

SEE AN EXPERT

Avoiding future trouble. If you think that there are issues in your family that might create conflict over who should serve as trustee, or if you own a family business or other complicated assets that require a trustee with specific expertise, consult an estate planning attorney. It's worth being careful about who you pick as trustee because the wrong trustee can wreck even the most well-thought-out plan. A well-meaning person who doesn't have the right skills could mismanage a trust's assets. A trustee who can't communicate well could end up arousing long-simmering resentments within a family. A trustee who isn't fair to all the beneficiaries can create family drama that might never be resolved.

Siblings

Here's one bad idea I hear fairly often: naming one child to be the trustee for younger siblings. It sounds like a nice idea, especially when there's a large age difference between your oldest and your youngest child, but it can be a terrible source of conflict. Even if the trustee is scrupulous about being fair to younger brothers and sisters and is careful to never benefit at their expense, it's a difficult position. If a younger brother or sister asks for money to fund a pet project or purchase a house or a business, and the sibling-trustee says no, there are bound to be bad feelings.

Grandparents

Another thing you need to think about is the age of the trustee. Naming your 75-year-old mother as trustee if you have a three-year-old isn't a terrific idea. Just do the math: If the trust is set up to last until that child turns 30, your trustee would be 102 when the trust ends. Your trustee is aging, right along with your kids. If you really don't have another first choice, go ahead and name your parent, but make sure that you also name a second choice who's in your generation, just in case. That way, if your trustee is unable or unwilling to continue managing the trust, the next person on the list can step forward for the job.

Remember, you can always revisit your choice of trustees a few years down the road. For example, if your sister (who you've named as trustee) has a major life change, like a divorce, and can no longer take on the job of trustee, you might want to find a new one. Or if your best friend becomes an investment wizard, she might be your first choice for trustee, replacing someone with less financial savvy. The point is you can always change your trustees.

Professional Trustees

If you can't come up with anyone you think is capable of, or interested in, managing money you are leaving children, consider choosing a professional money manager to serve as a sole trustee or as a cotrustee with a family member. Professional trustees are also known as trust officers and private fiduciaries. They work in the trust department of banks, at financial institutions, or independently. It is most common to name a professional trustee in wealthy families. But it can be a great idea for any family if the remaining family members would not be up to the task of managing a portfolio or there is likely to be conflict among family members over managing and spending funds. And, if you don't have any friends or family willing or able to serve as trustee, a professional is your only option.

Professional trust officers charge for their services, usually a percentage of the assets under their management. These fees vary depending upon the size of the trust being managed. As a rule of thumb, professionals charge an annual fee of between 0.75% and 1.25% of the assets being managed. One large trust company I'm familiar with charges 0.80% of the first $750,000; 0.70% of the next $750,000; 0.60% of the next $750,000; and 0.50% on all assets over $2.5 million. The larger the trust fund, the less the fee is as a percentage of the total trust, but the greater the dollar amount of trustee compensation. If, for example, you hired this company to manage a $1 million fund, the annual fee would be $7,500.

Some professional trustees will not accept the job unless trust assets are large, and all of them have a minimum trust amount that's required before they'll take on the job. The required minimum investment varies greatly, so make sure to ask what a firm's minimums are when you do your research.

There are a few disadvantages to using a professional trustee. Sometimes people worry that a professional trustee isn't personally enough involved with the trust or the beneficiaries to make the sensitive decisions that the job can require. For example, what if a trustee must decide whether or not a child is mature enough to use trust assets to buy a house, go to graduate school, or have a fancy wedding? Another drawback is that a trustee's financial institution, such as the local bank, might be purchased by another bank, and then another. Before long, a family is dealing with a trust department in another city, with people that none of them know.

Don't dismiss the possibility of hiring a professional trustee out of hand, though, if you think it might make sense for you or your family. It might be worth it to have a professional on the job. The money your estate spends in fees might be made up for because the trust investments do better than they would have if a family member were in charge.

 RESOURCE
Looking for a professional trustee? It isn't hard to find one. Many financial service companies and banks have trust officers who manage trusts for individuals and families. Your local bank, too, may offer such services. To find a private trustee, look at the Professional Fiduciary Association of California's website at www.pfac-pro.org for a listing of licensed professional fiduciaries.

If you decide that you do want to name an institution to serve as a professional trustee, make sure to check with them before you do so. The institution may have specific wording that they want you to use in your will or trust, or might even want to review a draft of your will or trust before they agree to offer their services. (The financial institution wants to make sure that you're giving the trustee the right powers to enable them to do the job properly and offering them sufficient protection against lawsuits if they do their job honestly.) If you want to name a specific branch of a national company, you can do so, but I always worry about being that specific—if the branch closes down or moves, you don't want your family left guessing about what to do. It's often better to name an institution and then appoint a family member, called a "trust protector," to select the particular branch to deal with.

See the sample Interviewing Professional Trustees Worksheet below, for good questions to ask when you are shopping around for potential trustees.

Interviewing Professional Trustees Worksheet

Ask trustees the following questions, as well as anything special to your situation.

Name and contact information of professional trustee: Suzanne Plummer, Western Trust Company, 666 Hawthorne Blvd, Los Angeles, CA 213-699-8862 SPlummer@WesternT.com

Date: 8/26/17

1. What is your investment minimum? $500,000

2. What are your fees? 1%

3. How are your fees calculated? assets under management

4. If my trust were approximately $500,000, what would the annual fee be at your institution? $5,000

5. What are the annual returns on trust investments over the last five years? 3%–4%

6. How do these returns compare with industry performance over the same five-year period? Competitive

7. How do you communicate with beneficiaries?

   Quarterly account statements.

8. What do your annual statements look like?

   She gave me an example statement.

9. Who would manage my trust account?

   I'd be assigned a manager in Los Angeles.

10. What is your firm's investment portfolio like for trust accounts?

    Balanced stocks and bonds

11. Would it be possible to speak with three trust customers about their experience with your trust services? She said she'd check.

NOTES:

FORM

Interviewing Professional Trustees Worksheet. The Nolo website includes a downloadable copy of the Interviewing Professional Trustees Worksheet for use in talking with professional trustees. See the appendix for the link to this worksheet and other forms in this book.

One Trust or Many?

Once you've selected a trustee, your next job is to decide how your trust should be structured. Really, the decision boils down to whether you want to pool your gift for the mutual benefit of your beneficiaries or create separate trusts for each child.

Pooling Trust Funds

If your beneficiaries are less than five years apart in age, pooling their funds sometimes makes the most sense. That way, the trustee can spend more money on the beneficiary who needs it the most, while remaining fair, of course, to the others. For example, one child might need expensive medications; a couple of years later, his sister might need to go to a special school. A pot trust could work well here because the trustee would have access to all of the trust's money and could distribute it as needed to the beneficiaries. When the trust ends, all the beneficiaries get an equal share of what's left in the pot.

Most parents, after all, do the same thing. They don't set apart identical sums to be spent on each child no matter what (even if some kids would think that perfectly fair). You use what you've got to give your beneficiaries what they need, and when they're grown and you're no longer around, they will share whatever's left.

EXAMPLE: Sasha and her husband, Jonah, establish a family pot trust in their wills for their three girls, aged three, five, and seven. In the very unlikely event that Sasha and Jonah die before all of the girls are at least 28, all of Sasha and Jonah's assets will go into a trust for the girls. They choose Jonah's sister, Charlotte, to serve as the trustee.

The trust states that money is to be used for anything that the girls need for their health, education, support, and maintenance. At age 23, or upon graduation from college, whichever happens first, each girl is to receive a gift of $20,000 from the trust. When the youngest daughter turns 28, the trust will end, and each girl will receive a third of what remains in the trust. That means that, if the trust were created when the children were young, the oldest girl would have to wait until she was 32 to receive her share. It also means that everyone would share what was left after college expenses had been paid out. If one child went to an expensive private college, one had gone to a community college, and one hadn't gone to college at all, they'd still all share what was left equally.

Creating Separate Trusts

If your beneficiaries are more than five years apart in age, or you want their ultimate inheritance to be affected by which college they attend, it may make sense to create separate trusts for each of them. Most importantly, having separate trusts makes the trustee's job of being fair to all children a bit simpler when it comes to the big-ticket items. If each beneficiary has his or her own trust, the trustee doesn't have to balance one beneficiary's needs against that of the others, or act like a referee if there's a conflict between beneficiaries over scarce resources.

If everyone starts out with the same amount of money when the trust is funded, older trust beneficiaries can go off to college—usually the single biggest trust expense—knowing exactly what their budget is. Meanwhile, younger children are assured that their older siblings aren't using more than their fair share.

With separate trusts, a child who goes to an expensive private school will have less trust money after graduation than a sibling who chooses a state school or doesn't go to college at all. Some people feel that a pricey degree is a reasonable investment of the money and don't worry about the child leaving school with less cash on hand.

Separate trusts make it easier to terminate each trust, too. If a trust ends when a child reaches 30, for example, and each child is to receive an equal share of the trust assets at that point, older beneficiaries aren't going to get their share until the youngest turns 30, because the trustee won't be able to calculate equal shares until then.

EXAMPLE: Kevin and Sharon have four children, aged two, six, ten, and 14. Because there's such a big age difference between their youngest and oldest, Kevin and Sharon decide to establish a trust that, if it's ever created, will divide into four equal shares. Each share will be managed by the same trustee, and the money in each can be used for health, education, maintenance, and support of that child. When a child reaches the age of 23, that child will receive $20,000 from his or her share. At 25, each child will receive 25% of what's left in his or her share, so that they can get some practice managing and investing money.

When each child turns 28, that child will receive the balance of his or her share. That means that, if the trust were created when the children were young, the oldest son would get his money when his littlest sister was only 16. It also means that each child began with an equal share, but that what they have left after college will be affected by where they choose to go. If one daughter went to an expensive private college, for example, she'd have less in her trust upon graduation than her sister who chose a state school or received a full scholarship.

How Long Should Your Trust Last?

It's not easy deciding when a children's trust should end. I've noticed that parents of toddlers tend to get dreamy-eyed when imagining the future financial acumen of their now-tiny children. Parents of teenagers, though, don't always have such a rosy view. Sometimes they even ask me if they can arrange it so that their kids *never* get their hands on the money.

I tell my clients to think back to when they were old enough to responsibly handle money. For some people, that's around 30, for others it's earlier, and for some it's later. Whatever the right age was for you, that's probably when the trust for children should end.

And trusts should end. Sooner or later, unless children have special needs or serious credit or substance abuse problems, they will want to manage and spend their money for themselves. I've heard several adult beneficiaries of trusts complain about having to wait too long to gain control of their inheritances. In one case, a woman wanted to buy a house after she graduated from college but had no access to the trust funds from her deceased father's insurance policy until she was 30. Of course, trust terms can give trustees discretion about such things, but this woman's trust did not.

Think about when you'd like children to begin managing and investing their money. That would be the age of your youngest beneficiary when the trust terminates, if you use a pot trust, or the age of each child if you use separate trusts for each child.

Giving Out Money Before the Trust Ends

Once you've figured out when your trust should end, you should look backward to college and see if you want to make any interim distributions to the beneficiaries. In other words, do you want the trustee to give a child a chunk of money at a certain age, or at a certain milestone, while keeping the rest in trust? Money that goes directly to the children would be under their control. Money that stays in trust is still available for the children's needs but remains under the trustee's control. The purpose of an interim distribution is to give children practice in managing money themselves, without turning everything over to them. You can even structure it so that no money is paid out to older kids until you're sure there's enough to get the younger ones through college.

If you give a child 25% of the trust money at the age of 25, for example, and that child immediately loses it all in a bad investment or spends it on a fabulous three-year trip around the world, the other 75% of their inheritance is still being safely managed by the trustee you selected.

EXAMPLE: Nareet and her partner, Emma, have two children, aged seven and nine. Their current net worth, including life insurance proceeds, is $1.5 million. The couple decides that their children's trust will be a pot trust, because the children are so close in age. They also decide that by their early 30s, their children will be as financially trustworthy as they're ever going to be. Here's how Nareet and Emma decide to distribute the trust over time:

Sample Trust Distributions: Nareet and Emma		
Age of Youngest Child	Trust Distribution	Why Do It This Way?
23 or graduates from college, whichever happens first	Each child gets $20,000.	No money is distributed directly to a beneficiary from the trust until the youngest finishes college. That way, the trustee can be sure that college expenses will be paid for first.
27	Each child gets 10% of the trust assets.	The other 90% of the trust assets are still being managed by the trustee for the benefit of the children. The children get to practice managing their 10%.
32	Each child gets half of what's left in the trust.	The trust ends, and each child manages her own money independently.

How Much Should You Control a Trust From Beyond the Grave?

Even though trusts offer you almost unlimited ability to restrict the use of the trust assets or direct investments, should you? Even if it would mean a lot to you for your daughter or niece to pursue a graduate degree in chemistry at your alma mater, Stanford, would it be a good idea to require that she do it as a condition of receiving her inheritance? Even if you're sure that a certain stock is going to be a long-term winner, should you require a trustee to invest in it?

Put bluntly, no. It's always a terrific idea to communicate your hopes for your beneficiaries, either directly or in a letter that you can write to them to be opened only upon your death. You can even write a letter to the children's guardian or to the trustee of your trust describing your hopes and dreams for these kids or their money. You might, for example, let your trustee know that you don't want your beneficiaries driving luxury vehicles or taking fancy cruises. You might set out an investment strategy that you hope that the trustee follows, like no more than 30% of the portfolio in bonds.

But inserting specific conditions in your trust can mean trouble for those who have to live by its terms. There's simply no way to know what the world will be like 20 or 30 years from now. What if your child has an incredible talent for poetry, not chemistry? What if they just don't have the grades to get in to Stanford? What if that dream stock tanks? If your trust is restrictive, and it no longer makes sense for a trustee to follow its directives, the trustee will have to go to court to change the trust's terms. This is expensive and time-consuming, and it might not even work.

A trustee's job is to exercise judgment and discretion. Let your trustee do it. Your trust can give the trustee freedom to give money to children for a wedding, to buy a house, or to start a business. But let the trustee decide whether any of those things is a good idea for a particular child at a particular time.

> **TIP**
>
> **There are limits on your power.** You're not allowed to require certain things in a trust or a will in California, because they would be considered against public policy. You couldn't, for example, make a distribution to your son on the condition that he commit a crime.

Your Backup Plan: Appoint a Property Guardian

Even though you've chosen a custodianship or a trust for your child's inheritance, as a backup, you also need to name someone (in your will) to serve as a "property guardian" for their property. A property guardian (under court supervision) manages any property that children might own after a parent's death that somehow isn't part of a children's trust or placed in a custodial account.

The odds of children owning property like this are quite low— most parents plan (if they plan at all) to leave all of their property to children in either a trust or a custodial account.

Still, children do sometimes end up owning property of their own. It could be stock given to them by a grandfather or a savings account left to them by an aunt. A more common situation, though, is when a parent or grandparent names a child as a beneficiary for a life insurance policy or an IRA, but doesn't name a custodian on the policy or plan. If the child inherits the money before age 18 and it's worth more than $5,000, a court must appoint a property guardian to manage the account. Until your children are legal adults, the property guardian can invest and manage the money on their behalf.

Mind you, the problem can be easily avoided by naming a trust that benefits a child as the beneficiary on these plans, or by designating a custodian to manage the asset for a child you name as beneficiary.

Whom should you pick? Most parents nominate the same person they've selected as trustee or custodian to serve as property guardian, should one be necessary. That's a sensible choice, because that's the person they've decided is the best money manager already. Most parents also name the same person to serve as property guardian for each of their children.

If there's only a small amount of money at stake, less than $20,000, your executor might be able to avoid a property guardianship, but that's up to the court on a case-by-case basis. In that situation, if the court permits it, the executor could appoint a custodian under the California Uniform Transfers to Minors Act as long as the will didn't forbid this. The custodian would manage the property for a child until age 25.

A property guardian is always accountable to the court that made the appointment. The property guardian must do a thorough inventory of a child's assets, submit it to the court, and seek court approval for any significant action, such as selling real estate. A property guardian must keep complete, accurate records of each financial transaction affecting the child's property and receipts for all purchases. The property guardian must also file periodic accountings with the court, listing receipts, expenses, income, and assets. The court may ask the guardian to justify some or all expenditures. The guardian must have receipts and other documents available for the court's review, if requested.

Most of the court-required documents are created by lawyers. That means high hourly fees. Property guardians can also request court approval for reasonable compensation for all the work they're doing. So having a property guardian can be expensive, and the fees are paid from the property children inherit. For all of these reasons, use a property guardianship only as a backup measure.

EXAMPLE: Cameron, a single father, names his only child, Alexa, who is 12, as the beneficiary of his $500,000 life insurance policy and names his sister, Caroline, as the custodian of the money. Caroline is also the executor of Cameron's will and Alexa's guardian. Cameron dies unexpectedly in a car crash. Caroline establishes a custodial account to hold the life insurance proceeds for Alexa's benefit until she turns 25.

A year after Cameron dies, Alexa inherits a $250,000 IRA from her grandmother, who named her as a beneficiary but didn't name Caroline as the custodian of the account for Alexa's benefit. Caroline must go to court and be appointed Alexa's property guardian in order to manage the account on Alexa's behalf until she turns 18.

Pull Your Plan Together

Once you've picked a person for managing money you leave to children and a method for leaving money, you can pull your plan together by filling out the Managing Money for Minor Children Worksheet (see the sample below). You can do so using what you've decided to create in a will or a living trust.

Managing Money for Minor Children Worksheet		
Use this worksheet to record your choices for money managers and methods. Just fill in the blanks that work for you, and skip the rest.		
How	**Who**	**For How Long**
Custodial Accounts	Custodians: 1. N/A 2. _____ 3. _____	Custodial account should end at age _25_.
Trusts	Trustees: 1. Jennifer Smith 2. Joseph Doe 3. _____ OR Cotrustees: _____ and _____	☑ Separate trust for each child. Trust ends when each child is _27_. OR ☐ Pot trust Trust ends when youngest child is _____. Interim distributions: _10%_ at age _23_ _20%_ at age _25_ _N/A_ at age _____

FORM

Managing Money for Minor Children Worksheet. The Nolo website includes a downloadable copy of the Managing Money for Minor Children Worksheet for you to record your choices for money managers and accounts (custodial accounts and/or trusts).

Keeping Your Ex Away From the Money

If you are divorced and are concerned about the ability of your ex-spouse to manage your children's money, be extra careful to set up either a trust or custodianship and put someone else in charge of these assets. You'll be happy to know that your ex-spouse or partner doesn't automatically get to be the guardian of your children's property. A judge can name anyone who will do a good job managing your children's money.

You can even request in your will that your ex not be named as your children's property guardian. If you have specific reasons to support your concerns, such as the fact that your ex has never paid required child support payments, you can state these, too. But remember that wills are public documents once you die, and anything in them will be open to public viewing.

Another option, which avoids public scrutiny, is to write a private letter (similar to what you might write to a guardian, except here you are sharing information that you are willing to be made public if necessary) detailing your ex's bad behavior and including supporting documentation, and give this letter to your executor. If your ex chooses to contest your wishes after you die, this letter can be introduced as evidence in a court proceeding—and may well be enough to avoid such a hearing altogether. One person I know (a lawyer) wrote such a letter and took out an insurance policy to pay for the legal fight she was concerned it might start.

Life Insurance Primer

Life insurance can be an important part of nearly every person's estate planning. If you've been reading this chapter with a sinking heart, feeling like you've got nothing left to give to the people that you love, life insurance can help provide cash to the people that you love.

It might be that all of your assets are either tied up in your house (which could be hard to sell) or your retirement plans (bad idea to liquidate). What you need then is a quick source of cash for kids in case of unexpected tragedy. It might be that you haven't been able to save much because living in California is expensive. The right kind of life insurance is one of the cheapest, most reliable ways to make sure that if you're not around, you can provide cash to the children you love most.

What Is Life Insurance?

Life insurance is a contract between you and an insurance company. At its most simple, the deal works like this: In return for your annual payments, called premiums, the insurance company agrees to pay out money, called a death benefit. For the insurance company, it's a bet—if you don't die before they have to pay out, they make money. If you die, and the insurance company has to pay out money, they don't. Of course, insurance companies issue policies to many people, so the risk of any one payout is spread out over a large pool of insured people. As long as enough people don't die while they are insured, the insurance company makes a tidy profit. (Earthquakes, hurricanes, and other catastrophes put great strain on insurance companies, for obvious reasons.)

The younger and healthier you are, of course, the better bet it is for the company. As you get older and your health declines, insuring your life gets riskier. The insurance companies know the odds. So it costs less to purchase insurance when you're young than it does when you're older. To put it another way, you get a huge discount for planning ahead. Many types of insurance policies have a level premium for the life of a policy, which means that you'll be able to lock in the lowest possible rate by buying the policy when you're younger.

People who put off buying life insurance pay more for it. A 45-year-old man will pay higher premiums for a life insurance policy worth $500,000 (about $700 a year) than that same policy if the man bought it when he was 30 (about $300). It makes sense if you think like an insurance company. They have to charge the 45-year old more to cover the company's risk of actually paying that $500,000. From the company's perspective, it's a lot more likely that the 45-year old man will die in the next, say, 20 years than it would have been had he purchased that same policy 20 years before.

Life Insurance at Work

Many people get life insurance as a work benefit. Often the coverage is equal to one or two times their annual salary. Someone who earns $50,000 a year, for example, might get a policy that would pay $50,000 to $100,000 as part of the benefits package. At some companies, you can even buy additional insurance for yourself or your spouse and have a small amount of your paycheck deducted to pay the premium.

There's nothing wrong with work-based life insurance; if it's offered by your company, take it. It isn't a good idea to depend on it entirely, though. If you get laid off or leave your job (and, let's face it, the odds of that happening are probably much higher than the odds of your dying while still in the workforce), you'll lose that insurance. Then you'll find yourself shopping around for a policy when you're older than you are now. And that means the policy will cost you more.

Do You Need Life Insurance?

Here's what life insurance can offer:

Immediate cash after a death. This money can be used for last illness and funeral expenses and to pay any of your remaining debts and taxes. If most of your assets are locked up in things that would be difficult to sell quickly (like a house, a business, or a collection of antiques) or in retirement assets that it would be a bad idea to liquidate, insurance money makes sense.

Tax-free money. The beneficiary doesn't have to pay income tax on life insurance proceeds except in certain, rare, circumstances.

Replacement of a lost income. If a working person dies, insurance can allow a stay-at-home partner to continue staying home.

Money for childcare and domestic services. This can allow a breadwinning partner to continue working while hiring help to take care of the children and household.

Probate avoidance. As long as you don't name your estate as the beneficiary of your policies (and you shouldn't), insurance proceeds aren't subject to probate court proceedings.

Money for children with disabilities. Insurance policies can provide money for the long-term care of children with special needs, as long as the proceeds are paid into a special needs trust for the benefit of the child, not to the child directly.

Estate tax reduction. If you're concerned about estate taxes, you can transfer your life insurance policies to a trust. The money will be paid to a surviving spouse or to children or other beneficiaries but won't be part of your taxable estate. Under current law, only about 2% of Americans die with taxable estates, so this isn't likely to be a concern for you.

What Kind of Life Insurance Is Best for You?

Depending upon your age and your health, you might be able to purchase a policy that will provide cash when it's needed.

Types of Life Insurance		
Type	**General Features**	**Variations**
Term	The policy lasts for a specified period of time, usually ten to 30 years, and pays out a fixed amount at the policyholder's death.	**Renewable.** You can extend the term without another medical exam. **Convertible.** You can convert your term policy to a permanent policy. That means that instead of the policy ending at a certain point, you can convert it to one that lasts your whole life.
Permanent	The policy lasts your entire life, as long as the premiums are paid up. Policies often include an investment component. Over time, a cash value for the policy builds up. Put another way, part of the premium you pay covers the risk of insuring you, and the rest is like an enforced savings account that the insurance company invests for you. You are usually able to take out loans against the cash value of the policy, and if you terminate the policy, you can cash it in for its "surrender value." As long as you don't take the money out, it grows tax free. When you die, these policies generally pay out only the death benefit. Some also pay your beneficiaries the cash value you've accumulated, but those policies cost more.	**Traditional whole life.** You pay a fixed premium for a fixed benefit. **Universal life.** The policy builds up a cash reserve, but you can vary the premiums and the benefits over time. **Variable life.** Your death benefit and the cash value of the policy vary depending upon how the company's investments perform. **Variable universal life.** These policies combine the ability to vary your premium payment and death benefit (like universal life) with the investment flexibility of variable life insurance. **Last survivor life ("second to die").** These policies insure two people but pay benefits only when the second one dies. They are generally used to pay estate taxes for wealthy families. **Single-premium whole life.** You buy the whole policy with one lump sum. This requires a large up-front payment, but it's useful if you want to give a policy to someone else and not worry about the premiums staying paid up.

Term Life Insurance

Term life insurance is the simplest form of insurance. You agree to pay premiums for a certain period of time (the term). The company agrees to pay your beneficiaries a certain amount of money (the death benefit) if you die during that term. If you don't die during the term, they pay nothing. If you do die during the term, your beneficiary gets the death benefit. For most term policies, the premium stays the same throughout the term, so you lock in the lowest rate if you buy it while you're young. If you stop paying the premiums, the policy lapses; you don't get your money back.

Because term life insurance is so simple and because the odds of young, healthy people dying are so low, it is cheap compared to policies that last your whole life and that also serve as an investment. These policies are usually sold in 10-, 15-, 20-, and 30-year increments. If you want to benefit minor children and provide for their education, consider buying a term policy that will last until your youngest beneficiary turns 21. After your youngest beneficiary is in college, life insurance will serve a different purpose in your plan—maybe providing for your surviving spouse or partner or equalizing your estate among adult children—or maybe none at all.

EXAMPLE: Loren and Sarah are in their 30s and have two children, Andy (age three) and Jenny (age six). Like many Californians, most of Loren's and Sarah's money is tied up in their house and their retirement plans. They have enough money in their savings account to cover three months of normal expenses. Loren and Sarah decide to purchase life insurance policies for both of them.

Loren would want to be able to continue working if Sarah died when the children were young, so Sarah's policy needs to pay out enough money so that Loren, at the very least, could hire enough childcare to take care of the kids during the day, Monday through Friday. Sarah would want to be able to stay home full time if Loren died first, so Loren's policy needs to pay out enough money to support the family for at least 15 years. Loren and Sarah also want to make sure that if they were both to die at the same time, there would be enough money to get both kids through a state college.

Loren and Sarah decide to buy term life insurance policies. Because their younger child Andy, is only three, they decide that 20-year policies makes the most sense. When Andy turns 23, his sister Jenny will be 26. By then the parents hope that both children will have made it through college. For Loren and Sarah, providing cash for young children is the primary reason to buy the policies, so they won't need life insurance once their kids are grown.

For advice on how much they should purchase, Loren and Sarah go see a financial planner. She advises them to get at least a $600,000 20-year term policy on Loren (this is ten times his annual salary) and a $250,000 policy on Sarah (ten times her annual salary).

Not completely satisfied with this recommendation, Loren and Sarah consult another planner, who has them fill out a financial worksheet. After discussing their plans to put both children through four years of college, keep the house, and allow Sarah to stay home for 15 years if something happened to Loren, and after evaluating their current assets and debts, this planner recommends a $1 million policy for Loren and a $500,000 policy for Sarah.

This makes more sense to Loren and Sarah, given their hopes for the future and how they'd like to take care of the other if one dies first. They decide that they can afford to pay about $75 a month to buy the policies recommended by the second planner.

Permanent Life Insurance

Okay, when might you want something other than term insurance? There are a couple of common situations. If you want a policy that lasts after your beneficiaries are adults, consider buying permanent life insurance or a term policy that you can convert to a permanent policy. If you like the idea of enforced savings, think about a permanent policy that allows you to pull money out later or borrow against the policy at a good interest rate to help you save money for the future. If you want to benefit a child with special needs and need to make sure that your policy will always be available to support them, you should purchase permanent life insurance. (See "If You Have a Child With Special Needs," below.)

How Much Life Insurance Is Enough?

Once you've figured out what sort of policy would work best for you, you'll need to decide how much of a death benefit you'd like to provide for your beneficiaries. In my years of practice, I've heard many different theories about the best way to figure out the best amount for any given family. Every insurance salesperson and financial planner seems to have a favorite calculator or ratio.

I think it's worth exploring some of the different approaches to insurance calculations here, but the real answer is, "Buy as much as you need. If you can't afford that much, buy as much as you can afford. As soon as you can." And feel good about it. If a $1 million policy would take care of your loved ones best, but you can only afford $500,000 worth of coverage, buy that. That's still $500,000 more for your beneficiaries than they had without any insurance in place.

Income-Multiplier Method

One simple way to calculate your insurance needs tries to replace lost income over a period of time. One figure I've heard frequently is six to ten times your annual salary. So if you earn $80,000 per year, you'd want $480,000 to $800,000 worth of life insurance. But this rule of thumb might not work for you. Maybe six to ten years isn't enough time for your loved ones to be supported by insurance. Maybe your current income isn't sufficient, so you wouldn't want to use it as a benchmark. And this model doesn't value a stay-at-home parent's work at all.

Online Calculators

Another approach takes a look at your overall financial situation, including your expected short-term and long-term expenses, current salaries, current savings, and educational needs for your children (if any). There are lots of online calculators that will help you do this. One that I like is on the Motley Fool website (www.fool.com). You can find it on their Calculators page, under Insurance Calculators, "How Much Life Insurance Do I Need?"

After you plug in basic financial data, the calculators compare your current funds with the total capital needed and calculate how much insurance you'd need to fill the gap between what you've got and what you'll need for as many years as you've specified. It's hard to tell what assumptions these calculators are making to come to their conclusions, or whether their estimates for investment returns and inflation are good ones. I used the same $80,000 salary figure mentioned above in several of these online calculators for 20 years of income replacement—and was told I needed from $625,000 to $1.5 million of insurance.

A Look at Your Lifestyle

Probably the best way to think about how much life insurance you need is to take a look at what you're spending now, and then think about how this would change if you or your partner were to die. You might spend less on food but more on day care, for example. The surviving partner might need to pay off the mortgage in order to continue staying home with the children. Someone working part time might have to find a full-time job. This analysis focuses, as I think you should, on what kind of life and lifestyle you'd want for your beneficiaries if you were to die. Once you get a rough idea of what it would cost your beneficiaries to live for a month, you can start figuring out how much insurance to get.

Several financial planners I know use variations on this last approach. They want their clients to get an insurance policy with proceeds that could generate enough income to pay off existing debts and cover the household's monthly expenses without dipping into the principal. A family with $50,000 in outstanding debts and $4,000 of monthly expenses, for example, needs $48,000 a year in income from investments to cover expenses, and more to pay off that debt. If they had $1 million invested at a 5% rate of return, that would generate $50,000 a year, less fees. If they got a policy worth $1.1 million, they'd be able to pay off the debts first and invest the rest. If they could get a better rate of return than 5%, they'd have more money to spend. If they could afford it, each parent should get a $1 million term life insurance policy.

If You Have a Child With Special Needs

If you want to take care of a child with special needs, none of the methods above really captures what you need to do with insurance, which is to provide lifetime care for that child. You might want to buy much more life insurance than any of the models would ordinarily call for. And because that child's needs are not going to diminish with time, a permanent life insurance policy probably makes the most sense. A term policy might terminate just when you need it most, and renewing it when you're older is not going to be cheap.

Most disabled adults rely on government benefits, especially Medicaid, and inheriting a large insurance payment directly may jeopardize their eligibility for these benefits. Creating a special needs trust (discussed earlier in this chapter) is the best way to make sure that money you've left behind will be used to supplement government benefits, not interfere with them.

Estate Planning Across Borders

Resident and Nonresident Aliens for Tax Purposes 165

Estate and Gift Taxation of Non-U.S. Citizens
  (Resident and Nonresident) 167

How Assets Are Taxed Worldwide for U.S. Taxpayers...............................169

Naming International Trustees and Executors...171

  International Executors of Wills...172

  International Trustees of Trusts 172

Naming Guardians for Minor Children Who Don't Live in the U.S......174

Estate Planning for a Noncitizen Spouse 175

Read this chapter if:

- You are a visa holder or permanent U.S. resident, but not a U.S. citizen, and live or work in the United States.

- You are nonresident alien and own property in the United States.

- You are married to someone who is not a U.S. citizen.

- Your close family members live abroad.

- You are a U.S. taxpayer and own assets in another country.

- You are a U.S. taxpayer and want to name a trustee, an executor, or a guardian who lives abroad.

P eople come from all over the world to live in California. Some of them stay here as nonresident aliens, some become permanent U.S. residents, and some of them become U.S. citizens or dual citizens. In our increasingly international world, people who live in California may also own property in other countries, or want to make gifts to family members and friends living abroad. And then there are children: Some parents have U.S. citizen children even though they are not themselves U.S. citizens, or some want to name guardians who live in other countries for their minor children.

All of this cross-border activity creates estate planning complexity. Where someone lives, where someone pays taxes, and where someone owns property each affect income and gift and estate taxation and IRS reporting requirements. Who to name as a trustee, an executor, or a guardian may raise questions that impact your estate plan, since naming someone who lives abroad for one or more of these jobs can create tax headaches, require the purchase of a bond, or simply not be allowed in California.

Addressing all of these topics in full is beyond the scope of this book, but what you will find here is an overview of these issues and why they matter. I will give you the basic information you need to prepare for meeting with a legal or tax professional, which, unfortunately, many Californians with international estate planning issues will need to do. Depending on your particular situation, this may be an accountant or tax preparer or an attorney, either in the United States or in the country where you or your spouse own property or have family.

Note: This chapter does not address how U.S. citizens living abroad should do their estate planning, or how persons living here illegally should address their estate planning needs.

California by the Numbers

California has more immigrants than any other state—more than 10 million people, which is close to one in four of the foreign-born population in the U.S. as a whole. See the introduction to this book for more stats on California's foreign-born residents.

Resident and Nonresident Aliens for Tax Purposes

People who are living and working in California legally, but are not U.S. citizens, fall into two categories for tax purposes: resident aliens (most often they have a so-called "green card") and nonresident aliens (they are not permanent U.S. residents and have a nonimmigrant visa if they are here legally). For both income and estate and gift tax purposes, resident and nonresident aliens are treated, and taxed, differently. In general, resident aliens are taxed in the same way that U.S. citizens are taxed on their worldwide income and assets, and nonresident aliens are taxed according to special rules. But the rules for who is a resident alien and who is a nonresident alien are different for income tax purposes and estate and gift tax purposes.

Since this book is focused on estate planning, I'm going to cover the estate and gift tax rules for resident and nonresident aliens in this chapter and leave income tax issues out, unless I need to explain them in order to make the estate and gift tax issues clear.

To keep things relatively simple, I'm also making some assumptions in this chapter—that is, a person with a green card, who intends to work and stay in the United States permanently, is who I mean when I say "green card holder" or "resident alien." That person would be treated, for gift and estate tax purposes and for income tax purposes, as a U.S. taxpayer. Conveniently, this is also a description of the vast majority of non-U.S. citizens that I work with in my estate planning practice. And this makes sense, because it is people who are living and working here permanently, and who have acquired significant U.S. assets, who are most likely to want to create an estate plan in California.

When I use the term, "nonresident alien," I am referring to a person who is in the United States for a temporary period of time, and either does not intend to stay here permanently or cannot, and is not a U.S. citizen. For the purpose of this chapter, I'm calling them visa holders, to describe people who are here legally for a specific purpose (like going to school) or working on a specific job.

 RESOURCE

To learn more about U.S. immigration procedures and rules, read *U.S. Immigration Made Easy,* by Ilona Bray; *How to Get a Green Card,* by Ilona Bray and Loida Nicolas Lewis; and *Becoming a U.S. Citizen,* by Ilona Bray, all from Nolo.

TIP

The rules for determining whether or not a non-U.S. citizen is a resident alien or a nonresident alien for estate and gift tax purposes are fact specific. The legal term is whether or not someone has a "U.S. domicile." A person is considered to have a U.S. domicile if they have no intention to leave the U.S. This is what's called a "subjective" test, which means it can depend on factors that are hard to predict. The IRS looks at the following factors:

- statements of intent to stay in the U.S.
- length of U.S. residence
- whether a person has a green card
- style of living in the U.S. and abroad
- ties to former country
- country of citizenship
- location of business interests, and
- place of church, club affiliations, and driver's license.

Seek expert advice from an accountant or other tax professional/ financial advisor if you are not a U.S. citizen and are not certain of your tax status for either income or estate and gift tax purposes.

Estate and Gift Taxation of Non-U.S. Citizens (Resident and Nonresident)

In Chapter 9, I'll go over gift and estate tax rules for U.S. taxpayers in more detail. Here's what you need to know for now:

- U.S. taxpayers (citizens and permanent resident aliens/green card holders) can give up to a certain amount, called the "federal estate tax exemption," to anyone, either during life or after death, free of gift or estate tax. Currently this exemption is $5 million, indexed to inflation ($5.49 million in 2017).

- U.S. taxpayers can make annual gifts of up to $14,000 free of gift tax, called "the annual exclusion" without using up any of that lifetime gift and estate tax exemption.
- Finally, U.S. taxpayers can also give an unlimited amount to their spouses, either during life or at death, which is called the "unlimited marital deduction," provided that the spouse is a U.S. citizen.

But these rules are different for nonresident aliens (visa holders). Here's how to make sense of these rules: The calculation of estate and gift tax looks at the status of the *donor* (the person giving the gift) first, and then, in the case of a spouse only, at the status of the *donee* (the person receiving the gift). If, for example, a U.S. citizen or resident alien (a U.S. taxpayer) wants to make a gift, either during life or at death, to someone (other than a spouse) whether the person receiving that gift is a U.S. citizen, a permanent U.S. resident, or a nonresident alien, that gift would fall within that U.S. taxpayer's annual exclusion ($14,000) or lifetime exemption ($5.49 million) from the federal gift and estate tax. If a nonresident alien wants to make that same gift to that same person (not a spouse), that gift (if it is real or tangible property located in the United States) would be subject to gift tax if it exceeds $14,000 or the estate tax if it exceeds $60,000. In each case, the same person is *receiving* the gift, but that gift has a different tax treatment because of the status of the person *making* that gift.

Nonresident aliens, then, are subject to taxes that U.S. taxpayers are not subject to, but guess what? These taxes only apply to gifts of real or tangible personal property (like a house, or paintings, furniture, and cash) located in the United States. Nonresident aliens are not taxed on gifts of nontangible personal property, like stocks and bonds made during life. And they are not taxed on their assets held abroad. U.S. taxpayers, in contrast, are subject to estate and gift tax on their assets worldwide. (Honestly, who makes this stuff up?!)

Estate and Gift Tax for Nonresident Aliens		
Type of Asset	**Estate Tax**	**Gift Tax**
Real estate	Yes, if in the U.S.	Yes, if in the U.S.
Tangible personal property (like jewelry and artwork)	Yes, if in the U.S.	Yes, if in the U.S.
Intangible property (like U.S. stocks and bonds)	Yes	No
Cash in bank	No, unless connected with U.S. business	Yes
Life insurance proceeds	No	N/A

How Assets Are Taxed Worldwide for U.S. Taxpayers

U.S. taxpayers, whether U.S. citizens or resident aliens, are subject to estate and gift tax on their assets worldwide. And, if they own property in other countries, they need to report that on their income tax returns as well. Worldwide assets, if they are over $10,000 at any time during the calendar year, must also be reported to the IRS, on a *Report of Foreign Bank and Financial Accounts* (FBAR) form and disclosed on the person's income tax return. For more information and relevant forms on FBARs, search for the topic on www.irs.gov.

The consequences of failure to file the FBAR can be severe—if you don't report foreign assets willfully (that is, if you knew or should have known that you were required to do so), the penalty can be the greater of $100,000 or 50% of the amount in the account at the time of the violation.

EXAMPLE: Frank and Caleb, a married couple, bought a vacation home in the south of France. They rent this home out when they are not using it. Every year, Frank and Caleb must report that rental income and that property on an FBAR form that they file with their joint income tax return.

When someone dies owning property in another country, those foreign assets are part of that person's taxable estate if they are U.S. citizens or resident aliens under the estate and gift tax rules. If estate tax is due in the U.S., the trust or estate must pay it. But if estate tax is also due in the other country, tax treaties may contain provisions that allow credits for tax paid in the U.S. (or the other country) so a person won't be taxed twice.

Countries With Tax Treaties With the United States

The U.S. has estate and/or gift tax treaties with 16 jurisdictions. These treaties can reduce or eliminate double estate or gift taxation.

Australia	Germany	Norway
Austria	Greece	South Africa
Canada	Ireland	Switzerland
Denmark	Italy	United Kingdom
Finland	Japan	
France	Netherlands	

Here's what I tell my clients who own property abroad: Keep your foreign assets out of your U.S. estate plan and make an estate plan in that country for those foreign assets.

EXAMPLE: Patrick lived in Sonoma. He is a divorced father of three children. He owned a house in Sonoma, a brokerage account, and a retirement plan. Patrick also owned a small farm in Ireland. He created a U.S. trust to hold his U.S. home and his brokerage account. Patrick named his adult children as beneficiaries of his retirement plan. He created a will in Ireland, leaving the farm to his children as well. Patrick reported the existence of the Irish farm on his annual tax return and filed the required FBAR forms.

What About Gifts From and to People Living Abroad?

If you are a U.S. taxpayer and *receive* a gift that is valued at $100,000 or more from a nonresident alien, you have to report that gift to the IRS on a Form 3520 (*Annual Return to Report Transactions With Foreign Trusts and Receipt of Certain Foreign Gifts*) which tracks receipts of large foreign gifts. If a gift is valued at less than $100,000, you don't have to report the gift.

If you are a U.S. taxpayer and *make gifts* to people living abroad, like your parents, the transfer is subject to the same gift tax rules that such a gift would be subject to if your parents lived here: You can use your annual $14,000 gift tax exclusion. For example, if you send your parents $1,000/month, for a total of $12,000/year, the gift does not need to be reported. If you send them $2,000/month, for a total of $24,000/year, you'd need to report the gift, but no gift tax would be due: The first $14,000 qualifies as the annual exclusion, and you would use up $10,000 of your lifetime $5.49 million gift and estate tax exemption.

 EXPERT

Get professional advice if you own assets in another country.
Make sure that you are reporting your assets properly on your income tax returns and get legal advice on the best way to handle this in your estate plan.

Naming International Trustees and Executors

Some of my clients struggle with whom to name as trustees or executors for their U.S. estate plans because their most trusted friends and family members live abroad. And they usually don't like my advice—that they need to find domestic friends or relatives, or a U.S. corporation with trust powers (like a bank or a trust company) to serve as trustees—or else face both increased income tax obligations and increased reporting requirements.

The problem really has to do with jurisdiction—a fancy lawyer word for whether the person serving as trustee would be subject to the authority of a U.S. court.

International Executors of Wills

Non-U.S. residents *can* serve as an estate's executor if they are named in a person's will, but because no California court would have jurisdiction over them if they broke the law (because they don't live here) they will have to purchase a bond to be appointed. A bond is like an insurance policy. It protects the heirs and beneficiaries if an executor breaks the law or doesn't follow the terms of the will and it normally costs a percentage of the value of the estate.

Just because you can name an executor who lives abroad doesn't mean that it is a good idea to do so. Probate (if necessary) takes time and the executor has to sign a lot of papers, so it may be a better idea to name someone who is both local and fluent in English for this job.

International Trustees of Trusts

Trustees need to be permanent U.S. residents (green card holders are fine, visa holders are not) because a trust needs to be *both* administered exclusively within the United States *and* subject to U.S. court jurisdiction to be considered a domestic trust. Or rather, thanks to the upside down way that many tax regulations are written, unless both of those things are true (U.S. administration and subject to U.S. jurisdiction), a trust is considered a "foreign trust," which triggers more income taxation and more reporting requirements.

Normally when one thinks of a foreign trust, some nefarious setup on an island nation, specifically designed to avoid U.S. taxation, comes to mind. And that's what the rules for foreign trusts were written to address—offshore trusts that hide income from U.S taxation. The problem is that run-of-the-mill living trusts, designed only to avoid probate at death, can become subject to these rules, even if all of the assets and all of the beneficiaries are in the U.S., if the named trustee lives outside of the United States, even if that person is a U.S. citizen, and even if that person is just named as a back-up trustee.

If a trust is classified as a foreign trust, distributions to U.S. residents that would normally not be subject to income tax under trust accounting rules (capital gains) are subject to income tax. Extra tax and interest may be charged on any income that was accumulated in the trust in prior years, and each of the trust's beneficiaries will have to file a special form with his or her tax return in any year that they receive a trust distribution. (The special form is IRS Form 3520, *Annual Return to Report Transactions With Foreign Trusts and Receipt of Certain Foreign Gifts*, mentioned earlier in reference to gifts a U.S. taxpayer receives from a non-resident alien.) Failure to file Form 3520 leads to a penalty that is equal to 35% of the distributions to that beneficiary for that year.

And a foreign trust that invests in securities or other financial interests may also have to register with the IRS and be subject to penalties for failure to disclose information about U.S. account holders. All in all, being a foreign trust by accident is a bad idea.

EXAMPLE 1: Padmini and Govinda are both green card holders, working in the tech industry and living in Palo Alto. Their two children are both U.S. citizens. The couple wants to name Govinda's mother, Indira, as the trustee of their trust and executor of their wills, but she lives in Delhi, India. When their estate planning attorney tells them that if Indira is named as trustee, the trust will have pay additional income taxes, Padmini and Govinda decide instead to name Padmini's friend, Sumiya, who is a U.S. resident and lives in Chicago, as trustee.

EXAMPLE 2: Arthur lives in the Central Valley. His son Robert lives in Chile. Arthur's daughter, Tina, lives in Idaho. Arthur would like to name Robert as his successor trustee, but does not want to trigger foreign trust status for his living trust. Arthur names Robert as successor trustee only if Robert is a U.S. resident at that time. If Robert is not a U.S. resident, the trust names Tina as successor trustee.

EXAMPLE 3: Ari and Naomi are green card holders living in San Francisco. They have three children. All of the other family members live in Israel. Ari and Naomi don't know anyone in the United States whom they want to name as trustee, but they want their living trust to continue to be administered and invested in the United States after their deaths because they expect that their children will continue to live there. Ari and Naomi decide to name a Bay Area bank as successor trustee. Because the bank is a U.S. corporation, and because all of the assets will be invested and administered within the United States, Ari's and Naomi's trust will not be considered a foreign trust after they both die.

Naming Guardians for Minor Children Who Don't Live in the U.S.

Unlike the job of trustee or executor, it is okay to name someone who lives outside of the United States to serve as the guardian for minor children upon one's death. Because there is no visa for guardians, though, unless a guardian has another reason to stay in the United States legally, minor children will usually have to go back to the guardian's home country to live.

Actually, if a minor child is left without a living parent, a court appoints a guardian. Appointment of a guardian in California is like an adoption process: It requires notice to family members, investigation into appropriate placement, and in the end it's up to the court to make an appointment that is in the best interest of the child. Children over 14 years old are allowed to let the judge know their preferences, which the judge will take into consideration. Parents nominate guardians in their wills, and judges take these recommendations seriously, but the judge, not the deceased parents, makes that final call.

An international guardian seeking to relocate a child to his or her country would need to come to California, petition for appointment as a temporary guardian, and post a bond. In that petition, the guardian would have to ask the court to permit him or her (the guardian) to travel back to the home country and get appointed as a permanent guardian there. Once appointed permanently, the guardian would then notify the California court of the children's new address, and ask the court to terminate the temporary guardianship in the United States.

Because it may take time for a guardian to travel to California, it usually makes sense for parents to also name a temporary, local, guardian to take care of their children until family members can arrive from abroad. I also tell parents to make sure that their children have passports, since they'd need them to travel abroad.

EXAMPLE: Eduardo and his wife, Consuelo, who live in Alhambra, want to nominate Consuelo's parents, who live in Colombia, as guardians for their three minor children. In their wills, they nominate Consuelo's parents as guardians, and also nominate their best friend and neighbor, Katherine, to serve as a temporary guardian should that be necessary. All three children already have valid passports because they regularly travel to Colombia to visit their grandparents.

Estate Planning for a Noncitizen Spouse

Married couples have some extra planning to do in case one or both members of the couple are not U.S. citizens. The reason for this is that only gifts to U.S. citizen spouses qualify for an unlimited marital deduction.

The marital deduction works like this: For tax purposes, the IRS treats a married couple (if both are U.S. citizens) as one economic unit. At the death of one spouse, no estate tax is due, even if the estate of the deceased spouse is greater than the federal estate tax exemption, if all of the assets are left to the surviving spouse, either outright or in a trust that qualified for the marital deduction. But there's a catch. At the second spouse's death, to the extent that there are assets left, the assets are taxed at that time—making the marital *deduction* more of a marital *deferral*.

EXAMPLE: Dylan and Louise were both U.S. citizens. Dylan died in 2003, with an estate of $6 million. He left it all to Louise and no estate tax was due because of the unlimited marital deduction. Louise died in 2017. Her estate was $5 million because she'd spent down her assets during the 14 years since Dylan's death. Because the value of Louise's total estate at her death in 2017 was less than the federal estate tax exemption of $5.49 million, no estate tax was due at her death.

Noncitizen spouses, though, are treated differently. First, gifts during life to a noncitizen spouse are free of gift tax up to $149,000 (this number is adjusted for inflation periodically). For gifts at death, gifts over the estate tax exemption (currently $5.49 million) are subject to estate tax. The IRS is worried that if they defer any estate tax due at the first death for couples with a surviving noncitizen spouse, the surviving noncitizen spouse might just return to his or her home country and die there, outside of the IRS's jurisdiction. If that happened, the IRS would never collect that deferred tax.

There's a work-around for this. And it's relevant only for couples with large estates and when one, or both, spouses are not U.S. citizens. Say the first spouse to die is a U.S. citizen or resident alien, and has an estate that exceeds the federal estate tax exemption, and the surviving spouse is not a U.S. citizen (and doesn't become one within nine months of the death). In this situation, the assets belonging to the first spouse to die that exceed that federal estate tax exemption (which would otherwise be subject to estate tax at the death of the first spouse) can be placed in what's called a qualified domestic trust (or "QDOT") for the benefit of the surviving noncitizen spouse.

Assets placed in a QDOT are not subject to estate tax until the survivor withdraws money from that trust (unless it's for an immediate need relating to health, maintenance, education, or support), or until that spouse dies. U.S. resident couples with nontaxable estates really don't have to worry about this because all of the deceased spouse's assets can pass free of estate tax, being less than the federal estate tax exemption. And if the deceased spouse's assets exceed the exemption amount, and the surviving spouse becomes a U.S. citizen within nine months of the death of his or her spouse, no QDOT is required. If, after a spouse dies, it turns out a

QDOT is necessary because the deceased spouse's assets exceed the exemption amount and the survivor doesn't want to become a U.S. citizen or can't do so, the surviving spouse can "reform" an existing trust or simply create a new QDOT to avoid the estate tax that would otherwise be due.

A qualified domestic trust must meet a few requirements:

- The surviving spouse must get all income from the trust.
- The trustee must elect QDOT status on the decedent's estate tax return.
- At least one trustee must be a U.S. citizen or a U.S. corporation.
- IRS regulations on QDOTs must be followed (mostly to do with special security requirements).

EXAMPLE 1: Liam is a citizen of Australia but a green card holder. His wife, Sylvia, is a U.S. citizen. When Sylvia dies in 2017, her estate is worth $7.49 million, which exceeds her federal estate tax exemption of $5.49 million. Because Liam, the surviving spouse, is not a U.S. citizen, he would be subject to estate tax on $2 million of the estate he is inheriting from Sylvia. The couple's estate plan, however, directs the trustee to allocate that $2 million to a qualified domestic trust for Liam's benefit. If Liam ever needs to withdraw money from that trust, he will have to pay estate taxes on those withdrawals.

EXAMPLE 2: Yuka and Toshi are both citizens of Japan and U.S. residents with green cards. Their total estate is $2 million. Even though they are both noncitizens, their estate plan doesn't need to have a qualified domestic trust because their estate is well below the current federal estate tax exemption and no estate tax would be due at either the first or the second death.

TIP

Options may vary by country. The U.S. has tax treaties with some countries which allow noncitizens to choose between using a qualified domestic trust or the provisions of a treaty. Couples with taxable estates and noncitizen spouses should definitely talk to an expert—either an attorney or a CPA.

Yours, Mine, and Ours: Estate Planning for Blended Families

Community Versus Separate Property 182

    What's Yours and What's Mine? 183

    What to Talk About..185

    Changing the Rules 186

    Why Sign a Property Agreement?...187

Community Property and Taxes...190

Planning Strategies for Blended Families..192

    Naming Successor Trustees..193

    Planning to Avoid Conflict If You Are Married.................................195

    Planning to Avoid Conflict If You Are Not Married.........................198

Planning for Children of Different Ages 199

Putting It All Together...200

Read this chapter if:

- You are in a second, or third (or fourth) marriage and have children from a prior marriage.

- You don't know if you own separate or community property, or both.

- You own property that you inherited or brought to your marriage and have kept separate.

- You are not sure if you need (or want) a premarital or postmarital agreement.

- You want to know why it might be a good idea to own property as community property instead of joint tenancy.

- You live with someone that you are not married to and may have children from previous relationships.

- You want to know how to balance the needs of your spouse or partner with the needs of your children from a prior relationship.

- You want to learn how to balance the needs of younger children with those of older children from prior relationships.

I t is hard enough to take the time to think through an estate plan when you are single or in a first marriage with mutual children. But it gets more complicated when you are in a second (or third) marriage, or are living with someone (but not married) and have children from prior relationships. If this describes your family, what's traditionally called a "blended family," this chapter is for you. I use the term blended family more broadly in this chapter to include couples, married or not, who bring children or assets to a relationship and need an estate plan that can address the issues that come with blending prior lives together.

While it is not universally true that blended families have more complicated estate plans, they often do, for these main reasons:

- Couples with children from prior marriages often want their assets to go to their respective children at their deaths. A husband and wife who married in their 60s, for example, each with adult children from a prior marriage, often want to take care of each other for their lifetimes, but want their respective children to inherit what's left of their estate after the death of their spouse.

- Couples may have mutual children that are many years younger than children from their prior marriages. If so, a couple may want their mutual, younger children, to get the bulk of their estate, but also want to make gifts to older children.

- Couples often come to a marriage with separate property that they want to keep separate. One partner might, for example, own the house that the couple lives in, but does not want their new partner to acquire any community property rights in that house.

- Unmarried couples do not get certain tax benefits that married couples do, and need to plan for that.

Estate planning for married couples in a blended marriage most often focuses on two key issues: *defining* clearly what property is separate property and what property is community property, and *controlling* where assets go after a person dies. These issues are completely related to each other, since you can't give away what you don't own.

Estate planning for unmarried couples most often focuses on understanding what will happen upon the death of the first partner with respect to taxes and the transfer of property; how best to take care of minor children; and, if each partner has children from prior marriages, how to balance the children's needs against those of a surviving partner.

Unmarried couples also need to plan for incapacity by putting durable powers of attorney and advance health care directives in place (see Chapter 11). While it is, of course, true that married couples also need to do this, for unmarried partners this kind of planning is especially important, since married couples sometimes get access to finances and medical information by virtue of the marriage, while unmarried couples often are required to show legal proof of their authority to act for one another.

None of the estate planning issues affecting blended families are insurmountable, but all of them require attention, focus, and, sometimes, a willingness to have uncomfortable conversations about topics that many people would prefer to avoid.

You Are in Good Company

If your household doesn't fit the traditional definition, here are a few statistics that are guaranteed to make you feel less alone:

- Recent U.S. Census data reported that less than a quarter of California households fit the description of the "nuclear" family—a married man and woman raising mutual children.
- According to a national study of the American family by the Pew Research Center in 2015, the share of children living in two-parent households is at the lowest point in more than 50 years: 62% of children live with two married parents. Only 46% of all children live with two parents who are in their first marriage. One in six kids is living in a blended family (defined in this study as a household with a stepparent, stepsibling, or half-sibling).
- Nationally, four in ten new marriages involve remarriage.

See the introduction to this book for more stats on California families.

Community Versus Separate Property

California is a community property state, one of only nine such states. All of the other states are called "common law" states. In a common law state, the name on an account or a deed to a house determines the ownership of that asset. In a community property state, all property acquired during marriage is presumed to be owned by both spouses equally as community property.

Community Property States		
Arizona	Louisiana	Texas
California	Nevada	Washington
Idaho	New Mexico	Wisconsin

* Alaska and Tennessee allow spouses to opt in to community property.

What's Yours and What's Mine?

California has specific rules for determining what property is community property and what property is separate:

- Separate property includes any property owned by one person prior to marriage or received by gift or inheritance during the marriage.
- Community property includes any and all income and assets acquired during the marriage.
- Quasi-community property includes all property acquired by either spouse that would have been community property if they'd acquired it in California. For example, if a married couple that lived in Santa Monica purchased a vacation home in Colorado, but then got divorced, that vacation home would be considered community property, owned one-half by each of them.

This all sounds simple enough. But in practice, things can get murky quite quickly. Most of my clients get confused about these rules, such as the following.

The name on a bank account or property deed doesn't determine ownership in California. The source of the funds in that account or the source of the funds used to purchase the property is what determines how property is characterized. So, for example, if Steven has a checking account in his name only, but the money in that account comes from wages he's earned while married, his wife, Carly, has a community property interest in one-half the value of that account.

If wages earned by one spouse during marriage are used to pay for real property owned by another spouse, both spouses gain a community property interest in the property with each payment on the mortgage. Here are a few examples for a fictional couple, Ella and Mike, both on second marriages:

- Ella moves into a house that her new husband (Mike) owned before the marriage. If Mike's house is subject to a mortgage, Ella acquires a community property interest in Mike's house with each monthly payment equal to one-half the equity gained each month (which is tiny, but adds up over time).

- Ella's father gives her an interest in the family business, and she continues to run that company with her new husband, Mike. By virtue of his labor, Mike is acquiring a community property interest in Ella's family's company over time.

- Mike came to the marriage with an investment account but continues to deposit money in that account after marriage. Ella, his new wife, owns some of that account with each such deposit.

For couples with such mixed-up property, estate planning can be a bit of a chore. It might be the first time they've ever thought about these issues and it often brings up some uncomfortable conversations. But estate planning can also be a real opportunity to clarify a couple's understanding of who owns what now, while they are both alive, and avoid conflict later on, when one spouse dies or the couple divorces.

Couples who live together, but don't marry, don't have to sort out the legal characterization of property. In fact, that's why many couples that I've worked with have chosen not to marry, but instead to keep their finances and property completely separate. Still, unmarried couples often face most of the other, thorny issues that come from trying to balance the needs of the surviving spouse/partner with the needs of children from prior marriages or relationships.

What to Talk About

Here are some things that many couples that I work with have discussed:

If married, what assets are separate and which ones are considered to be community? You might discover that you have different ideas about what you own together and what you own separately. You might discover that you don't even know how to characterize the property that you do have. If so, see a lawyer and work that out.

If a couple has children from prior relationships, would they like to make gifts to those children after the first spouse (or partner) dies? Balancing the needs of children with the needs of a surviving partner can be difficult, especially if there's not a large age difference between children of a first marriage and a new, younger partner. Sometimes life insurance can be used to provide adult children with assets after a parent dies while still ensuring that a surviving spouse/partner has sufficient assets to live on.

What would happen to the house when one spouse or partner dies? Would the survivor continue to live there? Would they be able to or want to do so? If that's the case, I advise couples to take a look at whether or not the survivor can afford to stay in the house—both in terms of maintenance and mortgages, but also property tax. (See Chapter 8 to learn about when property taxes go up.)

If stepchildren need to sell the house because it is their primary inheritance, where will the surviving partner then live? I advise couples to be realistic about the likelihood that stepchildren would permit a surviving partner to stay in a valuable house and to plan for the eventuality of that partner's having to move elsewhere.

How do you want to handle the furniture, furnishings, and other items of a personal nature at the death of one partner? Would stepchildren want some of their parent's things? Would giving them these things be disruptive for the survivor? Would stepchildren and the surviving partner be able to sort out which items belonged to which partner?

Couples sometimes leave lists of specific gifts of such tangible items to avoid fights about them. Couples also sometimes leave such tangible personal items in trust for the survivor, so it is clear to children that they can't just come over and take all the furniture after their parent dies.

Who do you want to name as beneficiaries for retirement plans and/or life insurance policies? Naming beneficiaries for accounts and policies is one way to transfer assets directly to children, or to your spouse or partner, but this requires filling out beneficiary forms with each institution, and, if you don't want to name a spouse as a beneficiary, that spouse needs to consent. For unmarried couples, it is especially important to name a partner as beneficiary for such accounts since they won't otherwise qualify as an heir.

RESOURCE

For more ideas, strategies, and estate planning solutions to common issues facing blended families, read *Estate Planning for Blended Families,* by Richard E. Barnes. For unmarried couples, *Living Together,* by Frederick Hertz and Lina Guillen, offers practical advice and downloadable forms for such things as buying a house, negotiating finances, starting a family, and raising children. Both books are published by Nolo.

Changing the Rules

While California has specific rules about who owns what, you don't have to be governed by them. California permits couples to come to a different understanding about what is community and what is separate property. To do this, a couple must clearly state how their property is owned. They must do so in writing; a handshake or an oral understanding won't do. Such a property agreement (called a premarital agreement if done before marriage, or a postmarital agreement if done after) must include express language stating that the characterization of property is being changed by the agreement.

Such agreements don't have to be complicated—they just need to be clear. As long as the pre- or postmarital agreement is in writing, and each party has it reviewed by a separate attorney (or waives their right to attorney review), the agreement will be valid as long as both parties have honestly and fully disclosed all of their assets.

RESOURCE
To learn more about prenup agreements and draft your own, see *Prenuptial Agreements*, by Shae Irving and Katherine Stoner (Nolo).

Why Sign a Property Agreement?

The value of signing a property agreement is that it helps makes things clear after the death of one or both spouses (and, of course, in case of divorce). And that's when the characterization of property (as either separate or community) really matters. First, clear characterization of property can avoid challenges to an estate plan that claim that one person gave away property that they didn't, in fact, own. In a blended marriage, where children are not mutual children, couples need to understand what they can, and can't, give away by will or trust.

EXAMPLE: Daniel and Nora had been married for more than 20 years. Nora had a daughter (Karen) from her prior marriage. Daniel had no children. The couple lived in Daniel's house in Stockton and he had also brought an investment account to the marriage. Daniel continued to add to the investment account during their marriage, and he and Nora had paid off the mortgage on the home. Daniel wanted to leave his property to Nora at his death, but he was worried that Nora's adult daughter, Karen, might claim some of the property as her own if Nora died first.

Daniel and Nora worked with a mediator to write an agreement that stated that the house and investment accounts were Daniel's separate property. Both Daniel and Nora had that agreement reviewed by their own attorneys. Daniel's estate plan leaves all of his property to Nora, or, if Nora doesn't survive him, to his sister, Angela. If Lisa dies first, her daughter, Karen, will have no claim on Daniel's property because it has been clearly designated as belonging only to Daniel. Karen can't argue that some of the house and some of the investment account should have belonged to her mother as community property.

Another benefit of having a property agreement is that it makes it easier for a person who wants to make certain that a particular piece of property, which may have been in his or her family for generations, stays in the family after he or she dies, and is not distributed to a spouse's family. Clarifying that the property is separate makes it simple to pass it directly to that person's heirs.

EXAMPLE: Felicity and Lance had been married for ten years. All of the property they acquired during the marriage was community property. Felicity's uncle died and left her a farm in Georgia that had been in the family for generations. The farm is Felicity's separate property because she received it as an inheritance. The farm is rented out and generates income that Felicity and Lance use to send their daughter, Camille, to school. Because Felicity wants to make sure that the farm will not have to be divided in a divorce, she and Lance sign a property agreement stating that the farm, and all income it generates, is Felicity's separate property. In the family trust, Felicity leaves the farm to Camille directly, if Camille survives Felicity, or to Camille's children if Camille does not survive Felicity. If Camille dies and has no children, the farm goes to Felicity's sister, Ginny. The community's assets all go to Camille, too. If Camille does not survive Felicity and Lance, and leaves no children of her own, the trust's community property assets are divided equally between Felicity's heirs (parents, siblings, nieces, and nephews) and Lance's heirs.

In the absence of any written agreement, heirs may have to sort out the nature of property at the death of one or both spouses. To do so, the survivor (or the ultimate beneficiaries) will look at the title to the property, the funds used to purchase that property, and any other evidence they have of gifts received. If a couple married when they had very little, and all the property was acquired during the marriage, that's not such a hard task. But, as I hope this chapter makes clear, that's not true for all families, and not defining the nature of property beforehand can make things complicated later on. That's why it's a good idea to discuss your understanding of how you own property together during life and create an agreement that makes this understanding explicit.

Unmarried couples don't need to create a property agreement, since their property is clearly separate, but they do need to discuss their intentions and plans with respect to how they will use that property to take care of each other (or not to) when one partner dies. For unmarried couples, estate planning can serve as a means to make these wishes binding and clear.

EXAMPLE 1: Layla and her partner, Vivian, are not married. Layla has two daughters from her first marriage. Vivian has two sons from her first marriage. Layla and Vivian live together but keep their finances separate. They own a home together—each partner owns one-half of the home. Layla and Vivian each create a separate living trust. Each trust leaves that person's trust assets to her partner, in trust for her partner's lifetime, and then whatever is left goes to that partner's children. Because Layla and Vivian are not married, their respective property is clearly separate, but they've used their estate plans to take care of each other with that property.

EXAMPLE 2: Harrison owns a lovely home in Monterey. He has three children from his two prior marriages. He now lives with Hilda, who is 15 years younger than Harrison and has two children from her prior marriage. They have chosen not to marry. Harrison would like Hilda to be able to stay in his home until she either chooses not to live there, or is not able to live there any longer. He creates a living trust that allows Hilda to live in the home for as long as she chooses to do so. At that point, the trust for Hilda will terminate and Harrison's children will inherit the house. Although Hilda has some assets of her own, Harrison is concerned that Hilda won't be able to pay for the expenses of that home, including property taxes and maintenance, so he purchases a life insurance policy that will cover these anticipated expenses and names Hilda as the beneficiary of that policy. Harrison leaves the rest of the trust's assets in equal shares to his three children. He tells his children that his plan allows Hilda to stay in the house for her lifetime so that they won't be surprised to learn this when he dies.

Community Property and Taxes

Married couples owning community property in California receive an enormous tax benefit at the death of the first spouse. All such property is revalued as of the date of the first spouse's death to the current market value. This is called a "step-up" in basis and it means that the survivor will not have to pay capital gains taxes on the increase in value of that property from the date of its initial purchase to the first death.

Property held as separate property, though, is only revalued when the owner dies. It's not hard to change property from separate to community. For real property, such as a house, a deed will do the trick. For all other property, a property agreement can do this. I'll discuss capital gains in more detail in Chapter 9, but for this chapter, my point is simply that owning property as community property reduces, or eliminates, capital gains taxes due after the death of the first spouse.

EXAMPLE 1: Adrian and Lucy, a married couple, purchased their home for $100,000 in 1995 and held title as joint tenancy. They did an estate plan in 2016 and changed the title on their home to community property during that process. Adrian died in 2017. The house was appraised at $1.1 million, and Lucy sold the house shortly thereafter for that amount. Lucy owed no capital gains taxes on the sale because she received a step-up in basis on the entire house. If Adrian and Lucy had sold the house before Adrian died, they would have owed approximately $165,000 in capital gains taxes: $1.1 million – $100,000 = $1 million of capital gains. Because it was their principal residence, the couple could have both used their $250,000 home-owner's exclusion to reduce the $1 million by $500,000, but would still have owned capital gains taxes on the remaining $500,000. Capital gains taxes are roughly 33%, so they would have owed approximately $165,000.

EXAMPLE 2: Dominic and Brian lived together, but never married. Dominic purchased a home for $100,000 in 1995, and took title to it as his separate property. Brian died in 2017, and the house was worth $1.1 million. Because Dominic was the sole owner of the home, it was not revalued at Brian's death (which means Dominic did not get a step-up in basis). If Dominic sold the house for $1.1 million after Brian died, he would owe capital gains on $1 million ($1.1 million – $100,000). Because the house was Dominic's principal residence, he could use his $250,000 homeowner's exclusion to reduce this to $750,000. Capital gains taxes are roughly 33%, so Dominic would have owed approximately $247,000.

Because of this step-up in basis, couples are sometimes eager to change separate property into community property as part of their estate planning process. This makes sense when you realize that a couple ordinarily isn't making an estate plan if their marriage is in imminent danger—they're not thinking about divorce at all. The problem is that things can change over time. And signing a deed or creating an agreement as to the status of property can come back to haunt couples if they subsequently divorce. For this reason, most estate planners refer couples to family lawyers to draft property (pre- or postmarital) agreements. This isn't a plot by lawyers to make planning more expensive. Instead, most estate planners feel that they must refer couples to family law attorneys to avoid any conflict of interest, since estate planners normally represent couples jointly. Because the spouses who are changing the nature of their separate property are giving up something of value by doing so, most estate planners think that those spouses should have their own attorneys to advise them on the consequences of their actions.

EXAMPLE: Craig and Lauren were married for 23 years. In 2004, they created a family trust. While working with their estate planner, Craig changed his Mendocino home from separate to community property by executing a deed transferring it from himself, as his sole property, to Craig and Lauren as community property, and then transferred it to the family trust.

Craig had purchased that home in the early 1980s, prior to his marriage to Lauren, for $75,000. In 2004, that property was valued at $475,000. Craig reasoned that at the death of either spouse, revaluing the house to current market value would eliminate hundreds of thousands of dollars in capital gains taxes when the home was subsequently sold. Their estate planner advised Craig of his right to work with separate counsel to make sure he understood what he was doing, but Craig declined to do so. In 2017, Craig filed for divorce. He was not happy to discover that, because he'd changed the Mendocino home to community property in 2004, Lauren was now entitled to a 50% interest in that home. Craig thought that he'd changed the nature of the property only in case of death, not divorce, but it doesn't work that way. Once you change property from separate to community, it applies to both death and divorce.

Planning Strategies for Blended Families

Every family, blended or not, creates an estate plan to benefit the people they love and hopes that the plan will work as intended when the time comes.

For married couples who create a living trust together, as most of my clients do, planning gets complicated because one trust has to accommodate both partners' wishes and, potentially, treat each of their respective children differently. For unmarried couples, the concerns are the same, but the planning can be a bit easier because each partner usually does a separate trust, which makes taking care of any children from different relationships more straightforward.

This kind of family planning often boils down to four key decisions:

- whom to name as successor trustee—this is the person who will administer the trust after you die or become incapacitated
- how to structure a trust at the death of the first partner
- how to distribute assets at the death of the second partner, and
- how to coordinate beneficiary designations so that they are consistent with the plan. (See Chapter 10 for more on retirement assets.)

Naming Successor Trustees

By the time most couples in a blended family get around to estate planning, they know their children and the family's dynamic pretty well. My advice: Don't sugarcoat it. If your stepchildren don't like their stepmother or her children from a previous marriage, don't pretend that they do. If you know that your son from Marriage One has always felt aggrieved and mistreated, don't fantasize that at your death, he will suddenly learn to play well with others—he won't. And if your idea of a family holiday is shuttling between households rather than eating dinner together, don't put together an estate plan that relies on clear communication and mutual goodwill.

Honesty beats fantasy every time in estate planning. A good plan works because it is well thought-out and carefully crafted. A good plan works when expectations are realistic and the rules for distribution are clear.

Blended families need to think carefully about whom to name as successor trustees. Typically, the surviving spouse will serve as trustee after the first spouse dies. It would be unusual *not* to name a surviving spouse in this situation, but I have worked with families that want an adult child of the decedent to work with the surviving spouse as a cotrustee, or who name a professional instead. Generally, though, the last thing a surviving spouse wants is to have stepchildren involved in the day-to-day management of their finances, or to give up control over their checkbook to anyone, especially after the death of a spouse.

Most of the time, the discussion turns on who to name as successor trustee after both spouses have died. And it's here that it is important to be ruthlessly honest. A child who has always been a procrastinator, or who is dishonest, or controlling, can wreak familial havoc if given the trustee's job. You, as the person creating the trust, are better off picking the best people for this job, regardless of family politics. You are going to need someone who can communicate well with everyone, who will be fair, and who is willing to address reality, especially when stepchildren don't get along.

For some blended families, none of the children will be able to serve as successor trustees. For other blended families, having one child from each family makes sense. For still other families, naming a professional fiduciary makes the most sense. There isn't one solution that works for everyone, but it is critical to treat family conflict with respect and not just hope that somehow longstanding grievances will magically disappear at the death of a parent.

EXAMPLE 1: Bette and George married when they were in their late 50s. Bette had three sons from her first marriage, all adults. George had a daughter and a son, also both adults. Although the five children were polite to one another, they did not consider themselves to be a family unit. Bette and George alternated holidays with their respective children, but they purchased a new home to live in together and considered it to be their home, not a family gathering place. In their estate plan, Bette and George decided that they wanted one child from each family to serve together as cotrustees after they both had died and required that all decisions be made by mutual agreement. They discussed this with their respective children and told them that they felt that this way, each side of the family would feel represented and listened to. Their adult children agreed to work together to settle Bette and George's estate when the time came.

EXAMPLE 2: Didi and Judith married each other after each had been divorced. Didi had two boys, one in high school and one in college. Judith had two girls, one in middle school and one in high school. Didi lived in San Francisco and Judith lived in San Rafael. They decided to not live together until all of their children left home, so they just alternated homes on weekends. In their estate plan, they named Didi's younger sister and brother to serve as successor trustee for Didi's assets and Judith's best friend from college to serve as successor trustee for Judith's assets. The couple felt that their children were all too young to take on that responsibility, but also that they wanted to keep their finances separate as much as possible. Didi's assets will pass to her boys; Judith's assets will pass to her girls. To make their plan work they also signed a property agreement that kept all of their assets completely separate.

EXAMPLE 3: Roselyn had three children from her first marriage. She then married Walter and they had two daughters together. Roselyn's son, Tony, was abrasive, unhappy, and angry about Roselyn's new family (and almost everything else). Roselyn and Walter decided to name a local bank to serve as successor trustee. They wanted a neutral professional to settle their estate and help shield their younger children from Tony's troublemaking nature.

Planning to Avoid Conflict If You Are Married

A well-designed estate plan can accommodate the sad truth that after a parent dies, relationships between stepparents and stepchildren may change. A common estate plan for a married blended family is to create two (and sometimes three) trusts at the death of the first spouse. One trust (the survivor's trust) holds the assets owned by the surviving spouse and the other trust (the bypass trust) holds the assets of the deceased spouse. If the deceased spouse's assets exceed the federal estate tax exemption (which is $5 million, currently 5.49 million since the exemption is indexed to inflation), the amount over that exemption may be allocated to a third trust (the marital trust). For most couples, though, two trusts are created.

This kind of estate plan used to be created for almost all married couples as a way to minimize estate taxes, but since families with less than $11 million don't have a taxable estate under current law, the main reason to consider such a structure now is really about control. By dividing assets into two trusts at the first death, the first spouse to die can be certain that his or her assets will be available to the surviving spouse, but, after the surviving spouse dies, the first spouse to die's assets will flow to their chosen beneficiaries. For couples with children from prior marriages, this can be an ideal way to provide for their current spouses and their children from prior marriages.

Both trusts are held for the benefit of the surviving spouse for his or her lifetime. The survivor can change the terms of the trust that holds their assets, but the terms of the trust that holds their deceased spouse's assets can't be changed; it becomes irrevocable at the first death. At the death of the second spouse, the assets of the first spouse to die go to that person's children and the assets of the second person to die goes to that person's children.

While that sounds simple enough, families sometimes balk at the complexity of it. But they shouldn't. Such a plan can really protect a surviving spouse's relationship with stepchildren and provide them with flexibility if that relationship doesn't work out as it was expected to after the death of the first spouse.

EXAMPLE: Sandy had two daughters from her first marriage. Her current husband, Ross, had three daughters from his first marriage. Sandy died first. Her assets were allocated to a bypass trust for Ross's lifetime benefit. His assets were allocated to a survivor's trust, also for his benefit. Ross was the trustee of both trusts. Five years after Sandy died, Ross amended the survivor's trust to add gifts to his two grandchildren. At Ross's death, the assets in the bypass trust were distributed to Sandy's two daughters and the assets in the survivor's trust were distributed to Ross's three daughters, with a gift to each of his two grandchildren.

Typical Estate Plan for a Blended Family

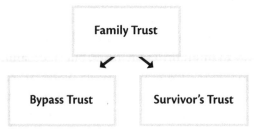

Sometimes It's Not About Trust

I once met with a client who really didn't want to create a bypass/ survivor's trust estate plan. She was concerned that her husband of more than 20 years didn't trust her enough to take care of his son from a previous marriage because he wanted to place his assets into an irrevocable trust at his death. To her, the fact that they'd been married for so long was proof enough that their estate plan should be simple—they should just leave everything to each other, without all the complications of creating two different trusts.

But from my perspective, there was another way to look at it: Creating a trust to hold her husband's assets for her benefit if he died first might be helpful to her, not harmful. To my mind, it wasn't about whether or not her husband "trusted" his wife, but rather whether or not he wanted to reduce the potential burden on her of dealing with his son for her lifetime. If her husband's assets were in an irrevocable trust for his wife's lifetime benefit, she would not be able to use any of that money for his son. Having a trust like this, I told her, can make saying "no" easier. Creating two trusts makes it clear to children that they only inherit after the death of the second spouse.

The truth of the matter is that, even in families that have managed to cobble together good feelings and create a blended family, all of that can change when the parental glue that holds it together disappears. And when it does, a trust structure that keeps each spouse's assets separate can be a good thing.

One family I worked with, for example, had been married for many years when they came to me. They each had children from prior marriages, and wanted to treat them all the same. When we met to do their estate plan, they spoke fondly of their blended family and how the children enjoyed each other's company and how they spent family holidays together. Their plan used a bypass/survivor's structure to divide into two trusts at the first death, even though they felt this wasn't really necessary. Their trust left an equal share to all five of the children equally from each trust.

Sometimes It's Not About Trust (continued)

Then, the wife died. And suddenly, her three children became suspicious and aggressive towards their stepfather, demanding personal items that had belonged to their mother and making him feel unsafe and unhappy. Within a year, he amended his survivor's trust to leave all of his assets to his two daughters, excluding his wife's three children, with whom he'd become estranged. Their estate plan allowed him the flexibility to amend his survivor's trust, but not the bypass trust. At his death, all five children will still share the assets left in the bypass trust equally.

Couples can also place restrictions on how a surviving spouse can use the assets held in the bypass trust. Typically, the restrictions are minimal and drafted to make sure that the survivor won't be taxed on the bypass trust's assets—the survivor can use these assets for health, education, maintenance, and support. But sometimes, families will place additional restrictions, such as use of income only; use of the family residence with no power to sell that home in the future; or use of principal only for health care expenses not covered by insurance.

Planning to Avoid Conflict If You Are Not Married

Unmarried couples who create separate living trusts often create plans with a similar structure to the one described above for married couples. When the first partner dies, his or her assets are held in trust for the benefit of the survivor. Once the first partner dies, that trust becomes irrevocable. In a typical A/B trust for a married couple it works the exact same way: At the first spouse's death, his or her assets are held in an irrevocable trust for the benefit of the surviving spouse. The survivor can use the trust's assets for his or her lifetime, but can't change the ultimate beneficiaries (because the trust is irrevocable), who are often the deceased partner's children from a prior marriage. The surviving partner has his or her own assets in a revocable living trust that functions like the survivor's trust in the example above. That trust is fully amendable and revocable by the survivor during his or her lifetime and keeps that person's assets separate from those of the deceased partner's.

What's different about an unmarried couple's plan is primarily tax related. Married couples (who are U.S. citizens) can leave an unlimited amount of assets to each other free of estate tax at death. Unmarried couples (who are U.S. taxpayers) can leave their partners assets up to the maximum federal estate tax exemption available at their death, currently $5.49 million dollars, free of estate tax. Very wealthy unmarried partners may have to pay an estate tax bill at death that spouses can defer if they own more assets than the federal estate tax exemption allows them to pass tax free. As discussed in Chapter 9, this marital deduction actually defers any tax due until the death of the second spouse, when such assets are subject to tax. But since very few people have more than $5.49 million, the estate tax isn't usually the focus of their plan. For the purpose of providing for a surviving partner, then making sure that your assets will go to your children or other beneficiaries after your partner dies, a two trust solution works well.

Planning for Children of Different Ages

At the death of the first partner, most couples choose to create an estate plan that takes care of the surviving partner only, opting to distribute assets to children or other heirs only after the death of the second spouse or partner.

But some blended families don't want to do this, for various reasons. For example, one partner, who has much older children from a previous marriage, will want to make sure that those children receive something from that parent, even if survived by a partner. Or a couple may want to direct more money towards their younger, mutual children who have yet to grow up or go to college.

To accomplish either goal, an estate plan can include a gift to older children at the death of their parent, and then leave the remainder in trust for the surviving partner, who, presumably will use some of that money to raise and educate the younger mutual children. Another way to take care of older children may be to purchase a life insurance policy, naming those children as beneficiaries, but leave trust assets to the surviving partner.

EXAMPLE 1: Greg had three adult sons from a prior marriage. His second wife, Jocelyn, was 30 years younger than Greg, and they had two children together. In their estate plan, if Greg dies first, he directs the trustee to distribute a gift of 50% of his assets directly to his three sons, in equal shares. The remainder is allocated to a bypass trust for Jocelyn's benefit. At her death, the remaining assets will pass to the two youngest, mutual children. In effect, Greg wants to make sure that his older sons receive their inheritance at his death, even if Jocelyn survives him. Since Jocelyn is only five years older than Greg's oldest son, Greg didn't want his sons to have to wait until Jocelyn's death to receive an inheritance.

EXAMPLE 2: Len had a 25-year old daughter, Eileen, from a relationship he had in college. Len married Sumita many years later. Len and Sumita's estate plan left everything outright to each other; they kept it simple. Len purchased a life insurance policy on his life and named his daughter Eileen as the beneficiary. Len paid for that insurance policy with his separate property, using a bank account that he owned before his marriage and that he kept separate from his joint account with Sumita. When Len dies, Eileen will receive $500,000 from that insurance policy and Sumita will receive all of the rest of Len's assets.

Putting It All Together

Blended families face planning challenges that are unique, but with enough humility, honesty, and willingness to grapple with the issues, there's no reason that you can't put together an estate plan that addresses your main concerns. As long as you are clear about the ownership of property and honest about the likelihood of your families getting along after you die, your estate plan can go a long way towards making it easier, not harder, after your death.

Estate Planning and Property Tax: What You Need to Know About Prop 13

Property Taxes in California and Prop 13..203

    A Little History...203

    What Prop 13 Did... 204

What Really Matters: Change in Ownership of Your Home.................... 206

Exclusions From Reassessment That You Have to Request 209

    Parent-Child and Grandparent-Grandchild Exclusions............................ 209

    Transfers Between Cotenants 213

    Purchase of a Replacement Residence by a Person 55 Years

        or Older..214

Automatic Exclusions from Reassessment 216

    Transfers Between Spouses and Registered Domestic Partners..........216

    Transfers Between Co-Owners That Don't Change

        the Proportional Interests..217

    Transfers Into and Out of Trusts..219

Reporting a Change of Ownership...220

    What If You Don't File a Claim for Exclusion from Reassessment?.....222

Read this chapter if:

- You own a house or other real property in California.

- You would like to pass your low property tax rate to your children, spouse, or partner at your death.

- You own both a residence and other rental properties and want to understand how to transfer these properties at your death without an increase in property tax.

- You own property as a cotenant with another person.

- You are over 55 and would like to downsize without triggering an increase in property tax.

One major way that estate planning in California differs from other states is the way property taxes are calculated. California used to calculate property tax the same way most states do it: The assessor looks at the value of your property in the current market annually and assesses property tax based on that value. That works well if property values remain relatively constant, or even go down—not something that's true in California historically. As you'll read below, in the late 1970s, California voters, struggling with paying property taxes on property that kept going up in value each year, fundamentally changed that system by passing a constitutional amendment, Proposition 13.

As a result of Proposition 13, today, your property tax rate is pretty much locked in when you purchase property. Your property tax can go up a tiny bit each year, but it won't be reassessed to reflect the current market value of your property until there's a new owner. To put this another way: It's a change of ownership, not a change in market value, that changes your property taxes. If you've owned your property for a long time, it's a sure bet that your property tax rate is far lower than a neighbor who purchased their house last year.

For individuals and families who want to preserve their low tax rate, knowing when there's been a change of ownership, and whether or not that transfer is exempt from reassessment, can save property owners a lot of money. Not knowing how these rules work can trigger a massive increase in property taxes that may come as an unexpected, and unwelcome, surprise.

This chapter explains how Proposition 13 works to keep property taxes low, when property taxes are reassessed to current market value, and how you can take advantage of the exceptions to the law to avoid reassessment for certain transfers of property during life or at death. You'll learn which exceptions to the law are applied automatically and which require you or your heirs to file a claim form to qualify for the exclusion from reassessment. You'll also learn what happens if a claim form is required, but wasn't filed within the required amount of time.

Property Taxes in California and Prop 13

Property taxes in California pay for local government services provided by counties, schools, and special districts (like water, sewage, and pest abatement). Property tax rates vary county by county in California, since local governments can create special, local tax assessments by popular vote. But state law sets the maximum tax rate allowed and limits the annual increases each county can require.

In California, property tax is collected by county assessors. Their job is to annually assess all taxable property in the county, which involves determining the proper taxable value for each property and sending out property tax bills to the property owners.

A Little History

In most states, property tax is calculated annually based on the fair market value (FMV) of the property being taxed—that is, what a third party would pay for that property if it were sold today. In many parts of the country, where property values have remained stable, or declined, over the years, this method isn't controversial. But in California, as land prices boomed in the 1960s and 1970s, property tax became a political issue. California's hot real estate market was a mixed blessing. For homeowners looking to sell, it was great. But for people who weren't selling their homes, rapidly increasing property values meant rapidly increasing property tax bills and the fear by many homeowners that they wouldn't be able to stay in their homes. In the late 1970s, the state also had a $5 billion tax surplus, making taxpayers even angrier at their escalating tax bills.

As a result, in 1978, fed-up California voters passed Proposition 13, an amendment to the state constitution that changed the way that California calculated property taxes from a system that used the *market value* of a property to drive the tax system to one that used the *value of a property each time it changed hands* to do so.

What Prop 13 Did

Proposition 13 rolled back most local real property assessments to 1975 market value levels, and then limited property tax to 1% of the property's value, called the property's "base year value." It then limited increases in a homeowner's tax bill to 2% of that base value each year.

The original base value plus these annual increases is called the property's "factored base value" or, in simpler terms, the assessed value of your property. As a general rule, the longer you own your house, the greater the difference is going to be between the fair market value and this assessed value. The result is that people who have owned property in California since the 1970s pay the lowest property tax rates of all.

When you purchase a house, the county assessor assigns your property a base year value based on your purchase price. Each year thereafter, your property taxes can't increase by more than 2% of that base year value—which means that your property taxes are predictable and modest (excluding special local assessments, such as school bonds).

If you remodel your house, the assessor is going to take those improvements into account, and your property taxes will increase. But unless you completely remodel or rebuild, the original base year value for your home does not change (that was determined when you bought it)—the assessor is going to value the square footage that you've added and add these to the base year value of your home.

If you tear the whole house down and rebuild it from scratch, then your property tax bill is also going to increase. The assessor is going to keep the base year value of the land you own, but they're going to reassess the value of the new home you've just built. What's going to happen is that the new construction is going to generate a new supplemental assessment, which is equal to the difference between what you had to pay before, and what's due now because of the new house. Your property tax isn't going to be as much as what a new owner would have to pay, because that new owner's land value would also be reassessed to current value (and in many areas, the value of the land is a huge part of the value as a whole); but your property is going to be assessed for more than what you paid before you knocked the old house down.

If you sell your home, the new owner's purchase price becomes the new base year value and their property taxes will be significantly higher than the ones you were paying on your home. The result is that property taxes can vary dramatically for nearly identical houses in the same neighborhood.

EXAMPLE: Olivia and Kim are next-door neighbors in Walnut Creek, with nearly identical houses, but very different property tax bills. Olivia purchased her home in 1968 for $23,000. In 1978, Olivia's property tax rate was rolled back to what her house was worth in 1975 ($50,000). Using a modest .974% property tax rate, Olivia's property tax bill started at $397 per year and her increases were limited to 2% increases after that. Olivia paid approximately $843 in 2017.

Olivia's neighbor, Kim, purchased her home in 1995 for $305,000. Using the same tax rate as Olivia's, Kim's property tax bill started at $2,422 per year and increased 2% per year thereafter. When Kim sold her home in 2017, she was paying roughly $3,671 per year. The new owner, Ed, paid $980,000 for Kim's house. Ed's tax bill was $7,781 (compared to Kim's $3,671 and Olivia's $843) and would increase thereafter by a maximum of 2% per year.

To find out your current property tax bill and the current base year value of your home, look at your most recent property tax bill. The bill lists the assessed value of your property (which includes the land and the improvements on it). This value will almost always be lower than the current market value of the property unless you've recently purchased the house or the market has gone down since you purchased it.

RESOURCE

For a handy property tax calculator, go to https://smartasset. com/taxes/california-property-tax-calculator. If you, like me, don't normally look at your property tax bill because you have added your tax bill to your mortgage payment, this calculator can be illuminating. You enter your location and the price that you originally paid for your house and see an estimate of your property tax rate based on your county. To see how your property tax bills would increase over time, go to www.calculatorsoup.com/calculators/financial/property-tax-calculator.php.

What Really Matters: Change in Ownership of Your Home

Since Proposition 13 limits annual property tax rate increases to a modest 2%, property taxes go up only when there's been what the assessors call a "change in ownership." The assessor looks at it this way: Whenever the "beneficial owner" of a property changes, that's a change of ownership, whether or not money ever changed hands.

The simplest change of ownership event (triggering a property reassessment) is when a new owner buys a property. But it turns out that you don't have to sell the property to trigger a change of ownership—and that's relevant to your estate plan. Here are some other situations (not an exhaustive list) when this (a change of ownership) may occur:

- You leave your house to your niece in your will.

- You give your child a partial interest in your house during your lifetime.
- Siblings jointly inherit a house and one wants to buy the others out.
- You place your house in a trust for the benefit of someone who isn't a spouse or a child.

EXAMPLE: Ruby had a living trust. She left her house in Chico to her church when she died. The church members became the "beneficial owners" of Ruby's house upon her death because they are now the people who have the right to use the property. The transfer of the house at Ruby's death is a change of ownership. There is no exclusion for the transfer of a house to members of a church. The property will be reassessed as of the date of Ruby's death.

A change of ownership will trigger a reassessment of the property tax due on a piece of property. Usually, this will result in an increase in property taxes. Of course, in a falling real estate market, a reassessment after a change in ownership can mean a reduction in property tax, but that's a rare thing in the Golden State.

But—and this is a big but—not all changes of ownership trigger a reassessment and the property tax increases that typically accompany a change in ownership. Many property transfers/changes of ownership are excluded from reassessment because of the people involved or because of the way that the property is held. I'll explain below the most common ways to transfer property (or change ownership) that are excluded from reassessment. Some of these exclusions were part of the original Proposition 13; others were added by constitutional amendment over the years).

Knowing when and whether an exclusion applies can save your family thousands of dollars in taxes. Taking these exclusions into account in your estate plan can save your family property taxes for generations. These may require that you or the person(s) inheriting your property complete and submit a specific claim form to avoid reassessment, or the exclusion may be automatic. See the following sections for detailed explanations of the various exclusions.

As a general rule, the way to approach a property transfer is to ask these three questions:

1. Will the property transfer trigger a change in ownership for Proposition 13 purposes?
2. If so, does an exclusion apply so that the property tax rate won't go up?
3. If an exclusion does apply, is it an automatic exclusion, or one that requires filing a claim to avoid reassessment?

Finding Out More About Proposition 13

Property can change hands in all sorts of ways in California: by gift or by sale of a house, or within an entity such as an LLC or corporation. And property tax reassessment will be an issue in all such transfers. A thorough exploration of all of these transfers is beyond the scope of this book. I am focusing in this chapter on Proposition 13 issues related to estate planning only and primarily for residences and rental properties you may own.

For more information on Proposition 13, check out the website of the California State Board of Equalization, BOE, at www.boe.ca.gov:

- For a good overview of exceptions to Prop. 13, see "Change in Ownership" under "Frequently Asked Questions" at www.boe. ca.gov/proptaxes/faqs/faqspropindex.htm.
- For information on Proposition 13 related to property transfers and transfers of property within entities like LLCs and corporations, see www.boe.ca.gov/proptaxes/proptax.htm.
- For a more detailed explanation of Proposition 13 rules, including a lot of helpful examples (if you want to go deep into the weeds), see *The Assessor's Handbook, Change of Ownership*, at www.boe. ca.gov/proptaxes/pdf/ah401.pdf.

If you have a complicated issue, however, these resources will only get you so far; this is not a customer-friendly legal topic. If you get confused, consult with an attorney who knows this area of law; often real estate attorneys are most helpful for transfers within entities, and estate planners know the most about transfers between people at death.

Exclusions From Reassessment That You Have to Request

Some, but not all, of the exclusions from reassessment require that the person receiving the property file a form that tells the assessor why they (the assessor) can't raise property taxes. These exclusions from reassessment aren't automatic. If a person doesn't ask for one of the exclusions discussed in this section, they won't get it. These are "use it or lose it" rules—and it's up to you and your heirs to know them. These nonautomatic exclusions include:

- transfers between parents and children
- transfers between grandparents and children (if the parents have died)
- transfers between cotenants who have lived in the property for the year proceeding the transfer, and
- the purchase of replacement property of lesser value by a person over age 55 in the same county (and certain other counties).

Since these exclusions are not automatic, the person inheriting the property will need to file a claim form to escape reassessment.

Parent-Child and Grandparent-Grandchild Exclusions

In my practice, the most common Proposition 13 exclusion to reassessment that comes up is hands-down the transfer of property from parents to children. Since I'm an estate planner, this makes a certain amount of sense. I also have grandparents who ask me if they can transfer property to their grandchildren; but, as you'll read below, this exception is only available in the relatively rare situation where the parents are deceased.

Parent-Child Exclusion

Proposition 58, a constitutional amendment passed in 1986, excluded reassessment on real property transfers from parents to children (and from children to parents) within certain limits. These transfers can be as a result of a gift, a sale, or an inheritance (such as through a will). Transfers via living trusts also qualify.

Here's how it works. Parents can transfer their primary residence to children with no value limit, plus an additional $1 million worth of other real property, such as investment property or a vacation home, to children without property tax reassessment. Before you start panicking about the family beach house, read on. That $1 million worth of real property is calculated using the assessor's factored base year value, which (if you've owned the property for a long time) is nearly always much lower than the current market value of the property.

EXAMPLE 1: Tom, a widower, died in 2017 and left his home in Fresno to his only daughter, Leticia, in his will. When the probate of Tom's estate was completed, Leticia inherited the home, which was appraised at $300,000. Leticia's property taxes were not reassessed, and she continued to pay the taxes that her father had paid prior to his death. Leticia's tax bill will continue to go up, but not by more than 2% a year of the factored base year value of the property, which is far below the market value of the house ($305,000 in 2017), since her father purchased the house in 1981 for $60,000. Leticia's property taxes would be roughly $1,107 per year; a new owner, who paid $305,000 for the house would pay $2,760.

EXAMPLE 2: Maya and Dave own a house in Palos Verdes that is worth $3.5 million dollars. They also own three rental properties in Los Angeles that they purchased in the early 1970s. Maya and Dave want to leave all of their properties in equal shares to their three children via their living trust. Their children will be able to inherit all four properties without any reassessment of property tax. Maya and Dave's principal residence can be transferred to their children free of reassessment because Proposition 58 allows the transfer of one primary residence of any value. Maya and Dave's rental properties are worth $2 million currently, but their base year value is only $435,000 altogether; this is because Maya and Dave purchased the rental properties in 1978, for $70,000 each, and the property tax increases have been limited to an annual 2% since that time.

EXAMPLE 3: Zoe owns a cabin in Auburn. Over the years, she and her husband find that they don't use it as much as they used to, now that their children have grown up and moved away. Zoe's mother, Audrey, loves the cabin and now that she is retired, she is ready to sell her home in the South Bay and move to the Gold Country. Zoe sells Audrey the cabin. Because this is a transfer between child and parent, it is excluded from reassessment and Audrey keeps Zoe's property tax rate. The cabin is not Zoe's principal residence, but its base year value is far below $1 million, so the transfer fits within Proposition 58's limit.

Grandparent-Grandchild Exclusion

Proposition 193, a constitutional amendment passed in 1996, excludes reassessment on transfers of real property between grandparents and grandchildren. But to qualify for this exclusion, all of the parents of the grandchildren receiving this property must be deceased as of the date of the transfer. The same limits apply to these transfers as to the parent-child transfers: one primary residence of any value and up to $1 million of other real property.

EXAMPLE: Luciana left her home in Santa Rosa to her deceased daughter's son, Mateo, when she died. The property passed to Mateo via Luciana's living trust. Because Mateo's mother died before Luciana transferred the home to Mateo, the grandparent/grandchild exclusion to reassessment applied, and Mateo kept Luciana's low property tax assessment.

The exclusion is not available if a grandchild's parents are alive—which makes a certain amount of sense. After all, if a parent was alive, a grandparent could give the property to that parent and that transfer would qualify as a parent-to-child transfer: Then, that parent could later transfer it to his or her own children, which would avoid reassessment again.

EXAMPLE: Nelson was ready to move to an assisted living facility in Modesto, near to his daughter, Gigi, and her family. He had lived in his home since 1954, and his property tax bill was a fraction of that paid by his neighbors, who had bought into the neighborhood in the early 2000s. Nelson sold his home to his grandson, Rob. Because Rob's mother Gigi was still alive, the transfer to Rob was not excluded from reassessment. Rob's new property bill was pegged to the purchase price he paid and was much higher than what Nelson had been paying. If Nelson had sold his house to Gigi, first, and then Gigi had sold it to Rob in a year or two, the family could have retained Nelson's very low property tax rate.

Who Counts as a Child for the Parent/Child and Grandparent/Grandchild Exclusion?

Applying these exceptions to real-life families can be tricky, especially in California, where there are so many blended families. Here's who qualifies as a "child" and "grandchild" for the purposes of qualifying for these exclusions:

- any child born of the parent making the transfer
- any stepchild, as long as the relationship of stepchild and stepparent exists
- any son-in-law or daughter-in-law of the parents
- any child adopted before age 18
- spouses of eligible children until divorce, or, if the marriage is terminated by death, until the remarriage of the surviving spouse, stepparent, or parent-in-law, and
- any grandchild who is a child of parents who qualify as children of the grandparents under the above rules.

EXAMPLE 1: Lew wants to leave his home in Anaheim to Constance, the wife of Lew's deceased son, Finn. Constance has not remarried. Constance qualifies as a "child" under the parent/child exclusion because she has not remarried after Finn's death and so she will be able to inherit Lew's home and retain his low property tax assessment.

EXAMPLE 2: Bonnie decides to leave her beach house in Malibu to the three children of her second husband, Ralph, at her death. Bonnie and Ralph are still married, this transfer qualifies under the parent/child exclusion and the beach house won't be reassessed when her stepchildren inherit it.

EXAMPLE 3: Logan wants to leave his condominium in Vallejo to his grandchildren, Tara and Chloe. Logan's daughter, Nancy, died three years ago. Nancy was married to Gabe, Tara and Chloe's father, when she died. Because Gabe is still alive, and has not remarried, this transfer would not qualify for an exclusion from reassessment under Proposition 193 and Tara and Chloe would be reassessed at the market value of Logan's property when they inherit it. Logan could leave his condo to Gabe, though, without triggering a reassessment under Proposition 58, because Gabe is his son-in-law and has not remarried.

EXAMPLE 4: Kristen wants to leave her Bakersfield home to her grandchildren, Brock and David. The children's father, Scott, died ten years ago, after he divorced their mother, Vanessa. Vanessa is still alive. Because Scott was not married to Vanessa when he died, the fact that Vanessa is alive doesn't matter for Kristen—her ex daughter-in-law is not considered her child for purposes of the exclusion—so Kristen can leave her home to Brock and David and they will not have their property taxes reassessed.

Transfers Between Cotenants

Transfers between unrelated people can be excluded from reassessment in certain circumstances, but the rules can make your head spin. The most common scenario that I deal with happens this way: An unmarried couple own a home together as either joint tenants or as tenants in common. Sometimes this is a couple who have been married to other people before and want to keep their lives financially separate or do not want to be married for some other reason. Sometimes two people buy property together and live in it as co-owners although they are not living together as a couple. In either case, transfers between such cotenants will be excluded from reassessment at the death of one of them provided that *all* of the following apply:

- The two cotenants together owned 100% of the property as either tenants in common or joint tenants.
- The two cotenants were the owners of record for the one-year period immediately preceding the death of one of the cotenants.
- The property was their principal residence for that one-year period.
- The surviving cotenant receives 100% of the interest in the property.
- The surviving cotenant signs an affidavit affirming that he or she continuously lived in the residence for that one-year period.

EXAMPLE 1: Paul and Matt own a home together in San Diego as joint tenants. They have lived in the home for 20 years. They are not married. When Paul dies, Matt will own the home as the surviving joint tenant and will not have property taxes reassessed because he and Paul lived there for the year prior to Paul's death, Matt owns 100% of the property, and it was their principal residence.

EXAMPLE 2: Stephanie and Jane purchased a home together as joint tenants. They used it as an investment property and rented it to students at San Francisco State University. When Jane died unexpectedly, Stephanie became the sole owner, but one-half of the house was reassessed. Stephanie didn't qualify for an exclusion from reassessment because the rental was not Stephanie's and Jane's principal residence.

Purchase of a Replacement Residence by a Person 55 Years or Older

Proposition 60, a constitutional amendment that passed in 1986, allows homeowners aged 55 or older to transfer the base year value of their principal residence to a replacement home, provided certain conditions apply. The new home must be:

- located in the same county as the original home
- equal to or less than the value of the original home
- purchased within two years of selling the original home, and
- sold to a new owner, who will be paying property tax on that sale value.

What that means is that if you downsize, you can keep your low property tax rate. This is a one-time exclusion from reassessment. If you purchase another home, your property taxes will go up.

This works for sure if you stay in the same county. In 1988, Proposition 90 passed, allowing counties to accept transfers of the base value from other counties. But as of this writing only 11 of California's counties accept such transfers (since that means the counties are foregoing property taxes that they could otherwise collect).

You might be wondering why this applies to estate planning. Here's why: If your heir inherits your low property tax rate, and is over 55, and would like to sell that house and move into a different house without losing that low rate, this exclusion might do the trick.

List of Counties That Accept the Transfer of Base Value for a Replacement Residence

This list is current as of the fall of 2017. To see if any counties have been recently added to this list, check out the list published by the California Board of Equalization. You can find it by going to their website at www.boe.ca.gov, then clicking on "Taxes/Property Taxes" and scrolling down to the "Frequently Asked Questions" section.

Alameda	Riverside	Santa Clara
El Dorado	San Bernadino	Toulomne
Los Angeles	San Diego	Ventura
Orange	San Mateo	

EXAMPLE: Nicole inherited her parents' home in the Berkeley hills in 2010. She was able to keep her parents' low property tax rate because it was a transfer from parents to child (her parents had purchased their home in 1979). Nicole and her family lived in that home for seven years, but, she decided to downsize the home after her children left for college in 2017. By then, Nicole was 58. She sold the Berkeley hills home to a nice young family and purchased a smaller house in the flatlands of Berkeley. Because her new home was purchased for less than what the Berkeley hills home was sold for, and because Nicole purchased her new home within two years of that sale, she was able to keep her low property tax rate for the new home.

Automatic Exclusions from Reassessment

In addition to the exclusions listed above (that all require a claim form), there are several automatic exclusions from reassessment that don't require that the new owner file a form requesting such an exclusion from reassessment. If an exclusion is automatic, once you notify the county assessor that it applies, you are done. You don't need to file an additional form requesting exclusion for reassessment.

Transfers that are automatic include those between spouses and registered domestic partners; between co-owners that don't change the proportional interest; and transfers into and out of trusts.

Transfers Between Spouses and Registered Domestic Partners

Transfers between spouses and registered domestic partners (that occurred after 2006) are excluded from reassessment. (Transfers between registered domestic partners from 2000 to 2006 are also excluded from reassessment, but the procedure is different.) This exclusion (meaning there is no reassessment of property tax) applies to transfers at death and during life, including the following situations:

• One spouse buys out the other as a result of a divorce.

- One spouse transfers separate property owned as a single person to his or her new spouse as community property.
- A couple transfers their property into or out of a revocable living trust.
- A couple transfers their property from joint tenancy to community property with right of survivorship.

EXAMPLE 1: When Wilma died, her 50 percent interest in the family home in Riverside was transferred to her husband, Adam, as the surviving joint tenant. This is a change in ownership of a 50% interest in the house from Wilma to Adam. Transfer of ownership between spouses is an exclusion from reassessment. Wilma's 50% of the house will not be reassessed. This exclusion from reassessment is automatic, so Adam does not have to file a claim form.

EXAMPLE 2: Amanda and Eric owned their home as joint tenants. When they went to see an estate planner, she suggested that they change this to community property with right of survivorship so that their entire house would get a step-up in basis at the death of the first spouse. Since transfers between spouses are exempt from reassessment, this change did not increase Amanda and Eric's property taxes.

EXAMPLE 3: Taylor and Robin owned a house as community property. When they created their revocable living trust, they transferred the house into the trust. Because transfers to or from revocable trusts for the benefit of the transferor and the transferor's spouse are exempt, this change did not increase Taylor and Robin's property taxes.

Transfers Between Co-Owners That Don't Change the Proportional Interests

Transfers between co-owners can trigger reassessments when they change the percentage interests each owner has. This is important for estate planning because families need to consider this when planning for the transfer of property with low taxes if their children will not inherit that property equally.

For example, if three siblings have inherited a house together from a parent and own it as cotenants, no property tax reassessment would have happened at the parent's death because of the parent/child exclusion. If, however, a year later one sibling buys the other two out of the house, two-thirds of the house will be reassessed because now one sibling owns the whole thing and there is no exclusion for transfers between siblings.

One way to avoid this kind of reassessment is to leave a house specifically to one child, and leave other assets of equal value to the other children. This, of course, only works when there are sufficient other assets to let one child receive the entire house as his or her share and when you know that one child wants the house but the others do not. The problem that many families face is that there are not enough other assets to make this work perfectly and so the sibling who does want to keep the house has to buy out a sibling, triggering a reassessment for the percentage of the house they purchased.

EXAMPLE 1: Owen has two daughters. One daughter, Liz, wants to inherit his home in Novato. The other daughter, Casey, lives in New York and doesn't want to inherit the home. Owen has $2 million in assets, and the house is worth $1 million. Owen's living trust directs the trustee to allocate his home to Liz's share, and an equal amount of other assets to Casey. Liz will inherit Owen's home without reassessment under the parent/child exclusion. The assessor will want to see proof that Casey received an equivalent amount of other assets and that the house was appraised at $1 million.

EXAMPLE 2: Leroy has two sons. One son, Steve, wants to keep Leroy's house in Santa Cruz. The other son, Victor, already owns a home. Leroy has $1.5 million in assets, and the house is worth $1 million. Leroy's living trust divides his assets in equal shares between Steve and Victor. When Leroy dies, Steve and Victor each inherit a 50% interest in the house. Steve sells his existing home and purchases a 50% interest in the house from Victor for $500,000 and now owns the entire house. Half of the house is reassessed for property tax purposes. The half of the house that Steve inherited from Leroy is not reassessed under the parent/child exclusion.

SEE AN EXPERT

Get legal advice. If you and your siblings are trying to transfer inherited property interests without triggering a reassessment, consult with an attorney before you file anything with your county assessor's office. The reason to take your time here is that you want to think through the consequences of what you are doing. If, for example, one sibling wants to purchase property from another sibling, it's a good idea to work through the details before you report the percentage of ownership each sibling has. Any subsequent change to those percentages will trigger a reassessment of the portion of the property that has changed hands.

Transfers Into and Out of Trusts

Transfers into and out of trusts are not by themselves triggers for reassessment. The assessor doesn't care that a trust owns property. The assessor cares about who will use the property—if that changes, property tax may go up. If necessary, the assessor will read the trust or will to determine who has the use of the property, whom they consider to be the new owner, which they call "the beneficial owner." But if the new owner falls within any of the exceptions to reassessment that I've described above, and files the necessary claim forms, property taxes won't go up.

The most common transfer into and out of a trust is the one that you would do if you created a living trust as part of your estate plan. If you transfer your home into a revocable living trust for the purpose of avoiding probate (more on that in Chapter 3), you are still considered to be the owner of that property and no reassessment will happen. The assessors know that revocable trusts are created for the benefit of the people who own the property, so there's not a "new" beneficial owner created just by transferring a property into a trust. They don't need to read your trust in this situation.

If you transfer your property out of a living trust, most commonly to refinance your property, or because you are getting a divorce and must divide up the property, the assessors understand that the same people own it after the transfer out of the trust. They just own the property in a different legal way—as husband and wife as community property, for example, or as an individual owner. Again, the transfer out of a revocable living trust back to the original owners doesn't trigger a reassessment because there's not a new beneficial owner. Again, they don't need to read the trust in this situation.

But when someone dies, then a new owner can take over the property. The assessor will ask for a copy of the trust or the will, and they'll read it to determine who will inherit the property. If a surviving spouse is the beneficiary of the trust for his or her lifetime, there's no reassessment (it's an automatic exclusion). If children are the beneficiaries of the trust, there's no reassessment (but they'll have to file a form requesting an exclusion from reassessment). And if, for example, a person without children leaves her assets in equal shares to her four nieces and nephews, there is going to be a reassessment because there's no exclusion for this transfer of ownership.

Reporting a Change of Ownership

You might wonder how the assessor figures out that property has changed hands at all, let alone whether an exclusion from reassessment applies or whether that claim requires a claim form or not. Here's how it works. When there's a change of ownership due to the sale of a property, the death of the owner of the property, or any other change in title that requires the filing of a new deed, such as the transfer of a home into or out of a trust, the owner (or, in the case of death, the trustee or executor) must file a change of ownership report within a certain time period.

If the change of ownership is a result of a death, the time period is within 150 days of the death and the form that's used is called Notification of Death of Real Property Owner. If the change of ownership is a result of a deed that transfers ownership of the property, you must file this report when you file the deed and the form is called a Preliminary Change of Ownership Report (a PCOR). In most trust administrations, you'd be filing both. The Notification of Death of Real Property Owner would be filed after a person has died. The Preliminary Change of Ownership Report would be filed later with the deed transferring the property as a result of the death (based on either the trust or a court order at the end of a probate proceeding) at the end of the trust administration or the probate process.

After you let the county know that there's been a change of ownership, you also must file the appropriate claim form to avoid reassessment within the earlier of three years from the date of the transfer or prior to the transfer to a third party if such a claim is required. If you file that claim within that deadline, your taxes won't be reassessed, going all the way back to the original date of transfer. If the transfer is because of death, the date of death (not the date when you recorded a deed) is the date that ownership changed hands.

EXAMPLE: Thomas inherited a house from his father in Placerville. He notified the county that his father had died by filing a Notification of Death of Real Property Owner with the county. This is a parent/child transfer, which requires a claim form. When Thomas filed an executor's deed, transferring the property from his father's estate to himself, he also filed a Claim for Exclusion from Reassessment with the El Dorado County's assessor's office. On that form he checked the box that said that this was a transfer between parent and child and therefore excluded from reassessment. He attached a copy of his father's will and sent that with the form to the assessor's office. Thomas's property taxes were not reassessed.

What If You Don't File a Claim for Exclusion from Reassessment?

If you (or your heir) don't file a claim for exclusion from reassessment, and one is necessary, but you do get a notice that your property taxes are being reassessed (called a Notice of Supplemental Assessment), you have an additional six months from getting that notice to file a claim for exclusion from that reassessment.

EXAMPLE: Michelle inherited a house from her mother, Blanche, who left Michelle the house in her trust. Michelle filed a deed transferring the house from the trust to herself. She forgot to file a Claim for Exclusion from Reassessment though. Six months later, Michelle got a property tax bill that was much higher than what Blanche had paid. The next day, Michelle filed the claim form, informing the assessor that Blanche, the former owner, was her mother and that therefore no reassessment should be done. Her property taxes were not raised, going back to when Blanche died.

If you haven't made a claim to avoid reassessment after that three-year deadline has passed, you can still file a claim, but if your taxes are lowered as a result of your claim (which would mean that your claim for exclusion from reassessment was granted), this will only apply to taxes due for the year in which you filed the claim and thereafter (not for those years prior to filing).

EXAMPLE: Michelle inherited the same house from her mother, Blanche, who left Michelle the house in her trust. But Michelle didn't file the required claim for exclusion from reassessment after Blanche had died. Even after Michelle received a higher property tax bill in the year after the transfer, Michelle didn't file a claim. But four years later, Michelle went to a seminar and found out about the parent/child exception to Prop. 13. She promptly filed a claim and was able to reduce her property taxes for the year in which she filed that claim and going forward. She didn't get a refund for the taxes that she'd paid for the previous years.

Death and Taxes:
Income, Gift, and Estate Taxes

Some Background on Death and Taxes 225

Income Taxes 226

    Capital Gains Tax 227

    Inherited Property Subject to Income Tax 234

    Gift and Estate Taxes Still Matter 236

Gift Tax 236

    The Ed/Med Exemption from Gift Taxes 240

    529 Plans: Saving for College 241

    Accounting for Gifts Made During Life as Part of Your Estate Plan 242

The Estate Tax 243

    What Assets Are Taxed? 244

    Portability of Estate Tax 245

Estate Tax Planning Strategy If You Are Single: Philanthropy 247

Read this chapter if:

- You own assets that have increased in value.

- You own assets, as your separate property, including stocks, bonds, or cash.

- You own an Inherited IRA or want to learn more about how retirement assets with be taxed for your heirs.

- You have received, or want to make, gifts.

- You are a surviving spouse.

- You have questions about the estate tax and whether it applies to you.

- You want to make charitable gifts in a tax-effective way.

M ost people come to see me to create or update an estate plan because they want to benefit the people or organizations that they love, and not just to minimize taxes. Except for the accountants out there, most people's eyes glaze over when we get into the tax part of our discussion.

But, honestly, taxes *do* matter to just about everyone in one way or another. In fact, there are several different taxes that can affect your plan: estate tax, gift tax, income tax, and property tax. Chapter 8 focuses on property tax and how your heirs can inherit your low property tax rate. In this chapter, I'll give you an overview of the other three taxes that can make an impact on your plan: income, gift, and estate taxes.

My goal here is to provide a helpful overview of tax topics relevant to estate planning, not explore the nuances. I hope that by reading this chapter you'll feel better informed and be better able to identify specific issues that may require expert help.

For those with complicated estates, or millions of dollars, this book is not a substitute for consultation with an estate planning attorney and/or an accountant who can provide specific recommendations for their situation. And for those with international assets or with loved ones who are not U.S. citizens or permanent residents, tax issues can become complicated quickly and I'd advise that they seek expert help before making an estate plan. (See Chapter 6 for an overview of these international issues.)

Some Background on Death and Taxes

Over the years that I have been an estate planner, the focus of most tax planning for estate plans has changed dramatically. Until 2012, most estate plans were designed to minimize the *estate* tax. Now, most estate plans (except for those created for the very wealthy) are focused instead on reducing *income* taxes. For Californians in particular, income taxes may turn out to be the biggest potential tax your heirs will face because they will inherit assets (like your house) that have increased in value over your lifetime. Planning to minimize income taxes is smart. Planning to minimize the estate tax, if your estate will most likely not ever pay it, isn't nearly as useful.

The reason for this change in focus is that the number of people who pay the estate and gift tax has declined dramatically. Prior to 2001, many people were subject to the estate tax. Now, few people are. Here's why. Estate tax falls only on estates that exceed what's called the federal estate tax *exemption*. This exemption is the dollar amount that a person can give away free of tax, hence the name: Gifts made at death that fall under this number are *exempt* from the tax.

The current federal estate tax exemption was set in 2012 at $5 million per person, as indexed annually for inflation. Today (2017) this exemption is $5.49 million dollars. Your taxable assets include all of your assets, including your equity in real property, stocks, bonds, cash, the value of your retirement assets, and any life insurance proceeds payable upon your death. If you are married, your taxable estate includes all of your separate property and one-half the value of your community property. (See Chapter 7 to learn more about what's community property and what's separate property.)

If you, like most Californians, own less than $5.49 million at death, no estate tax will be due and your estate is not required to file an estate tax return. If your estate exceeds the exemption, your estate must file an estate tax return. Only the amount of your estate that exceeds the exemption amount is subject to the tax and this may be reduced by any charitable deductions you have made. The maximum estate tax rate is 40%. Estimates are that less than one in 550 estates will have to file an estate tax return now—which works out to less than .2% of Americans (roughly two out of every 1,000 people who die).

But the estate tax isn't the only tax to consider. In fact, the income tax, and most specifically, the *capital gains taxes* that are levied on the difference between what an asset was purchased for and what that asset was sold for, is increasingly relevant for many Californians, especially for those with highly appreciated homes. Understanding how and when to make gifts during your lifetime (and when not to do so) can make a huge difference in how those gifts are taxed. And knowing that you can give away your assets without having to pay any gift tax on them might just spur you to be more generous than you thought that you could afford to be. If you want to benefit charities, understanding which of your assets are best to give away and why will increase the size of your charitable gifts. And, finally, even though most estates will never have to file an estate tax return, filing one anyway can make good tax sense for some Californians.

Income Taxes

Income taxes matter to Californians making an estate plan in at least three different ways:

- Capital gains taxes are levied on the sale of appreciated assets.
- Income taxes are levied on retirement account withdrawals.
- Gifts of appreciated assets to charities are free from capital gains, gift, and estate taxes.

In this section I'll explain how to take all three of these income tax issues into account when you are making an estate plan, or revising an old one. These taxes can influence the kind of estate plan you put together, the way in which you leave assets to your beneficiaries, and how and when to make charitable gifts.

Capital Gains Tax

Capital gains taxes are levied on the difference between what you purchased an asset for, called its "cost basis," and what you sold it for. For example, if you bought a share of stock in Newco for $10 a share in 2000 and you sold that stock for $110 a share in 2017, you will be taxed on your gain of $100 per share.

If you are a high income tax payer (earning over $200,000 per year) and you live in California, you can use 33% as a pretty good guess at the capital gains taxes you'll owe. The maximum federal capital gains rate is 23.8% (which currently includes a 3.8% tax on certain investment income that is part of the Affordable Care Act). California doesn't tax capital gains differently from ordinary income, and the maximum tax rate for income is 13.3%. So, our lucky investor would owe approximately $33 per share in taxes for the sale of that Newco stock.

Since real estate in California has mostly appreciated over the years, capital gains taxes are relevant for many homeowners. Homeowners are entitled (under federal law) to a $250,000 exclusion from capital gains when they sell their primary residence, if they've lived in that home for two of the five years prior to the sale. Married couples can combine their exclusion for a total of $500,000, as can unmarried couples who own a home together (because each has their own $250,000 exclusion). Better yet, there's no limit on the number of times you can use this homeowner's exclusion as long as you follow the rules. In most of the country, this means that people can sell their homes and not pay *any* capital gains tax. But not in many parts of California, where the average home price has soared to more than twice the national average.

If you and your partner purchased a home, for example, in San Luis Obispo for $100,000 in the early 1980s and sell that home for $2.1 million in 2017, you will owe capital gains taxes on that $2 million of gain. It's a good news/bad news story: Your home is worth a whole lot more than you purchased it for/but no one wants to write a tax check with six digits ($2 million gain - $500,000 (each of your home sale tax exclusion) = $1.5 million gain x 33% = $495,000).

Interesting, but how does this relate to estate planning? When a person dies, all of their assets, such as their home and stocks and bonds that are not held in retirement accounts, are revalued to their date of death value. Since most assets go up in value when they've been held for long periods, this is called a step-up in basis. And this step-up can save your heirs a lot of money.

EXAMPLE: Abby purchased her home in Menlo Park for $50,000 in 1976. At her death, the house was appraised at $1.865 million. Abby's son, Rudolfo, sold the house for $1.865 million three months after Abby's death. His basis in the property was $1.865 million, so Rudolfo owed no capital gains taxes at all.

If Abby in this example had sold that same Menlo Park house during her lifetime, she would have owed capital gains of $1.815 million (this is the difference between her basis ($50,000) and that same sale price ($1.865 million)). Abby's tax bill would have been approximately $516,450 after taking her $250,000 homeowner's exemption: $1.815 million - $250,000 homeowner's exemption x 33% (estimated capital gains tax) = $516,450.

The big idea here is that gifts made at death receive a step-up in value. But the sale of appreciated property during the owner's lifetime does not get that step-up. That's why Abby would have had a large capital gains tax bill if she had sold her house during her lifetime, but her son, Rudolfo, would not have a bill at all if he sold that same house after Abby's death. (The date of death value would be part of Abby's taxable estate, but since her total estate was less than the federal estate tax exemption, $5.49 million in 2017, no tax was due.)

Gifts of Appreciated Assets Are Always Appreciated

Owning appreciated assets can be frustrating. If you've done well, that's great; however, sometimes I work with people who own appreciated assets and don't want to sell them and trigger capital gains. But holding onto these assets (rather than selling them) does no good at all.

Here's some good news: If you have charitable intent, appreciated assets are great assets to donate. Qualified charities don't pay capital gains on the sale of appreciated assets. If Stewart, in the example below, *donated* $10,000 worth of Solarco stock to the VH1 Save the Music Foundation, he could take a charitable deduction of $10,000 in the year that he makes the gift. Assuming his tax rate is 28% and that he itemizes his deductions, that deduction saves Stewart $2,800 in taxes. The VH1 Save the Music Foundation sells the 400 shares of Solarco. It pays no capital gains taxes, so all $10,000 goes to the organization.

> **TIP**
> **If you own appreciated assets and want to benefit a charity,** ask that charity if it can accept gifts of stock or real property (most can) and seek advice from your accountant to make sure that you understand the tax consequences of such a gift.

The same rule applies for gifts made during life. Lifetime gifts do not get a step-up in basis. Instead the recipient receives the gifted asset at the donor's basis. This rule applies to all property that can appreciate—most often real estate and stocks. What that means is that if a person can keep such assets until death, not selling or giving them away, that will be beneficial for their heirs. (An exception would be making gifts of these assets to charity. (See "Gifts of Appreciated Assets Are Always Appreciated," above.)

EXAMPLE: Stewart owns 500 shares of Solarco stock that he purchased for $5/share. He decides to give that stock to his son, Todd, as a birthday present. Todd then owns the stock with a cost basis of $5/share because Stewart gave him the stock while Stewart was still alive. Since the stock is now worth $25/share, Todd will owe capital gains taxes on $20/share if he decides to sell the stock. If, instead, Todd had inherited that stock at Stewart's death, and the stock was still worth $25/share, Todd would owe no capital gains taxes if he sold the stock at that price.

When creating an estate plan, most Californians shouldn't worry about minimizing the estate tax. Instead, most Californians should worry about the best ways to minimize capital gains taxes for their heirs. Here are the things you should think about.

How You Own Property Matters

If you are married, the first thing to think about (when it comes to capital gains) is how you own property. Many of my clients own their homes as joint tenants with their spouses. There's nothing wrong with owning a house in joint tenancy with your spouse, but it comes with a huge tax drawback. If a couple owns a house in joint tenancy, and one person dies, only the deceased person's one-half of the house gets a step-up in basis. If, however, a couple owns their home as community property, at the death of one person, the entire house gets a step-up in basis. This is a big deal. (See Chapter 7 for how to determine what is community property.)

EXAMPLE: In the early 1980s, Donald and Helen purchased their home in Altadena for $100,000. They held title as community property. When Donald died in 2015, the house was appraised at $3 million. Helen, as the surviving spouse, got a stepped-up basis of $3 million for the house. When she sold the property two years later (in 2017) for $3.125 million, Helen owed no capital gains taxes at all. (She earned $125,000 of gain, but she had a $250,000 exclusion.)

Unfortunately, this step-up is only available to married couples. Unmarried couples who own property together do not get the same benefit—only the portion of the property that belonged to the deceased partner gets revalued up to the date of death value. I've had a few clients who decided to get married on this basis alone.

In the example, above, If Donald and Helen had owned that same house as joint tenants; Helen would have gotten a stepped-up basis on one-half the house (the half that Donald owned). If she had sold the house two years later for the same amount ($3.125 million), her tax bill would have been approximately $437,250! (Donald's one-half of the house had a basis of $1.5 million, so the gain on that half was $62,500. Helen's one-half of the house had a basis of $50,000, so the gain on that half was $1,512,500. Altogether, the gain was $1.575 million - $250,000 = $1.325 million x 33% = $437,250).

TIP

Find out how you are holding title to your house by getting a copy of the most current recorded deed. If you are married and own your home as joint tenants, change this to community property with right of survivorship. See Chapter 1 for advice on ordering a copy of your current deed and changing it if necessary.

The Type of Trust You Have Matters

If you have a living trust, the second thing to think about (when it comes to capital gains) is what *kind* of a trust you have. If you are married, and did your estate plan before 2012, you probably have what's called an "A/B" trust. In this kind of trust, assets are divided at the death of the first spouse into two trusts. The A trust, called the survivor's trust, holds the assets owned by the surviving spouse. The B trust, called the bypass trust or credit trust, holds the assets owned by the deceased spouse, up to the federal estate tax exemption.

How an A/B Trust Works

```
            Family Trust

        ↙           ↘

   Bypass          Survivor's Trust
   "B" Trust        "B" Trust
```

The primary tax purpose of the B trust is that none of the assets in that trust are counted as the survivor's assets when he or she dies. The survivor can usually use the assets in the B trust, but when he or she dies, none of those assets count towards the estate tax bill. This kind of plan is still relevant for couples with more than $11 million in assets or those in second (or third) marriages with children from prior marriages. (See Chapter 7 for planning strategies for blended families.) But for many Californians, an A/B trust isn't necessary now.

Making an estate plan designed to reduce estate taxes made a lot of sense in 2002, for example, when the federal estate tax exemption was $1 million, since that meant that many middle-class people with home equity and life insurance needed to plan to reduce the tax. Placing the decedent's assets into the B trust, up to the maximum available federal estate tax exemption, saved many families estate taxes.

EXAMPLE: Andre and Francine had a trust with $2 million in assets. When Andre died in 2002, the estate tax exemption was $1 million. Andre's trust assets ($1 million) were allocated to the B trust. Francine's trust assets ($1 million) were allocated to the A trust. Francine died in 2004, when the estate tax exemption was $1.5 million. Her total estate at that time was $1.3 million (this included the assets in the A trust and her retirement accounts which were not in the trust). Francine's estate was not taxable. If Andre's assets had been included in her taxable estate at death, her estate would have owed estate tax, since she would have owned $2.3 million. The A/B trust structure worked as planned, reducing the estate tax to zero.

The A/B trust doesn't make sense for many people now, unless they are either wealthy, in second marriages, or have concerns about dementia or other issues that might have an impact on distribution of the assets owned by the first spouse to die. Francine, in the example above, could have owned all $2.3 million in assets at her death in 2017 and owed no estate tax. The A/B structure protects most people against a tax they no longer have to pay (the estate tax). Worse, it now *creates* a tax burden for many families because the assets in the B trust do not receive a step-up in basis when the second spouse dies. Only the assets held in the survivor's trust get a step-up in basis at the second death. As a result, the A/B structure creates a capital gains tax burden that the family could avoid with a simpler trust.

EXAMPLE: Noah and Delia purchased a house together for $70,000 in Morgan Hill. When Noah died in 2001, the house was appraised at $600,000. One-half of the house was placed in the bypass trust/B and one-half of the house was placed in the survivor's trust/A. When Delia died in 2017, the house was appraised at $3 million. Julian, Noah and Delia's son, inherited the house and sold it for $3 million. Julian owed no capital gains tax on the property held in Delia's survivor's trust because that half got a step-up in basis to $1.5 million at Delia's death. But Julian got a tax bill for the half of the house held in the bypass trust/B because that half had a basis of $300,000 (the value it had in 2001, when Noah died). Julian's tax bill was approximately $396,000 ($1.5 million − 300,000 x 33%). Because the house wasn't Julian's primary residence, he didn't have a $250,000 exclusion, either.

If you are married and have assets valued at $5 million or less (and most Californians do) and you have a living trust with an A/B structure, it makes sense to simplify that trust to one that holds all assets in one revocable trust for the benefit of the surviving spouse—unless you are in a blended marriage and want to leave assets to children of different marriages, or are otherwise concerned about controlling how your assets are ultimately distributed if you die first (that is, before your spouse). In an all-in-one revocable trust, all of the assets held by the surviving spouse will receive a step-up in basis at the second death, reducing capital gains taxes for your heirs. While it is true that all of the assets in the survivor's trust do count towards the surviving spouse's estate tax bill, this doesn't matter if all of the assets don't add up to a taxable estate.

All-in-One Revocable Trust

EXAMPLE: If Noah and Delia (in above example) had an all-in-one revocable trust, their son, Julian could have sold the house for $3 million and paid no capital gains taxes at Delia's death. Julian would have received a step-up in basis for the entire house (not just half) because it was held in the survivor's trust. Because Delia's total estate was less than $5 million, it owed no estate tax either.

SEE AN EXPERT

If your estate plan was drafted before 2012 and has an A/B structure, and your total estate is less than $5 million, consider visiting an estate planning attorney to discuss simplifying your plan and updating it for tax purposes.

Inherited Property Subject to Income Tax

Tax-deferred retirement plans, like 401(k)s and IRAs, go to beneficiaries without a step-up in basis. And assets in retirement plans are also one of only a few types of assets your heirs will inherit that may be subject to income tax. That's because when your heirs withdraw money from these plans, they, like you, will have to pay income tax on the withdrawals.

Your heirs will have to start withdrawing money from such inherited retirement plans by the end of the year after your death. The plan administrator will give your heirs some options. Usually they can choose to withdraw the money out in one lump sum, over a period of five years, or slowly over their lifetime, based on their life expectancy. (See Chapter 10 for more information on retirement accounts.)

For the purpose of this chapter on taxes, the important thing to know is that your beneficiaries will have to pay income tax on your retirement plan assets. And that means that if you have a house worth $500,000 and an IRA worth $500,000, leaving the house to your daughter and the IRA to your son would mean that your son actually gets less, since he will have to pay tax on the withdrawal of that money. If you want your children to receive equal shares of your assets, it is a better idea to simply leave them half of each asset.

If you want to benefit charity, naming charities as beneficiaries for part, or all, of your retirement accounts is very smart. Charities do not pay any tax on withdrawals from these plans, so a gift of $100,000 from an IRA will transfer all $100,000 to the charity.

What About Roth Plans?

Beneficiaries who inherit assets from Roth IRAs and Roth 401(k)s also must begin withdrawing those assets by the end of the year after the owner's death, but no tax is due on these withdrawals (as long as the account has existed for five years or more) because the owner was taxed on the money before it went into these plans.

RESOURCE

Useful guide to inherited property. The IRS guide, *Distributions from Individual Retirement Arrangements* (IRAs) (Publication 590-B, available at www.irs.gov) does a good job at explaining the tax consequences and options that beneficiaries face.

Gift and Estate Taxes Still Matter

Even though income taxes are now the focus of most estate plans drafted in California, the gift and estate tax rules are still relevant. For one thing, many parents want to know how to make gifts in a tax-efficient manner. For another, the gift and estate tax rules are connected, so that gifts made during life affect the amount of estate tax exemption a person has available at death. Finally, understanding how the estate tax works is important for surviving spouses who need to decide whether or not to file an estate tax return to increase their available estate tax exemption.

Read on to learn about gift and estate tax rules.

Gift Tax

A section on lifetime gifting may seem a bit off topic in a book about estate planning, but it isn't. Life is expensive in California, and I've worked with many clients who would like to help their children to purchase a house, or help pay for their grandchildren's education or medical expenses while they are still alive. It's helpful to know that there's no tax penalty for doing so: If you are able to help, you can do so without paying a tax. And, let's face it, there's a lot of joy that can come from helping the people you love while you're still alive to hear them say "Thanks."

Gift tax falls, in theory, on all gifts made during a person's lifetime. Gifts can include the transfer of real estate, cash, stocks, bonds, and virtually anything of value, even such things as forgiving a loan or providing housing without charging a person rent. The IRS figured out a long time ago that people might try and give away their assets during life and then die penniless in an effort to avoid the estate tax. To prevent people pursuing that particular strategy, the tax code looks at gifts made during life and after death together.

Really the gift and estate tax are the same tax. The difference is *when* a gift is made; a gift made during life is subject to gift tax; a gift made at death is subject to the estate tax. The maximum tax rate for all gifts is currently 40%.

If a gift is made during life, then it may be subject to the gift tax. If a gift is made after death, then it may be subject to the estate tax. The words "may be" are the key words in both sentences because, these days, 99.8% of Americans are not currently subject to either tax.

That's because, as of 2017, only gifts or bequests that exceed $5.49 million (the lifetime estate and gift tax exemption) are subject to these taxes. That's a lot of money. If you give away less than this dollar amount (the lifetime estate and gift tax exemption), no tax is due. Ever.

In addition to this lifetime gift and estate tax exemption, each person is also allowed to give up to $14,000 (2017 figure) per year per person free of gift tax and without using up any of their gift and estate tax exemption at all. This is called the annual gift tax exclusion. It is also indexed to inflation, but only changes when the IRS announces a change. Your annual gifts don't need to be reported to the IRS as long as they don't exceed $14,000 per person per year.

You could, for example, give $14,000 to every single person in Detroit (and they'd be very happy to receive that gift), and report nothing to the IRS. More realistically, you could give your children annual gifts over many years—for example, ten years of such gifts to two children would transfer $280,000 of your assets with no gift tax due. If your children are married and you also give their spouses $14,000 a year, the total would be $560,000. (Double these amounts if your spouse is also gifting each person $14,000 per year.) As you can see, a long-term program of making annual gifts is one way to transfer a lot of money to your loved ones without using up any of your lifetime gift and estate tax exclusion.

EXAMPLE: Dawn gives each of her three grandchildren and their two parents $14,000 in 2017. The gifts total $70,000. Because none of the five gifts exceed $14,000, Dawn does not have to report any of them to the IRS. She still has a $5.49 million exemption from both gift and estate tax. Dawn plans to make these gifts each year for as long as she can afford to do so.

If the gifts in any one year exceed the annual threshold, though, you do have to report all gifts made in that year on a gift tax return, filed in April of the following year. Reporting a gift does not trigger any tax until you've used up all of your lifetime credit of $5.49 million. If, for example, you report a gift of $50,000, but have $5.49 million dollar's worth of exemption to apply towards that tax, no tax is due when that return is filed. Instead, you've now used up $50,000 worth of that exemption. And that's just fine, if you have more exemption than you'll ever need, which is the case for most people these days, even in California. These gift tax returns work like a running tab: By filing them you're documenting how much of your lifetime exclusion you're using. When you die, the IRS knows how much of your exemption you have left.

You can think of the lifetime exemption like a large basketball clock, with a lot of time on it. No time is used up by making annual gifts. Giving away larger gifts, either during life or after death does use up some time on your clock, because these gifts must be reported. But reporting these gifts isn't going to trigger any tax until you exceed $5.49 million, or use up all the available time. Or think about it like this: If you have a gift card for Starbucks worth $30, and you buy a fancy coffee drink for $4, you still have $26 left on the card.

EXAMPLE: In 2017, Cubby gives her son $84,000 to help with the down payment on a condo in Irvine. Because that gift exceeds the annual gift tax exclusion, Cubby must report a gift of $84,000 on a gift tax return the following year (2018). (The first $14,000 of that $84,000 gift is free of tax). Cubby owes no gift tax, but has used up $70,000 of her lifetime estate and gift tax exemption of $5.49 million and now has $5.42 million left to use. This doesn't bother Cubby because she has $2 million of assets altogether.

When a person dies, we total up their reported lifetime gifts to see what exemption amount is left. That's the "unified" part of the gift and estate tax system.

EXAMPLE: In 2012, Clifford gave $314,000 to his daughter, Barbara, to help pay for the UC college education of Barbara's twin boys. Clifford reported the $314,000 gift on a gift tax return (the first $14,000 of his $314,000 gift counted as his annual gift exclusion). When Clifford died in 2017, he had an available exemption of $5.19 million ($5.49 million − $300,000 that he'd used up in 2012). Clifford's total estate at death was equal to $3 million. No estate tax was due.

Gifts to Caregivers

If you are over 65, or someone who requires help with financial matters, and want to make a gift to a nonrelative who provides you with care (like cooking for you, cleaning your house, or driving you to doctor appointments), it's important to know relevant rules for doing so. California law (Probate Code 21380-21392) may require that a lawyer signs a document called a "certificate of independent review" that certifies that you are making a gift to a caregiver of your own free will. If you don't get this certification, your gift may not be made because it may be declared invalid. The law presumes that, unless you get this certification, such a gift to a caregiver was made under pressure and isn't valid.

This law applies to gifts you make to a caregiver who is not a member of your family and who provides you with help in exchange for money. Neighbors and friends who provide care for you without payment aren't considered "caregivers" if they have a personal relationship with you for at least 90 days before providing you with care. The law applies to gifts over $5,000 (less if your total estate is less than $150,000).

If you are over 65, or require help with financial matters, and want to make a large gift to a caregiver, see an attorney and get a certificate of independent review if necessary.

So, what does this mean if you are making an estate plan in California? It means that if you can afford to be generous, you are not limited to making gifts under $14,000 to avoid gift tax. Many of my clients don't realize this, and are relieved to find out that they can, in fact, make gifts to their children or grandchildren, without paying an additional gift tax and without triggering an estate tax at their deaths.

The Ed/Med Exemption from Gift Taxes

In addition to the annual gift tax exemption, there are two other ways to make gifts during life that don't use up a person's lifetime exclusion from gift and estate taxes. Called the "Ed/Med" exemption, this section of the tax code says that if a person makes a *direct* payment for education or medical expenses of another person, no gift tax is due, and none of that person's lifetime exemption from the gift or estate tax is used up. And these gifts are not limited to the annual $14,000 limit.

To get the tax benefit, these gifts must be made directly to an educational institution or health care provider. You can't, for example, give your daughter a check for her son's college tuition (as in the case of Clifford, in the example above, giving his daughter Barbara money for his grandson's college expenses). You have to write the check directly to the school to take advantage of the tax benefit.

EXAMPLE 1: Sven pays for his granddaughter's high school tuition by sending a check for $27,000 to her private school in Marin. Sven doesn't need to report this gift on a gift tax return in the following year. Sven still has his full lifetime exemption of $5.49 million.

EXAMPLE 2: Patricia pays for her son's medical insurance premiums and for his expensive prescription drug that isn't covered by that insurance. Patricia writes checks directly to the insurance company and the pharmacy. The $22,000 she pays each year is free of gift tax, does not need to be reported, and does not use up any of her lifetime estate and gift tax exemption of $5.49 million.

529 Plans: Saving for College

Another way that friends, parents, grandparents, and other relatives can help pay for educational expenses is by creating 529 college savings accounts for children. These accounts, which are essentially large mutual funds that are run by each state, allow people to save for qualified higher educational expenses. Money in these accounts can be withdrawn to pay for tuition, books, and room and board for college and graduate school expenses. And, as long as the money is withdrawn for such qualified expenses, these withdrawals are tax free. If a child doesn't use up all of the money in his or her 529 plan, it can be used for other family members' qualified educational expenses. Money can even be withdrawn from the plan altogether, but would then be subject to both a tax on earnings and a 10% penalty.

Contributions to 529 plans do not fit within the Ed/Med exemption because they are not made directly to an educational institution. But these contributions do count as annual gifts—so as long as they don't exceed $14,000 in any one year, they do not have to be reported. In addition, a person can make a donation equal to five year's worth of annual gifts at once, called "front-loading" without using any of their lifetime gift/estate tax exemption. This means that a single person can contribute up to $70,000, and a married couple can contribute up to $140,000 to a 529 plan. (They can't make any more gifts to the plan's beneficiary for the next five years.)

RESOURCE

Excellent source of information on 529 plans. Check out the Saving for College website (www.savingforcollege.com) where you can compare different state's fund performance and learn the ins and outs of using 529s to pay for college.

Accounting for Gifts Made During Life as Part of Your Estate Plan

If you've been able to make lifetime gifts, and you want to take these into account in your estate plan, that's easy enough. Your will or trust can say that, at your death, the executor (if you have a will) or your trustee (if you have a trust) should take all such lifetime gifts into account, and equalize the gifts your children or heirs receive.

EXAMPLE: Simone helped her daughter, Nan, purchase a house in El Cerrito in 1996, by giving her $50,000 towards the down payment. Simone's other daughter, Patsy, didn't need help to buy a house in Boston, where she lived. Simone amended her living trust to say that, at her death, the trustee should make sure that Nan and Patsy each received an equal amount of her assets, and Nan's share should include that $50,000 gift. When Simone died, her estate was $1.75 million. The trustee divided the estate this way: First, she added that $50,000 gift back into the estate, just to calculate the shares. This makes sense, because if Simone hadn't given that $50,000 to Nan in 1996, she would have had $1.8 million when she died. Then the trustee divided $1.8 million into two equal shares of $900,000. Patsy got $900,000. Nan got $850,000 (because of the $50,000 she'd received in 1996).

Of course, not every person wants to take such lifetime gifts into account at death. For some families, any previous gifts are simply water under the bridge and they just want the executor or trustee to divide up what's left at death. That's also just fine. I tell my clients that what's "fair" differs from family to family and that they need to consider what feels right for them. In a family, for example, where two children are doing well financially, but another child has needed periodic (or constant) help for years, parents might not want to equalize the gifts each child ultimately receives. That needy child, in fact, might well be the child who needs more, not less, when the second parent dies. While family harmony may suggest leaving equal shares to children, reality sometimes requires another distribution altogether. My advice to clients with families where children have divergent needs is to consider being open and transparent about the estate plan—that way, no one will be surprised when it comes into play.

The Estate Tax

The estate tax (assuming any is due) is paid by the estate of a person who died, if that person owned assets that exceed the estate tax exemption (which is $5.49 million currently). That's why it's called the "estate" tax. It is not a tax on the people who receive an inheritance; that would be called an "inheritance" tax. Some states do have inheritance taxes, but California does not. Although often called, for political reasons, the "death" tax, the estate tax really isn't a death tax. Everybody dies, but very few people pay the tax.

If there is an estate tax due, the estate pays the tax, and the beneficiaries inherit what is left after that. The tax can be paid directly by the estate or prorated against each beneficiary's share, but the basic idea is the same: The tax is paid and the beneficiaries inherit the rest. Currently, the maximum estate tax rate is 40%, so it's a heavy tax, but it doesn't fall on very many estates.

The Bad Old Days

In 2001, anyone with an estate over $675,000 had to pay the estate tax! That affected a lot more people. And the estate tax rate was 55%, so it was a heavier tax to boot. What that meant is that many Californians, just by virtue of the value of their homes, were likely to have to pay some estate tax at death.

What Assets Are Taxed?

What a person owns for the purpose of determining the estate tax includes everything a person owns, including life insurance proceeds, equity in a house, stocks, bonds, and cash, and the value of retirement plans like 401(k)s and IRAs. Because California is a community property state, a married person owns just one-half of all community assets, regardless of whose name is on title, unless there's a pre- or postmarital agreement that changes the default rules. (See Chapter 7 for more on community property rules.)

Married couples who leave everything to their surviving spouses also get the benefit of what's called the "unlimited marital deduction" if they are married to a U.S. citizen. (See Chapter 6 for what happens if you or your spouse is not a U.S. citizen.) What this means is that, if all assets are left to the surviving spouse, no estate tax is ever due when the first spouse dies, even if that spouse is wealthy and would otherwise have a taxable estate. But, when the second spouse dies, to the extent that he or she hasn't spent that money, the estate tax is levied then. The marital deduction should be called the "marital deferral" because that's what it is, really: The IRS just waits until the second spouse dies to tax the family's estate.

Before 2001, many middle-class Californians, just by virtue of the value of their homes, did have to take the estate tax into account and make a plan for how to pay it at the second death. This is why the A/B trust was used for years in California to reduce the estate tax due at that second death.

But for many Californians this kind of planning to reduce the estate tax due at the second death isn't necessary anymore. Really. Tax law can always change (and I'll alert you to changes on my blog), but for now, the vast majority of Californians can breathe a sigh of relief—the estate tax is not going to be an issue for them.

EXAMPLE: Jordan died in 2017. His wife, Joyce, survived him. At death, Jordan owned the following:

One-half interest in a home in Whittier	$800,0000
One-half interest in a bank account	$35,000
One-half interest in an IRA	$600,000
One-half interest in an annuity	$100,000
Jordan's Total Assets	$1.535 million

Jordan left all of his assets to Joyce. Because Jordan's total estate, $1.535 million, is less than his federal estate tax exemption of $5.49 million, Jordan's trustee, Joyce, does not have to file an estate tax return nine months after Jordan died. Because Jordan was married to Joyce, he left all of his assets to her and used the unlimited marital deduction to do so. Jordan didn't leave any of his assets to anyone else, and he had made no lifetime gifts, so he didn't use up any of his lifetime gift and estate tax exemption. At his death all $5.49 million of that exemption was unused.

Portability of Estate Tax

A new feature of the estate tax law, called "portability," allows a surviving spouse, like Joyce (in the example above), to request the use of their deceased spouse's unused estate tax exemption by filing an estate tax return and requesting that the survivor be able to make use of the unused tax exemption when he or she dies.

In the example above, if Joyce wants to use Jordan's $5.49 million dollar exemption at her death, she could decide to file an estate tax return for Jordan, even though he doesn't have a taxable estate. Here's how it would work. If Joyce files an estate tax return for Jordan, she could request the use of his $5.49 million exemption.

To file that estate tax return, Joyce would pay her accountant about $3,000 in preparation fees. She would also have to give her accountant account statements, appraisals, and other paperwork documenting the value of Jordan's estate.

If Joyce remarries after Jordan's death, she'd lose this extra $5.49 million dollars of exemption, because that's the rule. But, assuming she didn't remarry, at her death, her estate would have two exemptions from the estate tax: hers (whatever it is at her death) and Jordan's $5.49 million.

Why would Joyce decide it was worthwhile to request portability? If Jordan died young, and Joyce expected to live a long time afterward, and also expected her assets to appreciate during that time, she might want to have that extra exemption to protect her estate. Or, if Joyce's estate was larger than Jordan's, and, for example, she owned $5 million worth of property at Jordan's death, she would want Jordan's extra $5.49 million to cover any appreciation in those assets during her lifetime.

Joyce, however, might decide *not* to file an estate return and request portability. She, like many of my clients, might decide that her own exemption of $5 million plus an inflation adjustment, is more than enough to cover her estate. If Joyce and Jordan owned the same amount of property, she would own $3.07 million worth of property (because Jordan had left his one-half to her directly). If Joyce expects to spend most of that during her lifetime, especially her retirement assets, then she might decide that she doesn't need Jordan's unused exemption to shelter her estate. After discussing this with her financial planner or accountant, Joyce estimates that her total assets will be below the $5 million threshold when she dies, so she may decide that her exemption, alone, is enough to shelter her entire estate from the estate tax.

Whatever decision Joyce makes, she needs to make it within nine months of Jordan's death. That's the deadline for filing an estate tax return. If Joyce isn't sure whether to file the return at that point, she can request an automatic six-month extension to file it, but she needs to request that extension before that nine-month deadline. After that, it is too late. In other words, if Joyce didn't file an estate tax return and request portability for Jordan's unused exemption by the deadline, she couldn't request it later or make use of that exemption at her death.

EXAMPLE: Sara died in 2015. Her estate was worth $2 million. The estate tax exemption was $5.43 million at the time. Sara left everything to her husband, Raymond. Raymond owned property worth $3 million, including an apartment at Venice Beach which was going up in value quickly. Combined with Sara's assets, he now had a $5 million estate. Raymond filed an estate tax return for Sara's estate and requested the use of her unused exemption of $5.43 million. He spent $3,000 for the preparation and filing of that return. Raymond felt that the investment to prepare the return was worthwhile because he was worried that his apartment might go up in value so much during his lifetime that he might die with an estate worth more than the federal estate tax exemption. By requesting the use of Sara's additional $5.43 million's worth of exemption, Raymond would have at least $11.86 million of exemption available at his death (Sara's $5.49 million plus whatever his exemption would be when he died). As a result, Raymond was pretty sure that his children would not have to pay any estate tax at his death no matter how much his apartment continued to gain in value.

Estate Tax Planning Strategy If You Are Single: Philanthropy

Unmarried people can't use portability to increase the size of their available estate tax exemption. At their death, the calculation is simply totaling up all of a person's assets and comparing that to the available exemption for the year of death. If, for example, Sydney, a single woman, died in 2017, with a total estate of $3 million, her executor would not have to file an estate tax return for her estate.

The main estate tax planning strategy for reducing estate tax for a single person, or for a person with no children, is often to make charitable donations, either during life or after death. Such donations to qualified charities are fully tax deductible. Charitable gifts made at death reduce a person's taxable estate on a dollar for dollar basis. For example, if Peter, a single man, died in 2017 with an estate worth $8 million, but he had left his entire estate to his university, Peter's executor would have to file an estate tax return because Peter's estate exceeds the exemption, but no taxes would be due. Peter's charitable donation would have reduced his taxable estate to zero.

Naming the Right Beneficiaries: Retirement and Life Insurance

Alphabet Soup: Retirement Plans Explained...252

    Traditional IRAs...253

    401(k) Plans..253

    Roth IRAs.. 254

    Roth 401(k)s and Roth 403(b)s...255

What Beneficiaries Have You Already Named? 255

Retirement 101: The Basic Rules of Choosing Beneficiaries

    and Withdrawing Money... 258

    IRAs and 401(k)s.. 260

    Roth IRAs and Roth 401(k)s..261

Naming Beneficiaries for Retirement Plans...263

    Your Spouse.. 264

    Children 266

    Multiple Beneficiaries...267

    A Trust 268

    Charities..270

A Little Housekeeping: Cleaning Up Your Retirement Plans.................271

    Roll Over Those Old 401(k) Plans...271

    Consolidate Your IRAs..272

Filling Out the Forms Naming Beneficiaries...272

Naming Beneficiaries for Life Insurance...274

    Naming the Right Beneficiaries...275

    If You've Been Divorced, Check Your Insurance Policies.....................275

    Using Life Insurance to Reduce (and Pay) Federal Estate Tax.............278

Read this chapter if:

- You have 401(k)s from previous jobs that you haven't rolled over into IRAs.

- You have IRAs and wonder if you should convert them to Roth IRAs.

- You don't know, or aren't sure, how your retirement plans fit into your estate plan.

- You have retirement plans but aren't sure who you've named as beneficiaries.

- You'd like to use your retirement assets to benefit a charity but don't know how.

- You own a life insurance policy but aren't sure who to name as a beneficiary.

Retirement accounts offer tax incentives to help you squirrel away some of your paycheck for retirement. Congress, when it came up with these tax breaks, really wasn't thinking of retirement accounts as a way to pass money along to heirs. The idea was that you were supposed to save the money during your working life to spend during your retirement years, leaving nothing behind. Personally, I think that's an excellent plan. But it doesn't always work out that way: Many people work to an older age these days so they don't spend down their retirement as they had planned. Some people find that their other investments have done so well that they don't need to take more than the minimum required distributions required by their IRAs or 401(k)s. I have many clients who saved aggressively during their working years only to find out that they have more retirement assets now than they'll ever need. After all, every dollar they withdraw from these plans is subject to income tax, while their investment dollars are not taxed upon withdrawal. As a result, retirement assets are sometimes a large part of the inheritance a person leaves behind.

Life insurance, too, is often a large part of what a person leaves behind to their loved ones. But my clients often forget to mention it when we are making a list of their assets, because, to them, it's not "real" money. And, like retirement assets, life insurance passes only to those named as beneficiaries, not by the terms of a will or trust. In this chapter, I want to make sure that you understand how to include both kinds of assets in your overall plan and that you take the time to make sure you've named the right beneficiaries for both your retirement plans and life insurance policies.

Life insurance provides ready cash when it may be most needed. It can help pay down a mortgage or send children to college. There are complicated ways to use life insurance in an estate plan, but for our purposes, having enough and naming the right beneficiaries are the key issues.

Retirement accounts, though, are an important part of an estate plan for several reasons.

First, unlike the other assets you'll be leaving to your loved ones, most retirement plan money is going to be subject to income tax when the money is withdrawn.

Second, because retirement assets are the only assets subject to income tax that a person inherits, this is the last money you want your beneficiaries spending right away, because early withdrawals mean that the assets aren't growing on a tax-deferred basis. If retirement assets are a large part of your plan, educating your beneficiaries about how to manage them wisely should be part of that plan, too.

Last, but not least, as long as you handle your retirement accounts properly, these assets will be distributed after your death without going through probate.

Many books have been written on retirement plans. Many of them are huge or difficult to read—often both. Just the rules for taking money out of retirement plans (let alone the best way to put money into them) are complicated, and they change often.

But for now, here's all that matters: Someday, hopefully far in the future, your family, friends, or favorite nonprofit may inherit your retirement assets. So in this chapter, I want to focus on what you should do now (such as making sure that your retirement plans have the right beneficiaries, converting old 401(k)s to IRAs, considering a Roth conversion, and understanding how your retirement assets fit into your estate plan) to make the process as easy as possible for those who inherit your retirement accounts.

Since we'll be talking about beneficiary designations, I'm also discussing life insurance and how best to make sure that your policies support your estate plan. The main idea is that you want your estate plan to be coordinated with your retirement plans and life insurance policies, to help your beneficiaries to keep the money in your retirement accounts growing tax free as long as possible and to use your retirement accounts and life insurance policies to benefit charity.

Alphabet Soup: Retirement Plans Explained

Broadly speaking, there are three types of retirement plans that most people use to save for retirement: traditional IRAs, 401(k) plans (or 403(b)s if you work for a nonprofit or school), and Roth IRAs. All three offer significant tax incentives to encourage you to save money now so you'll have it to spend when you retire. Some employers also offer new forms of Roth plans (Roth 401(k)s and Roth 403(b)s). You might have more than one of each retirement plan on your list, especially if you've changed jobs a few times. Old retirement plans have a way of piling up if you're not careful (more on that later).

TIP

Get 'em together. A good way to keep track of all of your retirement accounts is to put each statement in a binder, one section per plan. That way, all of the relevant information is in one place. Also, if you get tired of filing so many different statements, that might nudge you to consolidate them into only one or two accounts.

Traditional IRAs

IRA stands for Individual Retirement Account. You can set up an IRA yourself to save and invest your earnings over your lifetime. At tax time, you can deduct the amount you contribute, up to a certain amount each year ($5,500 is the maximum for 2017, or $6,500 for persons over age 50), as long as you are not also covered by your employer's retirement plan.

EXAMPLE: Phil, who is 55 years old, contributes the maximum, $6,500, to his IRA. He is not covered by an employer's plan. He is able to deduct all $6,500 from his income.

When you withdraw your money from an IRA, it is subject to income tax. But by then you'll likely be retired, and your income tax rate will probably be lower than it is now. You may begin withdrawing money from traditional IRA plans when you are 59½ years old. If you withdraw the money early, you will generally be subject to penalties for early withdrawal, and then you'll pay income tax on top of that. You must begin to take money out when you turn 70½ years old. There are several kinds of IRA plans, but they are all variations on this theme.

401(k) Plans

Your employer usually sets these up and offers several investment choices. If you are self-employed and have no employees, you can set up a solo 401(k). You contribute pretax money, deducted from your paycheck. That way, your taxable income is reduced by the amount you contribute. Some employers even contribute matching funds. The money grows tax free in the account.

As with IRAs, you may begin withdrawing money from your 401(k) plan when you are 59½ years old, and you must begin to take money out when you turn 70½ years old. Early withdrawals are also generally subject to penalties. When you withdraw money, it is subject to income tax.

> ### 403(b) Plans
>
> If you've worked for a school or a nonprofit, you'll have a 403(b) plan. These are very similar to 401(k) plans except that they are governed by a different section of the federal tax law.

Roth IRAs

These are like traditional IRAs upside down. Like traditional IRAs, you can set these up yourself, but you make contributions with money you've already paid tax on. There's no tax deduction available for the contributions you make. And there's no mandatory withdrawal age. So what's so great about Roth IRAs?

When you withdraw money from a Roth IRA, you don't pay tax on it. You take the tax hit up front, but all the growth of the funds is tax free. A Roth IRA, if you can afford to create one, and you qualify to do so, can be a terrific way to pass money along to your loved ones. For people with large estates, converting a traditional IRA to a Roth IRA has two other benefits: First, Roth IRAs do not have required minimum distributions, so if you don't need to withdraw the money, you don't have to. Second, when you convert a traditional IRA to a Roth IRA, the taxes you pay reduce your estate—in effect, you are prepaying a tax for your heirs.

Currently (2017), Roth IRAs are available to married couples filing jointly with an adjusted gross income of less than $196,000 and to individuals filing separate returns with an adjusted gross income of $133,000 or less. These income limitations are set by the IRS and are indexed to inflation.

Roth 401(k)s and Roth 403(b)s

The newest options in the retirement planning world are the Roth 401(k) and Roth 403(b) plans. If your employer offers one (not all do), you can sock away a chunk of your salary and let it grow tax free. Like a Roth IRA, you'll put money into the plan that you've already paid tax on, but future distributions will be tax free. There are no income restrictions on who can participate.

What Beneficiaries Have You Already Named?

There are a million books and websites that can help you figure out whether you're invested in the right plan for yourself and your family and saving enough for your retirement (I include some of the best retirement resources later in this chapter).

But that's not the focus of our discussion. For estate planning purposes, the important thing is to understand who will get the money from your retirement accounts if you die before withdrawing it all.

First things first: You need to know what kind of retirement plans you've got at the moment and who will inherit them. I include a Personal Inventory form with this book (see Chapter 1), which includes a section for you to list your retirement accounts and life insurance policies.

I also include a Current Beneficiaries List so that you can list the beneficiaries of your retirement plans, life insurance policies, and other beneficiary-designated plans (see the sample below).

Current Beneficiaries List

I. Retirement Assets: Current Beneficiaries

Retirement Plan	Owner	Beneficiaries
Vanguard Roth IRA, Number 123–456	Hannah	Primary: Doris Secondary: Josh (age 21), Chris (age 25)
TIAA-CREF 401(k)	Doris	Primary: Hannah Secondary: Josh and Chris
		Primary: Secondary:

II. Life Insurance: Current Beneficiaries

Life Insurance Policy	Owner	Beneficiaries
West Coast Insurance Company	Hannah	Primary: Doris Secondary: Josh and Chris
Planters Beneficial Life	Doris	Primary: Hannah Secondary: Josh and Chris
		Primary: Secondary:

III. Any Other Payable-on-Death Accounts

Account	Owner	Beneficiaries
Savings Account #1234-6789-123	Hannah	Primary: Doris Secondary: Josh and Chris
		Primary: Secondary:
		Primary: Secondary:

FORM

Current Beneficiaries List. The Nolo website includes a down-loadable copy of the Current Beneficiaries List for you to use to create your own list of beneficiaries for your retirement plan, life insurance policy, and other plans. See the appendix for the link to this form and other forms in this book.

If you don't remember whom you named on your retirement plans, it's time to find out. Some companies let you view your beneficiary designations online; others require a phone call to either your HR department or the plan administrator (for example, Vanguard or Fidelity) directly.

If you don't remember who you've named, don't panic. My clients often can't remember whom they've named, or even what plans they have. We are all busy, and sometimes these plans, especially those from long ago, are easily overlooked and forgotten. The good news (the really good news) is that now is the perfect time to figure this out.

Each retirement plan asks you to name at least one beneficiary who would inherit the assets in the plan if you were to die with a remaining balance. You named this person when you filled out the form to create an IRA or enrolled in your employer's 401(k) or 403(b) plan. If you also own an annuity, that will have a beneficiary as well.

Your primary beneficiary is your first choice to inherit the money in the retirement plan. If that person dies before you do, your secondary beneficiaries, sometimes called the "contingent" or "alternate" beneficiaries, will inherit the money.

If you're married, you'll likely name your spouse as your primary beneficiary and your children (if any) as the secondary beneficiaries.

If you're not married, you can name a partner, your friends or relatives, or charities. If you are charitably inclined, naming charities as your beneficiaries is a great idea. Charities don't pay tax on these withdrawals, so they will receive 100% of the value. In contrast, if you name a person, like your brother, he will pay income tax on what he withdraws.

EXAMPLE: Dem names her local women's shelter as the beneficiary of her IRA. When she dies, the shelter withdraws the balance of $100,000 and uses it to build a new preschool for children staying at the shelter. If Dem had named her brother, Jed, as the beneficiary, he would have withdrawn that $100,000, and paid 28% of that in income tax, leaving him with the balance of $72,000.

Because your will or a trust won't control how your retirement assets are distributed, you should make sure that your beneficiary designations are correct and current. If you've been divorced or married since you opened up a plan, or had children since then, the chances are you've got outdated or incorrect beneficiaries listed. It's a good idea to double-check what beneficiaries you've designated even if no major life changes have happened. You might still have a new idea of whom you want to benefit.

If you need to change your beneficiary designations, don't worry —it's a piece of cake. I'll discuss it at the end of this chapter.

Obviously, you don't want to leave retirement plan assets to the flat-out wrong person. That would be a careless mistake. But even if you simply want to leave these assets to your spouse, child, or other loved ones, as most people do, it's worth understanding the best way to do so. Retirement plans have tricky rules about how money must be withdrawn and when. Worse, the rules are different for different beneficiaries.

Retirement 101: The Basic Rules of Choosing Beneficiaries and Withdrawing Money

It is critical to make sure that you have named the right beneficiaries to inherit any money you might leave behind in your retirement plans. Simple, eh? Well, for most people, it is.

But always keep the big picture in mind. First, if you have a will or a trust, ask yourself if the plan and your beneficiary designations match. Having a different set of instructions means that your plan won't work as you intended it to work.

EXAMPLE 1: Ronald's living trust leaves all of his assets to his partner, Jim. But Ronald's IRA names Martha, Ronald's sister, as his beneficiary. Ronald opened that plan in 2000, years before he met Jim. Ronald's estate planner asked Ronald to check on his beneficiary designations. Ronald had forgotten that he'd named Martha as beneficiary of his IRA.

EXAMPLE 2: Theresa's will names her godson, Tim, and her favorite charity, The Nature Conservancy, as her beneficiaries. But Theresa's 401(k) names Wilson, her now ex-husband, as her beneficiary. Theresa needs to update her beneficiary designations so that Wilson won't inherit the 401(k).

EXAMPLE 3: Brianna created a living trust for the benefit of her partner, Christian, for his lifetime, and then left the remainder to her three best friends. Brianna died. Six months later Christian died, too. After Brianna died, it turned out that she had named Christian as the beneficiary of her IRA (and not her trust). Since Christian died without a will and without any children, all $500,000 of Brianna's IRA went to Christian's sister, Madison, whom Brianna had never even met.

So, assuming that you've named the right beneficiaries, what happens when you die? Your beneficiaries will have some choices about how to withdraw that money. If you name a charity, it can withdraw the money with no tax penalty. But if you name a person, and if they are young, the most tax-efficient thing to do is to withdraw that money slowly, over their expected lifetime, so that it continues to grow on a tax-deferred basis. The older a person gets, the less value tax-deferred growth has, so they might decide to withdraw the money more quickly.

To allow your beneficiaries the luxury of tax deferral, you want to avoid doing anything now that will later trigger IRS rules forcing your beneficiaries to withdraw money quickly. As you'll see, there are a few mistakes you definitely want to avoid.

Different rules apply to traditional retirement plans (IRAs, 401(k)s) and to Roth plans. With traditional retirement plans, you must start withdrawing money after you've reached a certain age. These rules are there to make sure that you eventually pay the taxes you've been deferring, because you're taxed when you pull the money out. Roth plans, on the other hand, let you save for retirement with money that's already been taxed, so they don't require mandatory distributions for you (or for your spouse if you are married). When your beneficiaries inherit them, though, they'll be subject to mandatory distributions rules. Here are the basics.

IRAs and 401(k)s

You are required to start taking money out of your IRA, 401(k), or 403(b) by April 1 of the year after you reach the age of 70½. That's called your "required beginning date." The IRS allows you to defer paying taxes on the funds in your plan until then, but at that point you must start withdrawing money and paying income tax on it.

How much you take out is based upon your life expectancy. To simplify things quite a bit, you must take out a fraction of your account that's based on how long the IRS Uniform Lifetime Table says someone your age is likely to live.

If you die before you're required to start taking money out of your retirement plan, your beneficiaries (other than your spouse, if any) are going to have to start withdrawing money beginning in the year after your death. How much they must withdraw is based on their own life expectancies. Spouses, unlike all other beneficiaries, have an option to roll over Inherited IRAs.

EXAMPLE: When Miguel is 40, he inherits an IRA worth $150,000 from his Aunt Ethel who was 65 when she died. Miguel must start withdrawing the money the next year. The IRS tables say his life expectancy is 42.7 more years, so Miguel must take out $150,000 ÷ 42.7, or $3,512.88, that year (the year after his aunt died). Each year he must withdraw the current balance divided by a smaller number (the beginning denominator, minus 1 each year) until the account is exhausted. The second year, for example, Miguel would have to divide the current balance by 41.7 to get the required distribution.

If you die *after* you turn 70½, the rules are a bit different. A beneficiary who is not your surviving spouse must take the distributions that you would have taken in the year of your death. After that, these beneficiaries must take money out based on their own life expectancies, until the account is depleted.

Roth IRAs and Roth 401(k)s

Roth IRAs (and now, Roth 401(k) and 403(b) plans) are different from traditional IRAs. Remember, with these accounts, you pay the tax first, then invest the money. You don't get an income tax deduction when you contribute the money, as you do with traditional IRAs. The money, though, grows tax free, and there are no required withdrawals with Roth accounts. When you do withdraw the money, there's no tax on these withdrawals, provided the account has existed for at least five years and you are over 59½ years old. That means that if you don't spend this money, it can continue to grow tax free for your entire life, and you can leave it to whomever you wish.

Even though you don't have to withdraw money from your Roth account, your beneficiaries may have to. It depends on who's doing the inheriting:

- If you're married, your spouse can roll the money into his or her own Roth IRA and keep saving the money tax free. Surviving spouses are not subject to any required minimum distribution rules and will pay no tax on the money once it's been withdrawn.
- Other beneficiaries, including your children (if any), will be subject to the same required distribution rules that apply to IRAs and 401(k)s. This means that, provided the plan permits it, they will have to begin taking money out one year after your death, but these payments will be stretched out over their expected lifetimes. Again, the money can continue to grow tax free until the funds are exhausted, and no tax is due when it's withdrawn. What's really great is that if your beneficiaries need to pull the money out to buy a house or deal with a medical emergency, they can do so, with no tax penalty.

EXAMPLE: Jonathan contributes to a Roth IRA for the last ten years of his life, without ever withdrawing any money from it. He names his wife, Faith, as the primary beneficiary of the account. At Jonathan's death, Faith rolls the inherited Roth IRA into a Roth IRA in her own name. She lives another 20 years and never withdraws any money from the account. She names Tamar, her daughter, as the beneficiary.

When Tamar inherits the account, she must begin withdrawing funds. She is 35 when she inherits the money, so Tamar's life expectancy is 48.5 more years, according to the IRS tables. She must start taking out a small fraction of the account's total value each year for the rest of her life. No income tax is due on these withdrawals. And if Tamar needs more of the money, it's hers, tax free.

Naming Beneficiaries for Retirement Plans

I really can't imagine who writes IRS regulations, but I'm pretty sure they're not originally from this planet. Get this: You can designate your spouse (if you're married); your children (if any); another relative or a friend; a trust; or a nonprofit—basically any person or organization that you wish as a beneficiary. But—and this is a big but—only certain beneficiaries get to withdraw the money from your plan slowly, over time, which is generally what you want them to do if possible. Withdrawing money slowly over time, which is called "stretch-out" planning, is beneficial because the money in the IRA continues to grow tax free over a longer period of time. The more slowly this money is withdrawn, the more money there is left in that account to grow over time.

These lucky beneficiaries, who can stretch out distributions based on their life expectancies, are called "designated beneficiaries," and only the IRS can tell you who they are. These include a spouse and children, well as any "natural person," (such as a friend, a distant relative, or any other human being).

But organizations and businesses don't qualify as designated beneficiaries under IRS rules. They'll have to withdraw all of the money within five years.

EXAMPLE: Lucille had an IRA. She saved close to $600,000 over her 30 years of employment. When Lucille died, she named her church, her nephew, and her sister as beneficiaries of that IRA. Because the church is not a "designated beneficiary" under IRS rules, the plan administrator said that the church had to withdraw its share of the money over the next five years.

Name Somebody!

Your worst option is naming no one. If that happens, a quick payout will be required. If you die before you are 70½, and name no one as a beneficiary of a retirement plan, the beneficiaries of your estate must withdraw all of the money within five years of your death. If you die after you are 70½, the beneficiaries of your estate will have to withdraw the money based on your age (which probably means they will have to make withdrawals from your retirement plan a lot more quickly than they would have if you'd named them directly).

That means your retirement plan assets won't be able to keep growing tax free. Quite the contrary, there will be steep income taxes to pay when the withdrawals are made. Worse, the money will go to your estate, which means a probate proceeding will be necessary to transfer the assets.

Some plans use your spouse (if any) as a default beneficiary if you don't name one. But don't rely on that option. If your plan doesn't have this default rule, the money would go to your estate.

Your Spouse

If you are married, it makes sense (both financially and emotionally) to name your spouse as the primary beneficiary. Spouses get special benefits that other beneficiaries of inherited retirement assets don't. Only spouses can defer withdrawal of the retirement plan assets until they turn 70½ and name new beneficiaries to boot. Unless they need the money right away, this continued tax deferral is a terrific benefit. (Because all of these rules are a matter of federal law, they don't apply to registered domestic partners, whose rights are recognized only by certain states, including California.)

Surviving spouses have two options that no one else gets. They can:

- **Keep the plan in the name of the deceased spouse.** This way, the survivor can take distributions over his or her own life expectancy, but beginning in the year that the deceased spouse would have turned 70½.

- **Roll the assets into the survivor's own IRA and defer any withdrawal until the survivor turns 70½.** The survivor can also name new beneficiaries of the rollover account.

A Spouse's Rights

If you are married and want to name someone other than your spouse as the primary beneficiary of your retirement plan, you must get your spouse's consent in writing. Here's why:

- **IRAs.** IRAs are governed by state law. Since California is a community property state, your spouse owns half of the money in your IRA even if you don't name him or her as the beneficiary—if those funds were earned during your marriage (and if you don't have a pre- or postmarital agreement changing California community property rules). A spouse who doesn't consent to a beneficiary designation could claim half of the account when the first spouse dies because that's their property under California law.
- **401(k)s.** Under federal law, your spouse is entitled to inherit all of the money in your 401(k) or 403(b) plan unless your spouse signs a waiver consenting to your choice of someone else as a beneficiary.

SEE AN EXPERT

Spouses who inherit retirement assets should seek professional advice before they take over the accounts. The rules governing retirement assets are complex, and there are deadlines for making some decisions. Worse, a spouse who accidentally fails to take a required distribution within a certain period of time may be deemed to have decided to roll over an account, even if that was never intended. Start by talking with the plan administrator, who can explain your choices for rollover or withdrawal of the assets in the retirement plan.

Children

Who comes next, after your spouse (if any)? Most parents want to leave their retirement plan assets to their children. People without children may want to name a godchild, or family friend, or a grandchild, or niece or nephew. Here's where it can get a little complicated.

If your children are under 18, they can't own these assets directly. If you just write down their names as beneficiaries, and then you die, a court will have to name a property guardian to manage your retirement account for the children until they're 18. After that, the children would be able to do financially unwise things, like take out all of the money in the account. It would then be taxed as ordinary income. Then, they might blow the money on something silly. Ouch.

Here's where having a coordinated estate plan really helps. Rather than naming your children directly, you can follow one of these strategies:

- Name a custodian for your children, under the California Uniform Transfers to Minors Act (as explained in Chapter 5). That will provide management of the assets until age 25.
- Better yet, if you've created (in your will or living trust) a trust to manage the children's money, name the trust as the secondary beneficiary. Under IRS rules, the age of the oldest beneficiary, usually your oldest child, will be used to figure out how much each beneficiary must take out of the plan each year, and then the distributions will be divided among the kids (if the trust has more than one child as beneficiary) according to the trust's rules.

! CAUTION

Check your plan's rules. Even though leaving your retirement plan to a trust for children or other minor beneficiaries would allow them to stretch out withdrawals over the lifetime of the oldest child by IRS rules, some plans still might require the trust to withdraw all the money within five years. Plans can be more restrictive than what the IRS rules allow. Be sure that you know how your retirement plan handles this.

Multiple Beneficiaries

It's generally not a good idea to leave a retirement plan to more than one person at a time directly—say, to three adult children. (It's okay to leave the plan to a trust that benefits more than one person.) If you do, your good intentions could create a headache for them. Here's what happens: If your beneficiaries don't split up the account by September 30th of the year following your death, then the age of the oldest beneficiary is the one that they all have to use to determine the required distributions. That means the money must be pulled out more quickly than it would be if each beneficiary could use his or her own life expectancy.

EXAMPLE: Melody (age 45) leaves her IRA, worth $300,000, in equal shares to her much older partner, Mason (age 65), and her two daughters, Angie and Kaylee (ages 8 and 10). She names Mason as the custodian for Angie and Kaylee's shares. Melody unexpectedly dies the next year (when she's 46).

Melody's IRA plan allows beneficiaries to use the life expectancy rule when distributing the money. Because Mason is the oldest beneficiary, the account must be distributed over his life expectancy. He will be 67 in the first distribution year, making Mason's life expectancy (from the IRS tables) 19.4 more years. So to calculate the required distribution from the account, the beneficiaries divide the account balance ($300,000) by 19.4 years. That yields a result of $15,463.92, which is how much must be withdrawn in that first year.

If instead, Angie, Kaylee, and Mason had each inherited separate accounts, Angie's required distribution would be $100,000 ÷ 72.8 years = $1,373.63, and Kaylee's would be $100,000 ÷ 70.8 years = $1,412.43.

It's possible for the beneficiaries to avoid this problem. If they get timely advice from an experienced financial adviser, accountant, or tax attorney, the beneficiaries can split the account(s) up before September 30th of the year following the date of death. If they do that, the beneficiaries can base required withdrawals on their own life expectancies.

You can also prevent problems by splitting up your accounts now and leaving each beneficiary a separate account. The downside to doing this is that it will cost you more in administrative fees, because each account will be administered separately.

> **TIP**
> **Don't name a charity along with someone else as beneficiaries of an IRA or 401(k).** Because the charity isn't a "designated beneficiary," the other person will be subject to the five-year withdrawal rule unless the charity withdraws its share by September 30 of the year following the date of death. The issue here is that in order to get the benefit of stretch-out planning (the ability to take the money out slowly over your expected life span), all the beneficiaries of the trust must be what the IRS calls designated beneficiaries and charities don't qualify.

A Trust

Married couples often name a trust for their children as the secondary beneficiary of their retirement plans. (They name each other as primary beneficiaries.) Single parents often name a trust for their children as the primary beneficiary. That's generally a good plan (as discussed under "Children," above). I've written trusts for single people who name a trust created for other minor beneficiaries as well—often nieces and nephews.

A trust for your spouse is a different thing altogether. Naming a trust for your spouse as the primary beneficiary of your retirement accounts, instead of your spouse directly, is not something to do casually. If done with the help of an estate planning attorney and coordinated with a carefully drafted estate plan, it can be a way to maximize a couple's ability to save or defer estate taxes at the death of the second spouse. But most people don't need to worry about estate tax—under current law, federal estate tax isn't a concern unless you plan to leave more than $5 million (indexed each year to inflation, currently $5.49 million) to your children.

In my practice, there are only two situations that warrant naming a trust instead of a spouse: either to control where the plan's assets will go after the spouse dies, or to make sure that the assets are managed by a third-party trustee. For example, if a husband has a large retirement account and two adult sons from a previous marriage, he might name the trust as the beneficiary instead of his second spouse. That way, the second wife can use the assets during her lifetime, but what is left will go to her husband's sons. Or if a wife was concerned about her husband's ability to manage the assets, she might name the trust, but name a third-party trustee, such as a trusted family friend or a bank, as trustee.

Naming a trust as a beneficiary has some serious drawbacks:

- **No rollover.** Even if your spouse is the beneficiary of the trust, he or she will not be allowed to roll over plan assets into his or her own IRA and defer distributions until he or she turns 70½. (It's possible that a surviving spouse could take plan distributions and roll them over into an IRA, but that's why this is an area fraught with difficulties.)

- **No splitting.** If there are multiple trust beneficiaries, they won't be able to split the account into several individual accounts after your death. This means that they can't each use his or her own life expectancy to determine minimum distributions; instead, the oldest trust beneficiary's age will determine the required minimum distributions for all of the beneficiaries.

- **Complexity.** If someone other than your spouse is the beneficiary, that person will have to take out minimum distributions over his or her expected lifetime (or over five years, depending on the plan), and then the money will be subject to the trust's terms (unless the trust has special provisions directing the trustee to immediately distribute all plan proceeds to the trust beneficiaries).

Charities

Charities are *not* designated beneficiaries under IRS rules. Again, that means that the money will have to be taken out within five years after it's inherited and won't be able to keep growing tax free over the long term. But that's just fine because the charity is going to cash out the IRA and use the money for their charitable purposes. Since they don't have to pay income tax on these withdrawals, naming charities for your IRAs is a great idea for those with charitable intent.

 TIP
Naming a donor-advised fund as a beneficiary of an IRA or Roth IRA (or other retirement account) is another great way to benefit charity. A donor-advised fund is an account that you can open at a community foundation or many financial companies (like Schwab and Vanguard). You open the account, and fund it with cash or stock. You will receive a charitable deduction for the assets you use to fund the donor-advised fund. Then, you can direct the manager of the fund to send charitable donations in your name (or anonymously). A donor-advised fund is like a dedicated charity account that you can use to make donations at any time after you've funded it. If you name a donor-advised fund as a beneficiary of an IRA or other retirement account, those funds will go to the fund, to be distributed according to your instructions (which you'd leave with the fund's manager).

EXAMPLE: Brad opened up a donor-advised fund in 2017 with an initial contribution of $5,000 worth of stock that he purchased for $1/share in 2001. The stock was worth $5/share when Brad donated it to his local community foundation, so he transferred 1,000 shares of stock. Brad received a tax deduction for $5,000 for doing so. The foundation sold that stock and paid no capital gains on the $4,000 of gain that Brad had earned. In 2018 and 2019, Brad directed the foundation to use some of that $5,000 to make grants to the Sierra Club, the SPCA, and the American Cancer Society. If Brad wants to, he can make additional donations to the fund. He also named that donor-advised fund as the beneficiary of 50% of his IRA. At Brad's death, the IRA assets will be transferred to the donor-advised fund and be distributed according to a list of organizations that Brad has on file with the foundation.

A Little Housekeeping: Cleaning Up Your Retirement Plans

A great thing to do now to avoid headaches for your loved ones later is to consolidate your retirement plans.

Roll Over Those Old 401(k) Plans

First, roll your old 401(k) plans into an IRA. Many people do this routinely when they leave one job and start another. But many don't.

I have clients who have three or four 401(k) plans out there. If you roll them over during your lifetime, you'll gain control over where and how to invest your money. If you don't roll them over, your old company will continue to invest these funds in its 401(k) plan, which may be limited to a small group of funds and may be heavily invested in the company's own stock. Worse, you may discover that the company's moved the entire account somewhere else and neglected to tell you.

EXAMPLE: Gabrielle had a 401(k) from a former employer that was managed by a large brokerage company, Old Reliable Investing. Ten years after Gabrielle left that job, her former employer moved the 401(k) account to a different company, New Advantages Investment. Gabrielle learned about the transfer only when she got an account statement that showed her Old Reliable balance as zero.

After repeated phone calls to her former employer, Gabrielle was told that the account had been moved to New Advantages, but not what her account number was. Her former employer promised to contact New Advantages so that it would forward Sarah the forms for a rollover, but never did so. Finally, Gabrielle hired an attorney to help her move her money to an IRA that she could control.

You can roll 401(k) money over into Roth IRAs, provided you qualify under the IRS's income limits. (See "Alphabet Soup: Retirement Plans Explained," above.)

If having control over your money isn't a big enough incentive to get your old accounts cleaned up, consider this: By rolling your old 401(k) accounts over now, you'll also make it easier for your spouse (if any) to roll them over into his or her own IRA if you die first. If the funds are still in an old 401(k), your family or other beneficiaries will have to work with plan administrators in a company that they may have had no dealings with for many years. The company may no longer even be in business—in which case it probably transferred management of its 401(k) plan to another company entirely. By transferring your old 401(k)s now into IRAs, your heirs won't have as much to do when you die. The company that manages the IRA now can continue to manage it when your heirs inherit the IRA and has an incentive to keep them happy to avoid losing the business.

Consolidate Your IRAs

Also consider consolidating your existing IRAs into one or two accounts. This will make it a lot easier to figure out how your investments are doing. You'll also save yourself duplicate fees and lessen the onslaught of mail you receive each month. And you'll make it easier for your surviving beneficiaries to consolidate and manage their inherited accounts. It's surprisingly easy for survivors to entirely overlook an account if there are a lot to keep track of.

Filling Out the Forms Naming Beneficiaries

Plan administrators all have their own forms for you to use to designate your primary and secondary beneficiaries. You can also get a form to change your current beneficiaries. If you need that one, you can often download it from a company's website.

Every company's forms are a little bit different. But they're all trying to get you to name a primary beneficiary and a secondary (backup) beneficiary. "Completing a Beneficiary Form," shown below, is a cheat sheet that you can use to make sure you're naming the right people in the right way.

Completing a Beneficiary Form	
Beneficiary	**How to Fill Out the Form**
Spouse	My spouse, Jessica E. Jones, born on January 13, 19xx
Children	If as a custodial account:
	To my children, Zachary J. Jones and Evelyn M. Jones, in equal shares. Any benefits becoming distributable to a child under the age of 25 years shall be distributed to Rosalie L. Smith, as custodian under the California Uniform Transfers to Minors Act.
	[*You can name a different custodian for each child if you wish.*]
	To the trustee of the Jones Family Trust, created by my will dated April 4, 20xx
	OR
	To the trustee of the Jones Family Trust, created on April 4, 20xx

By the way, if you're married, it's always a good idea to name your spouse by name (not just by writing "my wife," for example). You could, after all, have a different spouse someday, and you don't want any confusion over whom you meant to name.

On many beneficiary forms, there's a box that you can check to add something called a "per stirpes" stipulation or "Right of Representation" to individuals you name as contingent beneficiaries. This means that if the named person doesn't survive you, but leaves behind children, those children would share the deceased parent's share, equally. I think it's a better idea to write down exactly what you want to do and not use their check boxes.

Resources on Retirement Plans and IRA Withdrawals

For a terrific (and easy-to-read) overview of retirement plans, good advice on retirement planning, and all the rules for taking the money out of these plans, see *IRAs, 401(k)s & Other Retirement Plans: Taking Your Money Out*, by Twila Slesnick and John C. Suttle (Nolo).

Other useful resources on IRA withdrawals include:

- **www.irs.gov.** See the "Individual Retirement Accounts" section for lots of helpful advice, including information for beneficiaries of retirement accounts.
- **www.finra.org.** The Financial Industry Regulatory Authority (FINRA) has helpful resources for beneficiaries of retirement accounts at www.finra.org/investors/alerts/inherited-iras-what-you-need-know.
- **www.aarp.org.** Check out the "Savings and Investing" section of the AARP site for information on IRAs and retirement planning, including how to handle inherited IRAs.

Finally, make sure to check with the plan administrator for your own IRA or 401(k) for advice on inherited plans. Not all plans offer the same withdrawal options to beneficiaries of inherited accounts. The IRS rules are still the rules, but an administrator that decides to offer more restrictive options can do so.

Naming Beneficiaries for Life Insurance

For most people, life insurance is the other major asset (after retirement assets) that they own that passes to their loved ones by beneficiary designation. (See Chapter 5 for advice on the benefits of life insurance and how to buy it.) For all of the reasons that I've discussed above, it's also important to make sure that your beneficiary designations for your life insurance plans are up to date and that you've named the right people or organizations to receive the policy proceeds at your death. Thankfully, this isn't usually complicated, but it does bear some thought.

Naming the Right Beneficiaries

When you buy a new insurance policy, you name a primary beneficiary and a secondary (alternate) beneficiary. You do it on the enrollment forms that the company sends to you after it's approved your application for coverage. The primary beneficiary gets the money when you die. If that person dies before you do, or at the same time, the secondary beneficiary gets the money.

EXAMPLE: Wyatt bought a life insurance policy on his own life and named his wife, Zelda, as the primary beneficiary. He named his brother, Gavin, as the secondary, or alternate, beneficiary. When Wyatt and Zelda die together in a yachting accident, Gavin receives the insurance proceeds.

If you already own a policy but want to change your beneficiaries, ask the insurance carrier for a change of beneficiary form. Fill it out and send it back. Be sure to keep a copy for your records.

Remember, it's really important to name the right people on these forms. Your will or trust has no effect on who gets your insurance proceeds. The beneficiary form that you fill out is what determines who inherits this money.

Use the Current Beneficiaries List included in this book (see the sample, above) to list the names of the primary and secondary beneficiaries of your life insurance policy.

If You've Been Divorced, Check Your Insurance Policies

If you've been married before, make extra sure to check all of your beneficiary designations.

If your divorce settlement agreement mandates that you name your ex-spouse as a beneficiary under an insurance policy for a certain number of years (a common practice), then you can't change that. If you are on good terms with your ex and raising minor children together, you might want to keep your ex as the beneficiary of your policy so that the children can be provided for.

But if you've simply forgotten to take your ex-spouse off the beneficiary form, your current spouse or partner could be in for a nasty surprise if you die unexpectedly. California law does *not* automatically revoke beneficiary designations of life insurance policies (some states do). In fact, California law (Family Code Section 2020) requires this notice be given on any petition for dissolution of marriage:

> "Dissolution or annulment of your marriage may automatically cancel your spouse's rights under your will, trust, retirement benefit plan, power of attorney, pay on death bank account, transfer on death vehicle registration, survivorship rights to any property owned in joint tenancy, and any other similar thing. It does not automatically cancel your spouse's rights as beneficiary of your life insurance policy. If these are not the results that you want, you must change your will, trust, account agreement, or other similar document to reflect your actual wishes."

My advice: Review the designations on your life insurance policies and change them if they don't reflect your current wishes.

Primary Beneficiaries

Here's how to fill out most forms for primary beneficiaries :
- If you have a *will*, and you are in a relationship, name your spouse or partner as the primary beneficiary of your life insurance policy. Your spouse will get the money directly. Example: "Natalie R. Reynoso, my spouse."
- If you have a *living trust* and you are married or in a partnership, name that trust as the primary beneficiary if the trust names the people that you want to give your assets to. It depends on the terms of the trust, but, if you are in a relationship, your spouse or partner would be the beneficiary of the trust when you die, so they will have full access to the money. Whatever your spouse/partner doesn't spend will stay in the trust, avoiding probate when that spouse dies, and be managed for your children or other beneficiaries if they're still young. Example: "The Johnson Family Trust, executed on January 4, 20xx."

- If want to give your life insurance assets to someone other than the trust's beneficiaries, name that person or organization directly as a beneficiary. Example, "the Girl Scouts of the United States of America" or "my dear friend, Sam Jacobs."

Secondary Beneficiaries

Here's how to fill out most forms for secondary beneficiaries:

- If you have a *will* that creates a trust for children or other minor beneficiaries, name that trust. Example: "the Rudolph Children's Trust, established by my will, executed on January 4, 20xx."
- If you have a *will* that doesn't create a trust for children or other minor beneficiaries, name a custodian for them under the Uniform Transfers to Minors Act. Example: "Gail Smith, as custodian for Joseph Sherman, under the California Uniform Transfers to Minors Act."
- If you have a *living trust*, you don't need to name a secondary beneficiary. Even after you pass away, your trust will continue to exist. It will be there to serve as the primary beneficiary. The money from your life insurance policy will pass into the trust and go to the beneficiaries of the trust the way you decided it should be distributed when you created the trust.
- If you want to leave your insurance policy to an organization or other person that's not a trust beneficiary, name that organization or person directly as a secondary beneficiary (example, "Marin Coastal Land Trust," or "Mary Rudolph").

EXAMPLE 1: Pedro fills out the beneficiary form for his new life insurance policy by writing in Camila as his primary beneficiary. For his secondary beneficiary, he writes "the Sanchez Family Trust, as established by my will, executed on December 4, 20xx." If Camila is alive when Pedro dies, she will receive the death benefit. If she dies before he does, or at the same time, the money will go to a trust established by Pedro's will for the benefit of his children.

EXAMPLE 2: Mila and Claudio Berner have a living trust. They purchase two term policies for $500,000 of coverage. On each policy they write in "the Berner Family Trust, created on November 15, 20xx," as the primary beneficiary. They don't list a secondary beneficiary because the trust will survive them. When either Mila or Claudio dies, the trust will receive the death benefit. All of the money will be available for the survivor's use. At the survivor's death, if there's any money left in the trust, it will pass to the couple's children, in trust, and avoid probate.

Using Life Insurance to Reduce (and Pay) Federal Estate Tax

People with taxable estates (only those with more than $5 million or more in assets, indexed for inflation, so currently $5.49 million) can use insurance benefits to pay their estate tax bill. This is done by transferring a life insurance policy to a separate trust. This trust is usually called an irrevocable life insurance trust, or ILIT.

The ILIT becomes the legal owner of your policy. It's okay for you to pay the premiums, but the whole thing works only if you don't have any legal control over the policy itself. After your death, the insurance benefit is paid to the ILIT. Because you didn't legally own the policy, none of the money it paid out is part of your taxable estate. The trustee of the insurance trust can then use the proceeds to purchase assets from your estate (real estate or a business, for example), and the money from the sale can be used to pay the estate tax. Many people purchase second-to-die insurance policies to fund these trusts.

This is high-end stuff. If you think it might make sense for you to set up an ILIT, see an estate planning attorney. ●

Advance Health Care Directives & Powers of Attorney for Finances

Health Care Directives 281

    Your Right to Decide About Medical Treatments...283

    Making End-of-Life Choices...285

    Your Health Care Agent's Duties..291

    Picking Your Agent 292

    After You've Picked a Health Care Agent: Time to Talk 293

    Making Your Health Care Directive Legal 297

    Changing Your Mind About Your Health Care Directive 298

Durable Power of Attorney for Finances 298

    What Your Agent Can Do..300

    When a Power of Attorney Takes Effect..301

    Whom Should You Choose as an Agent for Your
        Durable Power of Attorney for Finances?..303

    Making a Power of Attorney for Finances Legal..304

    Where to Get a Durable Power of Attorney 305

    Changing Your Mind About Your Durable Power of Attorney 305

Read this chapter if:

• You don't know what an advance health care directive or a durable power of attorney is or don't have one.

• You don't know whom to name as your agent for health care decisions.

• You don't know what a POLST and a DNR are, or how these documents are different from an advance health care directive.

• You don't know what to say about end-of-life care.

• You don't know whom to name as your agent for finances.

• You would like to know the difference between a durable power of attorney and a springing durable power of attorney.

I f you died unexpectedly, your loved ones would rely on your will or your living trust to put things in order to pass along your money and property to the right people. (If you don't have either a will or living trust, California's intestacy laws, described in Chapter 2 will determine who gets your assets.)

But if you became incapacitated (either seriously ill or injured or confused and unable to make decisions), those documents wouldn't do your loved ones any good. They would need two legal documents that gave them the legal authority to act on your behalf:

• **Advance health care directive.** This allows you to name an agent to act on your behalf with respect to medical decisions. If you could no longer communicate with your doctors, your agent would speak for you and manage your care. You may also state your wishes for end-of-life care, to direct your doctors and your agent.

• **Durable power of attorney for finances.** This lets you name someone to manage your finances if someday you couldn't—for example, if you were hospitalized or otherwise unable to write checks or manage your accounts on a temporary basis, or if you suffered from dementia or some other mental impairment that rendered you unable to do so on a permanent basis.

Do people like you need these documents? Yes. After all, anyone can be injured in a car accident or require hospitalization unexpectedly. If you're unable to manage your daily affairs or communicate with your doctors, your loved ones will rely on these documents to do both. And at the end of life, if you are not able to speak for yourself, your advance health care directive provides you with a place to make a clear statement of your wishes concerning life-sustaining treatment, such as artificial nutrition and hydration or artificial respiration—keeping this agonizing decision within your family circle of loved ones and out of court.

Health Care Directives

Your right to control your medical treatment comes from the U.S. Constitution. In 1990, the United States Supreme Court ruled that if you state your wishes about end-of-life treatment in a clear and convincing way, your wishes should be respected by hospitals, physicians, and family members. This is sometimes called a constitutional "right to die," free of government intrusion into the intimate matter of how and when one's life should end.

In California, the document you use to state these wishes is called an advance health care directive. (In some other states, such as Alaska and Missouri, the term "living will" is used for the document in which you state your wishes for end-of-life care.)

The advance health care directive actually allows you to do two things:

- state your wishes regarding the use of life-sustaining medical treatment, and
- designate a health care agent for making health care decisions short of the decision to end life support, such as what doctor, what procedure, and what medications you might need.

Your end-of-life instructions apply only when medical treatments may prolong your life for a limited amount of time but not help you recover, and when not receiving treatment will lead to your death. Doctors, usually two of them, have to determine whether or not you are at this point.

Finally, you might find it comforting to know that choosing to forgo life-sustaining treatment doesn't affect your medical treatment at all when you are in a situation that is not life threatening.

Doctors who receive a properly signed and witnessed or notarized advance health care directive stating your wishes for medical treatment are legally bound to honor your wishes or transfer you to the care of another physician who will honor them. At least, this is true in theory. At some hospitals, your agent might have to fight hard to get your wishes honored—all the more reason to choose someone who would be a strong advocate.

What Health Care Directives Do

- Appoint someone to make decisions for you if you can't communicate for yourself.
- Name the doctor that you'd like to supervise your care.
- State whether or not you'd like to receive end-of-life medical treatments that would prolong your life artificially, such as artificial respiration or nutrition supplied by a feeding tube if you are unable to swallow on your own.
- State your wishes regarding pain medications or other aspects of your medical or personal care.
- State your wishes for organ donation after death.
- Provide a written document that outlines anything else important to you, such as the kind of care facility you'd like to be placed in if you can't live at home; the kind of environment that you'd like to be in at the end of your life—such as whether or not you'd like visitors, music, or a particular color or scent; the kind of spiritual care that you'd like to receive (or not receive).

It's not hard to find an advance health care directive form. They are widely available, usually for free, and they are easy to fill out and make legally valid. (See "Advance Health Care Directive Forms and More Information," below.)

You absolutely don't need an attorney to create your health care directives. If you're working with a lawyer to draft an estate plan, though, these documents should be created for you as part of that plan.

Once you fill out an advance health care directive, keep the originals, but give copies to your doctors and health care provider, such as an HMO, and the people that you've named as your agents. This is a document that your loved ones will need to have handy in an emergency.

Your Right to Decide About Medical Treatments

Completing your advance health care directive requires you to make some decisions about what medical treatments you would, or wouldn't, want if you were unable to speak for yourself.

You have the right to state your wishes concerning medical treatment that serves only to prolong your life by artificial means. This is often called life-sustaining treatment. To put it another way, you have the right to choose to die by declining certain kinds of health care at the end of your life. If you want all medical procedures used to prolong your life as long as it is medically possible to do so, you can say that in your advance health care directive instead.

You've probably given little thought before to this issue, but don't be intimidated. There are excellent resources available to you on the Internet and in books if you want to educate yourself before making a decision. (See "Advance Health Care Directive Forms and More Information" below.) Because your right to make such choices comes from the U.S. Constitution, you're not limited to the forms that are available. If there's something you feel strongly about, you can attach your own statement of medical wishes to the form you're using and ask that these wishes be respected.

Before you fill out an advance health care directive, here are some things to consider:

- If you become terminally ill, would you like doctors to treat you as long as it is medically possible to do so?
- Are there certain treatments that you would want to receive?
- Are there certain treatments that you would *not* want to receive, such as antibiotics, dialysis, or blood transfusions?
- If you could not eat or drink independently, would you want doctors to give you nutrients and water through a feeding tube?
- If you could not breathe independently, would you want doctors to use respirators to prolong your life?
- Would you want to be kept as pain free and comfortable as possible during a final illness?

EXAMPLE: Trudy, a resident of Palm Springs, wants to put together her advance health care directive. In it, she states that she does not want her life to be prolonged by extraordinary means or by artificial nutrition or hydration if someday her doctors determine that her condition is terminal and incurable or if she is in a persistent vegetative state. Trudy also identifies her husband, and her two adult children to serve as her health care agents to make any other required medical decisions for her if she is unable to make such decisions herself.

Trudy may also attach her own additional directions to her advance health care directive, such as her statement that she wishes to die in her home, surrounded by her friends and family, and to receive all available relief from pain and discomfort. Trudy will sign this document in front of two witnesses or have it notarized. Trudy will then give this signed document to her husband and her two children, as well as to her primary care physician. When Trudy goes to the hospital for elective surgery, she also gives them a copy of her advance health care directive.

Making End-of-Life Choices

My clients have had all kinds of reactions when we start talking about health care directives:

- Many people get a bit giddy and make jokes about "pulling the plug."
- Others get very serious and worry that requesting no life-sustaining measures now might rob them of the chance to take advantage of future medical advances.
- I've heard more than a few people worry that if they sign up to be organ donors, they won't receive adequate care.
- Occasionally, I meet someone who is most concerned with draining the family's resources unnecessarily.
- Finally, some people I've worked with just want to skip doing an advance health care directive and let their partner or their children decide what to do if it's ever necessary.

If that last option (doing nothing) is the most appealing, take a deep breath and try to imagine your loved ones having to make an agonizing decision about whether or not to continue life-sustaining medical treatment for you. Imagine how much better they would feel knowing that you took the time to tell them what you'd like them to do. And if your loved ones can't agree, your doctors will have written evidence of what you would have wanted. The tragic cases that make the news, and sometimes the courts, are almost always situations in which a person left nothing in writing. That means it's left to California state law and the courts to determine who, if anyone, is authorized to make the toughest end-of-life decisions.

Court-Appointed Conservatorships: An Undesirable Alternative

If you don't create a health care directive and durable power of attorney for finances before you're unable to manage your own affairs, your loved one will have to go to court and ask to be appointed as your conservator. A conservator is a responsible adult appointed by a judge to care for an adult who is unable to manage either finances or personal care (or both). That's the only way that another person can step in and manage things on your behalf. Establishing a conservatorship is expensive and public—and unnecessary if you get the job done now by preparing an advance health care directive.

EXAMPLE: Javier, a young father of three, was in a tragic motorcycle accident one rainy night. Like most people, he'd never completed an advance health care directive or a power of attorney for finances. Javier suffered severe brain damage in the accident and faced a long period of recovery and an uncertain future. Although he was able to physically sign documents that were placed in front of him, Javier couldn't understand what he was signing or why his loved ones needed to have the power to make medical and financial decisions on his behalf.

Valentina, his wife, asked an attorney to draft an advance health care directive and a power of attorney for finances for Javier. The attorney told Valentina that it was too late for Javier to sign such documents and that she'd have to ask a court to name her as Javier's conservator instead.

Choosing to forgo life-sustaining treatments doesn't mean that your doctors won't ease your pain or try to make you comfortable in other ways. This is called "palliative care," which focuses on providing quality of life for a patient and their loved ones. (See "How Palliative Care Can Help," for details.)

How Palliative Care Can Help

Those who administer palliative care focus on providing a patient with dignity and comfort, not in trying to cure a disease or prolong life just because it is medically possible to do so. Not all doctors have been trained in palliative care, but it is getting increased attention from the medical community, and it is worth discussing with your doctor and your agent if it is important to you. If you are trying to advocate for someone in a hospital that isn't focused on palliative care, it can be frustrating and difficult to get doctors to listen. If you are in that position, my advice is to reach out to the hospital social worker and the nursing staff and ask for support in seeking palliative care. Often, social workers and nurses can be your best in-house advocates for such care.

When my father was dying, the ICU doctors kept ordering invasive testing that was not going to help prolong his life or make him more comfortable. The social worker and the nursing staff helped me to find an ICU doctor who understood what our family wanted and was able to discontinue the aggressive (yet useless) treatment and get my father discharged to a skilled nursing facility where he was able to rest and receive comfort care only. We needed the social worker's and nurses' support and guidance to navigate the hospital system. You might need such help, too.

You may receive palliative care at home, in a hospital, or at a hospice. For more information, see https://getpalliativecare.org.

What's a POLST?

Struggles with doctors who don't respect patients' choices in the advance health care directive led patient's rights advocates to pass laws authorizing another form, called a POLST, that creates a medically binding order with respect to end-of-life choices. POLST stands for Physician Orders for Life-Sustaining Treatment. You fill this out with your physician, nurse practitioner, or physician's assistant, and both of you must sign the POLST for it to be valid. It is usually printed on bright pink paper and will stay with your medical record once you've completed it. (California wants to create an electronic registry for these forms, but as of 2017, it's only a pilot program in Contra Costa County and the city of San Diego.)

At home, it is recommended that you place your POLST in a visible location (like your refrigerator) so that emergency medical people will see it if they are called to your home in an emergency.

The POLST form requires you to specify whether or not you want:

- attempted CPR
- use of high-intensity treatments, such as a ventilator to help you breathe, or
- use of artificial nutrition and hydration by a tube.

A POLST form isn't something you do *instead of* an advance health care directive, but rather something you might do *in addition to* an advance health care directive. They serve different purposes. The advance health care directive is a legal document that allows you to appoint agents to make medical decisions for you and in which you state your end-of-life choices. The POLST form is a medical document that you create with your physician, nurse practitioner, or physician's assistant when facing a serious illness that is binding on all doctors who subsequently treat you. Younger, healthier people should definitely complete the advance health care directive. Only people facing a serious or chronic illness need to complete a POLST.

RESOURCE

To get a POLST form, you can ask for one from your doctor, or download one from POLST California at http://capolst.org.

What's a DNR?

A do-not-resuscitate or DNR order is different from an advance health care directive and a POLST. Like a POLST, a DNR is a form that you sign with your doctor. But it is narrower in scope than a

POLST. It just tells emergency medical personnel that you don't want to receive cardiopulmonary resuscitation (CPR) if there's a medical emergency. CPR is used to restart your heart and get you breathing again. If you simply want to make sure that you don't receive CPR, a DNR is all you need.

But if you also want to make it clear that you don't want other measures taken, the POLST is a broader statement of your wishes concerning other life-sustaining treatments. (The POLST form contains instructions on CPR, so if you complete the POLST you don't also need a DNR.)

A DNR, like a POLST, should be placed in a visible place in your home so that emergency medical people will know what you do, and don't, want.

California's End of Life Option Act

California's End of Life Option Act allows patients to choose to end their lives by taking medication prescribed by doctors after going through a controlled process designed to make sure that this decision is a considered one. When it passed, California joined five other states which have made this legal, and the law is modeled after Oregon's law, passed in 1997.

Because the state's End of Life Option Act is a new law (it just became effective in 2016), its implementation is taking place gradually, and as I write this book, it is still very much a work in progress.

Here's what we do know: The law requires that two doctors determine that a patient age 18 or older has six months or less to live before the lethal drugs can be prescribed. Patients also must be mentally competent to make medical decisions and be able to swallow the medication themselves, and they must affirm in writing, 48 hours before taking the medication, that they will do so.

California's End of Life Option Act (continued)

To find out more about California's End of Life Options Act, and how it is being implemented, these organizations lead the way in tracking the new law:

- **Compassion & Choices,** one of the advocacy groups that supported the law's passage, has a website (www.compassion andchoices.org/california) with information about the law and finding care health care providers who will honor your values (see the "Find Care" tool). You can also contact the organization by phone at 1-800-247-7421.

- **The California Medical Association (CMA)** has published legal guidance for doctors and patients in a question-and-answer format that is available for free from its website, www.cmanet.org (search "End of Life Issues" in the CMA Legal Library).

- **The California Academy of Family Physicians** has published a guide for family doctors (www.familydocs.org/eol/end-of-life-option-act) that includes detailed information on such things as who can make a request for aid in dying; what are the proper procedures to follow in making such a request; who can properly respond to such a request; the proper procedures that a physician must go through in complying with the request; how to document and report the procedure; and what forms are required and where physicians can find them.

RESOURCE

To get a DNR form, you can ask for one from your doctor, or download the form at the California Emergency Service Authority's website at www.emsa.ca.gov/DNR_and_POLST-Forms.

Your Health Care Agent's Duties

Your advance health care directive allows you to designate an agent to act on your behalf. This person is called your health care agent or attorney-in-fact. No matter what the job title, this person's job is to act in your best interests and make the decisions required for your health care. You should name alternate agents in case your first choice is unwilling or unable to act for you.

As long as you can understand and communicate in some way, your decisions will be the ones that doctors respect. If your directive says so, your agent will act on your behalf only if you are unable to make your own health care decisions. You can make an advance directive effective upon signing, in which case your agent could make decisions for you at any time thereafter—but that's not the choice most of my clients make, because most of them would prefer to control their own health care decisions as long as they are capable of making them. You could be unable to make medical decisions because you are unconscious or because you are too confused to understand your choices—for example, if you are on a ventilator, you won't be awake or able to talk and your agent would need to make decisions for you; if you are awake, but too confused or disoriented to understand the risks or benefits of a particular procedure, your agent would have to decide for you.

In addition to naming an agent, you can, in your advance health care directive, define how much authority your agent may have over such things as medical care or services, the choice of doctors treating you, and the release of confidential medical information about you. Your agent has the right to act on your behalf in the following ways, unless you choose to limit them:

- to consent, or refuse to consent, to any medical treatment, including mental health treatment (but not electroconvulsive "shock" therapy, which has separate requirements)
- to select or discharge health care providers and institutions
- to approve or disapprove diagnostic tests and surgical procedures

- to direct that life-sustaining treatment or procedures, such as CPR or dialysis, be used, withheld, or withdrawn, and
- to authorize anatomical gifts or autopsy and to authorize your agent to direct for the disposition of remains.

Picking Your Agent

Obviously, picking the right person to serve as your health care agent is critically important. You're giving this person broad powers to act if someday you're no longer able to act for yourself. You are truly putting your life in his or her hands. Most couples choose their partners, but you are not required to do so. You could choose a close friend or relative, or an adult child.

In California your agent:

- must be at least 18 years old
- cannot be your health care provider or the owner or operator of a care facility (unless the person is also your spouse, domestic partner, or close relative), and
- cannot be an employee of a health care provider (unless the person is also your spouse, domestic partner, or close relative).

When trying to choose an agent, here are some things you should ask yourself:

- Would my agent be a good advocate for me?
- Does my agent really know what I would want?
- Would my agent respect my wishes?
- Could my agent be with me in the hospital (or would this be difficult if they live far away)?
- What would my agent do if my loved ones disagreed with my wishes?

Like picking a guardian for your children, there's no magic way to find the best person for the job. You certainly don't have to pick the same person that you choose for your agent for finance. I've had clients pick close friends who are health care professionals, in the hopes that they'll best be able to advocate for them. I've had clients specifically NOT pick their parents, because they felt that their parents would simply not respect their written wishes but would substitute their own. I've had clients choose their adult children, and others who want to shield those children from this burden and responsibility. The right person for you is the person who you feel is best able to act on your behalf and to carry out your wishes.

You should always try to pick one agent and one alternate. I wouldn't recommend choosing two people to serve together. If you give two people equal authority as your agents and they disagree over what to do, the whole point of your planning will be defeated. If you're not sure whom to pick and are worried about offending someone, talk to everyone and see if together you can come up with one person to serve as the agent and another as the alternate.

EXAMPLE: Ayala, a single mother, struggled with whether to pick her younger sister, Ilana, or her older sister, Phoebe, as her health care agent. She was close to both of her sisters and didn't want to offend either of them. Over the holidays, the three sisters discussed Ayala's concerns and decided that because Ilana lived much closer to Ayala, she was Ayala's best first choice. Phoebe agreed to serve as Ayala's alternate choice, just in case Ilana couldn't do it.

After You've Picked a Health Care Agent: Time to Talk

Once you've decided whom to pick (including an alternate), make sure that those persons know it (and are willing to take on this responsibility). You don't want your agent to be surprised by the job—the very best thing you can do is sit down now and discuss your health care wishes and concerns. If you don't choose your partner or child as your health care agent, it's advisable to let them know this and why. It's a good idea to avoid surprises here, since this document is likely to be used in a crisis.

The more your agent knows about what you would or wouldn't want, the better job they'll be able to do for you. Filling out your health care directive is a good first step, but having a serious discussion about your values, goals, and concerns about medical treatment is really important, too.

It's not always easy to have that kind of a discussion with a close friend or family member or doctor, but it's at least as important as the legal document you'll end up with. No document, no matter how detailed, can capture the dimensions of what you care about, what you're worried about, what you're willing to tolerate, and what you just couldn't live with. Talking about these things now can avoid misunderstandings later.

You'll also want to make sure that your agents have a copy of your properly signed health care directives and easy access to the originals. They'll need them should you become incapacitated. My clients usually keep their original directives with their other estate planning documents (in a safe deposit box or safe at home) but also give copies of their directives to both their named agents and their doctors.

EXAMPLE: Abe, a single parent, names his brother Tyson to serve as his health care agent. He names his sister-in-law Helena as his alternate agent, in case Tyson is unable to serve as his health care agent.

If Abe were to become ill, he would of course be in charge of discussing his condition with his doctors and making decisions about what to do. If Abe should become unable to communicate, though, it would be Tyson's job to make health care decisions on his behalf. Helena would be the backup agent.

Abe, Tyson, and Helena discuss Abe's concerns about treatment, and Abe gives Tyson and Helena a copy of his health care directives. Abe also tells them that he has the original in a fireproof box in his office and gives them the combination to the box.

As part of organizing your estate plan decisions, be sure to record your choice for health care agent (and alternate). You can use the Fiduciary Worksheet included in this book to do so (see the sample below).

Fiduciary Worksheet

Use this worksheet to record your choices for trustee, executor, and agents under your Durable Power of Attorney and Advance Health Care Directive. These are your "fiduciaries," people who will act in your best interest.

Trustee

First choice: Jennifer Rose Smith

Second choice: Joseph Arthur Doe

Third choice (optional): Sam Thornton

Executor

First choice: Jennifer Rose Smith

Second choice: Joseph Arthur Doe

Third choice (optional): Sam Thornton

Agent/Durable Power of Attorney for Finances

First choice: Jennifer Rose Smith

Second choice: Jane Powell

Third choice (optional): Larry James

Agent/Advance Health Care Directive

First choice: Jennifer Rose Smith

Second choice: Jane Powell

Third choice (optional): Lisa Greland

FORM

The Nolo website includes a downloadable copy of the Fiduciary Worksheet for you to record your choices for trustee, executor, and agents for advance health care directives and durable power of attorney for finances. See the appendix for the link to this and other forms in this book.

Advance Health Care Directive Forms and More Information

You can get health care directives at hospitals, nursing homes, and senior centers, and from your doctor. The federal government requires every facility that receives Medicare or Medicaid to provide information about health care directives to newly admitted patients and to record a patient's health care directives as part of his or her medical records.

Nolo has several useful resources, including:

- *Quicken WillMaker Plus* software, which, in addition to creating a will, can generate a valid California advance health care directive, and

- *Living Wills & Powers of Attorney for California*, by Shae Irving, which explains how to create your own advance health care directive.

There are also excellent resources on the Internet if you want more guidance on how to approach health care directives and California's form. Here are four of my favorites:

- **www.compassionandchoices.org.** This organization educates and advocates for choice and care at the end of life. You can download a health care directive that comes with helpful questions about your goals for medical treatment and your values.

- **www.caringinfo.org.** This is the website of the National Hospice and Palliative Care Organization. You can download health care directives here and they do an excellent job at helping you work through your health care concerns and values.

- **www.agingwithdignity.org.** Aging With Dignity is an organization that has developed Five Wishes, an advance directive that they say meets the legal requirements of 39 states (including California) and the District of Columbia. Even if you end up using a California-specific form, the Five Wishes form can be a great starting place for working through your feelings about end-of-life care and beginning a discussion about these issues with your loved ones and friends. I regularly share Five Wishes with my clients when they are looking for ways to understand what they do and don't want at the end of life.

> ### Advance Health Care Directive Forms and More Information (continued)
>
> - **www.disabilityrightsca.org.** Disability Rights California offers an advance health care directive that offers specific instructions for mental health care at www.disabilityrightsca.org/Pubs/508801.pdf. Also helpful are these sites:
> - **www.growthhouse.org.** This site has terrific resources for life-threatening illnesses and end-of-life care, including the *Handbook for Mortals*, a book that you can read online that has lots of useful information on end-of-life choices.
> - **www.cmanet.org.** The California Medical Association offers an easy to understand and complete advance health care directive kit that you can purchase for $6.00.

Making Your Health Care Directive Legal

You can either sign your advance health care directive in front of two witnesses or have it notarized; either will do in California. After you sign, make copies and give them to your designated agents, your family, your doctor, and any hospital in which you are likely to receive treatment. If you have your directive witnessed, you can't have a witness that is the person you named as your agent or alternate agent, your health care provider, or an employee or operator of a health care facility. Also, at least one witness has to be someone who isn't a family member or who receives anything from your estate. I always notarize directives when my clients are signing their other estate documents; it's just easier.

Changing Your Mind About Your Health Care Directive

You can revoke your health care directives at any time. You can simply rip up your existing document and make a new one. You should, of course, also notify your agent and your doctor that your old documents have been changed. Make sure that all copies of your old documents have been destroyed.

I think the safest thing is to sign a formal revocation of your old document, just to document that you no longer want it ever to take effect. This can be a simple written statement that you are revoking the document that you signed on a particular date. I'd advise having it notarized, that way there can be doubt that it was you who signed it. Then make a new directive and give copies to your agents and your doctor.

Durable Power of Attorney for Finances

A durable power of attorney for finances is another document that you should have as part of your estate plan. It authorizes your agent to act for you with respect to money and property. This is usually a general power of attorney that applies to all of your assets when it becomes effective, but you can create powers of attorney for specific transactions (like buying a house), for certain assets (like a specific account) or for a certain period of time (if you are traveling).

With a valid durable power of attorney, if you were in the hospital for a few weeks, your agent could pay your bills, hire someone to come in and clean your house, manage your investments, and make other financial decisions on your behalf. Without a durable power of attorney, your family members or other loved ones would run into a brick wall when they attempted to act on your behalf.

If you look at it from the point of view of a bank or an insurance company, it all makes sense. Imagine that your brother needs to use your money to pay your medical bills. He can't sign your checks. And if he asks your bank to deliver $1,500 from your checking account, the bank won't do it without something proving that your brother is authorized to act for you. After all, they don't know he isn't trying to steal your money to go to Las Vegas.

A durable power of attorney for finances gives institutions the assurance that they need to work with someone who's acting for you. If you don't take the time to create one while you're competent to do so, the only alternative your loved ones will have is to go to court and ask that someone be named your conservator—which is expensive, restrictive, and public. (See "Court-Appointed Conservatorships: An Undesirable Alternative," above.)

Some couples have joint checking accounts. If so, your spouse or your partner could still write checks for you, if necessary. But that's not a substitute for having a durable power of attorney in place as well. Couples who travel together can both be injured at the same time, and they need to name backup agents to take care of money and property in that case. And married couples don't have unlimited rights to deal with property that's owned jointly; without a power of attorney, one spouse can't sell property or cars without the consent of the other, or withdraw money from their partner's retirement account to pay for medical care or assisted living. In addition, couples who own property separately need a durable power of attorney for finances to allow each other to act with respect to it.

But I Have a Trust!

If your estate plan includes a living trust, and the trust holds your property to avoid probate, it's true that you're ahead of the game. Your successor trustee, the person you named in your trust to take over management of the assets someday, can step in. But you still need a durable power of attorney so that someone can manage the property that's outside of the trust, such as small bank accounts, your life insurance policies, and your retirement accounts. Your power of attorney can even authorize your agent to transfer property into your trust, which can make a huge difference to families who need to do last-minute estate planning when someone's terminally ill.

Finally, when someone is ill, there's more to deal with than just writing checks. Sometimes stock or other property must be sold, houses or apartments must be cleaned up or vacated, or nursing homes must be found and paid for. To do any of those things you need the authority granted by a durable power of attorney for finances. Without this document, you can't even talk to your partner's insurance company or retirement administrator to find out anything about the account or policy, or work with a real estate broker to sell property.

What Your Agent Can Do

You have control over what powers your agent has. These can be quite broad or very narrow—it's up to you. When you're creating a durable power of attorney as part of a comprehensive estate plan, the broader the powers you grant, the better. You want your agent to be able to take whatever action is necessary if you're unable to act for yourself.

Using most durable power of attorney forms, you can give your agent authority over some or all of these things:

- using your assets to pay your everyday expenses
- handling transactions with banks and other financial institutions
- buying, selling, maintaining, and paying debts and taxes on property
- filing and paying your taxes
- managing your retirement accounts
- collecting government benefits owed to you, such as Social Security
- investing your money in financial markets
- buying and selling insurance policies for you
- operating your small business
- making gifts on your behalf
- transferring your property to a living trust that you've already set up
- filing legal actions on your behalf, and
- paying for your personal care and supporting your family.

Your agent under a durable power of attorney, can't, sensibly enough, revoke your will, get married for you, adopt a child on your behalf, or do something that you aren't allowed to delegate, such as serve as a director of a corporation.

In using the authority you've granted, your agent must act only in your best interest and never for personal benefit. The agent must keep careful records and never mix your assets with anyone else's. Your agent must avoid conflicts of interest, such as purchasing your property for his or her own use, unless your durable power of attorney specifically grants the right to do so.

The power of attorney that you sign will state when and how your agent can be liable for breaking the rules. Generally, an agent who acts badly on purpose can be liable to repay the economic harm that results. But your agent is not liable for ordinary acts that don't work out well—say, an investment in a credible company that didn't do as well as expected.

When a Power of Attorney Takes Effect

You have a choice about when your agent's authority takes effect. You can give your agent power to act as soon as you sign the documents or specify that your agent's authority will begin only if you're incapacitated.

Most powers of attorney created by young, healthy folks are written so that they take effect only if someday the principal is no longer able to manage their own affairs. That way, as long as you are healthy and capable, you retain complete control over your property. This is often called a "springing" power of attorney, because it springs into effect only if the principal becomes incapacitated.

Proving incapacity usually requires that at least one doctor sign a statement that says that the principal is unable to manage his or her own affairs. This isn't a problem for someone facing major surgery, but it can be a problem for families when someone they love is facing a long-term degenerative disease, like dementia or Parkinson's disease. In such situations, families can disagree about whether or not someone is incapable of managing daily affairs (or the principal can disagree about his or her own capacity) and then it is difficult to use a springing power of attorney to help.

It can also be a problem because federal law makes doctors liable for giving out confidential health care information without a patient's consent. This can create a chicken-and-egg problem: An agent needs medical information (a doctor's statement of incapacity) to take charge under a durable power of attorney, but the doctor can't give that information without a patient's consent, and the patient either can't or won't give it.

For this reason, most estate planners get their clients to sign a consent form for the release of medical information along with a durable power of attorney for finances. Another way to avoid both issues is to make your power of attorney effective as soon as you sign it. That way, your agent will have immediate power to act for you, and no doctor will have to determine your capabilities or lack of them. My older clients, who already have adult children helping them with finances, often sign durable powers of attorney that are effective upon signing.

But even though there's nothing legally wrong with a power of attorney that's in effect right away, because these documents give others so much power, I'd recommend their use only sparingly when you're young and healthy. If you do so, only choose someone you trust completely. And if you want that person to be able to act immediately, be really sure that you know why you want them to have that authority now.

TIP
Get your financial institution's own power of attorney form. If you deal heavily with one institution, such as a bank or a brokerage firm, ask if it has its own, in-house power of attorney form, just for the assets that it holds for you. Even though institutions are legally required to accept valid powers of attorney, I've found that it never hurts to fill out theirs, too. It can make things a lot easier in a crisis.

Whom Should You Choose as an Agent for Your Durable Power of Attorney for Finances?

For obvious reasons, it's very important that your agent is someone whom you trust completely. You are giving this person a blank check and the power to sign it. If you are choosing agents while also doing your will or trust, you've already thought hard about the people you trust to make financial choices on your behalf. But the agent's job is different from the job of trustee and executor because it is effective at a different time: Your agent is going to act for you while you are alive, but in need of help.

Dating myself completely, I often tell my clients that the power of attorney for finances (and the advance health care directive) are "not dead yet" documents—eliciting a laugh from those old enough to have watched *Monty Python's Flying Circus*. Still, my point is that the agent's authority ends when the principal (you) dies—and that might make a difference in who you pick for the job. Sometimes this means choosing a friend or relative who lives close by instead of a trustee who lives far away but has more investment expertise. Sometimes this means choosing one child who has more time and energy now to help with day-to-day details than another child who would do a fine job on the task of settling your estate, hopefully further away in the future. And it's fine to choose the same person you've named as your health care agent—but when the health care agent has specific medical expertise they're not always the right choice for the finance agent.

Couples often choose their spouse or partner as a first choice. That's usually the best idea: Otherwise, you'll run the risk that the healthy spouse/partner could struggle with the ill spouse's agent for control over jointly held assets.

Single people sometimes struggle with whom to name. Many of my clients choose nieces or nephews, or trusted family friends for this job. Others choose professional trustees and executors, and name that same person or institution as agent (but not all professional fiduciaries will serve in this capacity, though many do).

For a second choice, people often choose the same person that they've already chosen as a second-choice trustee or executor.

You can name two people to serve jointly, but that will require them to agree on every action that they take on your behalf. That can be cumbersome at the least—or lead to a lawsuit at the worst. You can give them the authority to act separately, but that creates problems, too. Really, as with your health care directive, it's probably best to choose just one person to act for you. If you're worried about how your loved ones will feel, talk with them about it, and see whether you can all agree on what would work best.

Most agents serve without compensation, though they can be reimbursed for any expenses that they pay on your behalf. You can, however, provide (in the power of attorney document) for payment.

Whomever you choose, discuss your decision with loved ones or family members—and, of course, the person you've chosen as agent (and as alternate)—before you sign the power of attorney document. If you think your loved ones or family members will object to your choice, that's an even better reason to let them know about it in advance.

See the sample Fiduciary Worksheet, above, for recording your choices for power of attorney for finances.

Making a Power of Attorney for Finances Legal

You should sign your durable power of attorney in front of a notary public. California residents can choose to have their forms witnessed or notarized, but most financial institutions prefer notarized forms and most attorneys notarize them as well because any durable power of attorney that may affect real property has to be notarized so that it can be recorded if necessary.

Once you've signed your form, make sure that your agents have a copy of the signed document and know where to find your original in case they ever need to find it. I'd advise you to keep the originals with your other estate planning documents. That way, if you later revise and replace your durable power of attorney, you don't have to worry about originals floating around in the world that should no longer be valid.

Where to Get a Durable Power of Attorney

You can find durable power of attorney forms for finances in many of the same places that have the forms for advance health care directives: senior centers, state government offices that work with the elderly, and financial institutions. For some reason, though, they aren't as easy to find on the Internet as health care directives are. One good source for forms is Nolo's *Quicken WillMaker Plus*; using its simple question-and-answer format, you can easily create powers of attorney for California (as well as create a will and a health care directive). Another good source is *Living Wills & Powers of Attorney for California*, by Shae Irving (Nolo), which includes forms that you can download and fill out.

Changing Your Mind About Your Durable Power of Attorney

You can always revoke your power of attorney. You can sign a document that's called a "notice of revocation," or you can destroy all the copies and the original of the existing documents. It's always safer to do both, really. That way, your intent will be clear to everyone, and you won't worry that somewhere someone has the old version.

If you recorded the original durable power of attorney document with your county, make sure to file the revocation as well. If you used *Quicken WillMaker Plus* to make your power of attorney, you can use it to easily create a revocation form. If you used a form that you got somewhere else, you might have a hard time finding a revocation form. You can just write down your intent to revoke the power of attorney and sign it in front of a notary public. (The law actually says that you must revoke it as specified in the document itself, but just to be safe, notarize this.)

TIP

Don't leave your ex-spouse or -partner in charge. If you get divorced or dissolve a domestic partnership, make sure to update your power of attorney. In California, your ex-spouse's (or registered domestic partner's) authority is automatically revoked by divorce, but why take a chance that your bank doesn't know you've gotten divorced? And why wait till that divorce is final? You can revoke your existing durable power of attorney before you are legally divorced, and make a new one, naming someone you trust as your agent anytime. By the time the divorce/dissolution begins, most of my clients really don't want their soon-to-be exes making decisions for them. Don't rely on state law. Just update your documents.

Managing Your Plan and Keeping it Current

What's in Your Plan 309

Storing Your Estate Plan 310

Digital Estate Planning Issues 310

Whom to Give Copies of Your Estate Planning Documents To 312

Keeping Your Plan Current 313

   Change in Marital Status 313

   Changes Involving Children 314

   Changes Regarding Pets 315

   Changes Regarding Guardians, Trustees, or Executors 315

   Your Financial Situation Changes 316

   You Move Out of California 316

How to Make Changes to Your Estate Plan 317

   Updating Your Will 317

   Updating Your Living Trust 318

   Updating Powers of Attorney and Health Care Directives 320

   Updating Beneficiary Designations and Insurance 320

Read this chapter if:

- You want to know where and how to store your estate planning documents.

- You'd like to know when you'll need to update your plan.

- You want to know how to make changes to your estate plan.

Even the best designed estate plan needs revisions over time. Tax laws change from time to time; as I write this chapter, Congress is planning to discuss a major tax overhaul. In 1983, Congress completely restructured the estate tax as it related to married couples. In 2001, the amount you could give away at death free of tax was raised from $1 million to $3.5 million over ten years. In 2012, the amount you could give away free of tax went to $5 million, indexed to inflation. So, things do change now and then.

But, most often, my clients come back to revise their estate plans when their lives change: They've become wealthier, or less so; their guardians have gotten divorced or moved away; their children have grown up and can now become trustees and executors; my clients have gotten divorced or remarried; their parents have died.

And all estate plans need to be reviewed periodically to make sure that they list current assets and name the right people as beneficiaries.

This chapter will give you a helpful set of instructions for what to do after you've made that first estate plan and how to keep it up to date over time.

 TIP

Keep up to date with legal changes affecting estate planning. Check out the Legal Updates section of www.nolo.com (under "Wills, Trusts & Estates"), and read my blog, Life/Death/Law for updates (find my blog at www.lifedeathlaw.com or on www.lizahanks.com).

What's in Your Plan

Here's a list of what documents are in a typical plan and why you have each one.

Handy Estate Planning Summary	
Here are the documents you may have in your estate plan and why you have them.	
Will	If your plan just uses a will, this is the document that says who inherits. If you have minor children, it will also name guardians for minor children.
Living Trust	Holds your assets so that they will pass to your loved ones without having to go through probate.
Advance Health Care Directive	Names an agent to make health care decisions for you if you are incapacitated; states your wishes for end-of-life care.
Durable Power of Attorney for Finances	Names an agent who can take care of your property if you're incapacitated.
Beneficiary Designation Forms: Retirement and Life Insurance Policies (You'll have copies; originals go to the institutions that manage these assets.)	Name your primary and alternate beneficiaries
Property Deeds	If you've transferred your assets to a trust, you should have the deeds that you recorded to transfer your real property.
HIPAA Authorizations	You might have signed authorizations to allow physicians to share confidential health care information with your family or friends.
Personal Inventory	Some people keep an updated list of all of their assets. This is very useful for your trustee and executors.

Handy Estate Planning Summary (continued)	
Plans for funeral, cremation, or other final arrangements	You might have a prepaid contract with a funeral home or cemetery. If so, keep that with your important papers.
Letters to guardians, executors, or trustees	You might have written a letter, to be opened only upon your death, explaining your choices.
Records of outstanding loans or gifts	If your will or trust forgives loans or gifts, or asks the trustee or executor to take them into account, you should leave written records of these transactions with your plan.

Storing Your Estate Plan

You'll need a safe place to store your estate planning documents. You might not want to store your will or trust in a bank's safe deposit box, because it would be difficult for your family to get into the box after your death if they aren't on your signature card at the bank. Instead, you might want to put your original signed documents (and copies of your beneficiary forms) in a fireproof box. You can buy these at office supply stores and big-box retailers. Then tell your family where it is—and how to open it.

Digital Estate Planning Issues

We all store important things online these days. I give my clients a thumb drive with scans of all of their executed documents, and some of them store this in a safe deposit box, or give copies to their loved ones. Other clients store their scanned documents in the cloud, using Box, Dropbox, or some other form of cloud storage. That works, too, but then you have to make sure that your loved ones have access to that storage account after your death. For that, you'll need to make sure that they have your passwords, and, if possible, give them permission to access such accounts.

But getting access to digital assets after someone dies, including an estate plan, has been difficult up to now. Federal law prohibits service providers, like Google, Yahoo, and Facebook, from giving anyone access to the content of your electronic communications without either your consent or a valid court order. So after you die, companies can't reveal your emails or documents, even at the request of your executor or trustee, without either a court order or your prior permission. This federal law has created big headaches in the estate planning world.

There are lots of reasons why your executor or trustee might need to have access to your electronic records: You might be running your business online; you might have financial records that they'll need to settle your estate; your estate plan might be stored online. Your executor and trustee have access to all of your other assets after you die, why treat digital assets differently? For these and many other reasons, many states have been working on laws to make this all work better.

California recently passed a new law that gives your trustee and executor the right to receive your digital assets as long as they can prove that you've given them permission. Some service providers, like Google and Facebook, offer online tools that let you say who should have access to your digital information after you die. Google provides an Inactive Account Manager that lets users specify what they want to have happen after they haven't used their account for a period of time that you select. Facebook users can appoint a "legacy contact," who can download your photos and other posts, but cannot access your messages and other account information. If you haven't used such tools, or if there is no online tool to use, then the new state law looks to your will, trust, or power of attorney to see if you have given anyone access to your accounts. Virtually all up-to-date wills, trusts, and powers of attorney now give the appointed executor, trustee, or agent the right to access your digital records for this reason.

The law is evolving rapidly in the area of digital estate planning. For now, making sure that your loved ones have passwords to your accounts, that you use online tools to give them access to your accounts if they exist, and that your estate planning documents provide your executor, trustee, and agent access to your digital assets is a good start.

RESOURCE

To learn more about digital estate planning, you can download a free ebook, *Estate Planning for Digital Assets*, at my website: www.lizahanks. com/estate-planning-for-digital-assets.html.

Whom to Give Copies of Your Estate Planning Documents To

While it's not required, it's a good idea to give copies of your will and trust to the executor of your will and trustee of your trust if you feel comfortable sharing these documents. Not all people do. You should at least make sure that your family and loved ones know where to find them. It will certainly make it easier to settle your estate to leave an updated personal inventory (such as the one discussed in Chapter 1) with your documents, but that's a personal preference as well.

I also recommend giving copies of your health care directives and your durable power of attorney for finances to the agents you've chosen for health care and property. If you're in a car accident or another emergency, they'll need those documents right away. Also give a copy of your health care directives to your doctor, so that it will be in your medical records file. If you have completed a POLST form with your doctor, make sure that it's somewhere in your home where emergency medical folks will see it—the refrigerator door is often the place for that.

California law requires third parties, like banks and insurance companies, to accept an excerpt of a living trust, called a "certification of trust," while you are alive, instead of the whole trust. The certification just states your name(s), the name of the trust, and the provisions that name trustees and their powers. It says nothing about your children or your assets, so that information can remain confidential during your lifetimes. For more information, read California Probate Code Section 18100.5, which spells out exactly what a certification of trust must include and the penalty for not accepting it (damages plus attorneys' fees).

Keeping Your Plan Current

You'll need to review and revise your plan occasionally—probably every three to five years, or when something major happens in your life or the lives of your guardians, executors, or trustees. Even though you've worked hard to make good decisions, the odds that you'll never have to review or revise your estate plan during your lifetime are practically zero.

EXAMPLE: Samuel and Lina made an estate plan five years ago. Since then they've had a baby, bought a house, and started a business. It's time for them to revise their existing plan.

Here are a few of the most common reasons that people revise their estate plans.

Change in Marital Status

Getting married, or getting divorced, are moments when your life is changed by the law. It's a good idea to review your estate plan, or make one, when your marital status changes.

You Get Married for the First Time

Getting married is the time to consider whether or not it makes sense to create a prenuptial agreement that specifies what property is separate and what property is community. If you are uncomfortable talking about money, you might get curious as to why. You might be thankful that you have those discussions at the beginning of a marriage, as difficult as they can be.

You Get Divorced or Remarry

In either case, you'll have to review your will, trust, beneficiary designations, and life insurance needs. When you begin the divorce process, you will most likely want to create new powers of attorney and health care directives. You might want to create a new will. You can create a new living trust, but you can't fund that trust until the divorce is final. You can't change your beneficiary designations without your spouse's consent during the divorce process. After it ends, change them right away.

Your Spouse Dies

Obviously, the death of a spouse is a huge change. If you already have an estate plan, you'll need legal advice on what you'll need to do next and you will most likely want to update your documents. If you don't have an estate plan yet, now's the time to make one.

Changes Involving Children

Children are likely to be the change agents for your plan. They get born. They grow up. Sometimes (sadly) they die or have mental issues that require new planning.

You Have (or Adopt) a Child

Your existing documents may include children born after you created your documents. But you probably will want to add your new child to your plan explicitly. This can require an amendment to a trust, a codicil to a will, or brand new documents. It depends on what other changes you want to make.

You Have More Children

Asking someone to be the guardian of one child can be different from asking them to raise two or three children.

Your Children Get Older

As they do, your choices for guardians are likely to change. Perhaps your children want to stay closer to home; perhaps they've grown close to a relative you didn't name as guardian when they were little; perhaps your guardians are getting too old to handle teenagers.

A Child Dies

If your child dies, you may want to change the way your plan manages assets for your remaining children, or include grandchildren in a different way.

You Have Grandchildren

You may want to make gifts to grandchildren once you have them. You may want to make sure that they don't inherit anything if you don't approve of their life choices.

Changes Regarding Pets

If you've left money for the care of a pet, and that pet dies, you will want to update your documents. (I try to draft documents that aren't so specific, to make it easier for my clients to have multiple pets over the years. I once, though, wrote a plan naming a specific parrot, because the parrot was likely to outlive my client.)

Changes Regarding Guardians, Trustees, or Executors

Life happens. I tell my clients to expect to revisit their plans over time. Changing any of these people requires an amendment or restatement of trust and a new will or a codicil to a will.

Guardians, Trustees, or Executors Move Far Away

When the people you've chosen to take care of things move away, you might need to choose people closer to home.

You Have a Falling Out with Your Guardians, Trustees, or Executors

Friendships end; siblings quarrel. Sometimes that means you have to make new choices.

Your Guardians Get Divorced or Remarry

If your guardians change their family situation, you might want to rethink your choices.

Your Financial Situation Changes

You inherit money. Your company goes public. You get fired. You go bankrupt. You buy a house. You buy a business. You sell your grandmother's silver set that you had promised your niece. You get new benefits at work. Good or bad, a big financial change usually means that you should review your estate plan to see whether your choices still make sense.

You Move Out of California

Laws vary greatly from state to state. You want to make sure that you have a will or trust, as well as a durable power of attorney and a health care directive that are valid where you live.

Here are two state-specific issues to watch out for if you move out of California:

- **Custodial gifts to minors.** A couple of states haven't adopted the Uniform Transfers to Minors Acts (discussed in Chapter 5), so you might need to revise how you've left minors money in the care of a custodian. And different states require custodianships to end at different ages.

- **Marital property.** If you move from California (a community property state) to a common law state and don't intend to leave half of everything to your spouse, you will need to get an attorney's help to make sure your plan is drafted properly under your new state's rules.

How to Make Changes to Your Estate Plan

When you need to make changes to your will, trust, or other estate planning documents you can't just cross out a name, write in a new one, and initial the margin. Judges hate that. They won't know who made the mark, when it was made, or whether you really intended to make that change. Instead, you need to formally make changes and revoke your old documents. After you've created new documents, make sure to give them to the people you gave copies of the old one to, and get them to destroy the old documents as well.

Updating Your Will

If you decide to make changes to your will, you can probably do so easily. If you've done your own will, just make a new one. If a lawyer drafted your will, ask them to make you a new one. The second sentence of a will usually says that you revoke any previous wills. That means that your most current will is the only valid one. Make sure to destroy your old wills, so there's no confusion about which one is the newest version.

Another way to update your will is to add what's called a "codicil" to it. A codicil states the changes you want to make to the original will. Because you must sign and witness a codicil, it's almost always a better idea just to make a new will. It's not much more work, and that way your changes are integrated into one document, which makes it easier to read and harder to lose.

EXAMPLE: Hunter and Bella wrote a will after their first child was born, naming Bella's sister Scarlett as the guardian. When Hunter and Bella have twins five years later, they decide that they need to pick a new guardian. Scarlett, by then, is a single mom with two children of her own, living in a small apartment in Berkeley.

Hunter and Bella write a new will, naming Hunter's younger brother, Jeremy, as the guardian for their three children. Jeremy has one child of his own and a 20-acre ranch in the wine country, so they feel that Jeremy would be better able to take on three more children. Hunter and Bella also increase the value of their term life insurance policy so that there would be more money available to raise all three kids.

Updating Your Living Trust

If you've got a living trust, you can sometimes amend just the sections of it that you want to change. To change a paragraph that makes gifts to your grandchildren, or change your successor trustees, an amendment is often just fine.

But if you want to make a lot of small changes, or a few big ones, it works better to do what's called a restatement. You might restructure your trust for tax reasons because you've become more wealthy, or less so. You might decide that your children's inheritance should be kept in trust longer, add new beneficiaries, or set up a trust for a parent. For those kinds of changes, restatements work better. When you restate a trust, you keep the old name and the original date that you signed it, but you get a whole new trust that reflects your current wishes and is updated to current law. Assets already held by the trust stay there. Even better, no one ever sees what the old trust says. If you amend the trust, your beneficiaries will see both the trust and the amendment, so they'll see what you changed. If you've changed something sensitive, like who inherits or who you've named as trustee, you might not want people to know what your trust used to say. Also, it is hard to read a trust if there are lots of small amendments—you have to keep track of what's changed. It's often easier to restate a trust so that your trustee and beneficiaries have the whole story in one place. (It's more trouble to revoke a trust than it is to revoke a will, because if you make a new trust you have to transfer property out of the old one and into the new.)

If You Did Your Trust Yourself

If you did a trust yourself, the software or book that you used should also include an amendment form that you can print out and sign in front of a notary. You'd then keep the amendment with the original trust document and make sure that anyone who has a copy of the trust also gets a copy of the amendment.

If a Lawyer Did Your Trust

If you worked with an estate planner, ask that lawyer to make the amendment. Most estate planners charge on an hourly basis for amendments. If all you're doing is a simple change of a trustee or something similar, an amendment shouldn't take more than a few hours of the lawyer's time. (Revising the trust will require a new pour-over will, or a codicil to the existing one, because the will and trust share an important cross reference, so when you update the trust, you also should update the will.)

 TIP

Sometimes a simple amendment can cost more than you think. If you ask an attorney to amend a trust that he or she didn't draft in the first place, you might find it's an expensive proposition. A new lawyer must thoroughly review an existing document before making even a simple change. That's because a lawyer who amends a document is on the hook for any mistakes in the original. So, you'll be paying for at least a couple of hours of a new lawyer's time. It's always less expensive to go back to the lawyer who wrote the trust the first time.

Updating Powers of Attorney and Health Care Directives

Keeping your powers of attorney and health care directives up to date usually means making sure you're still comfortable with the agents you've chosen and that your documents are valid for the state where you now live (in case you've moved out of California).

If you need to make new documents, just make sure to revoke the existing ones and shred or tear them up. A revocation can be a simple document stating that you are revoking your existing durable power of attorney or health directive, dated [, *20xx*], and executing a new one. (See Chapter 11 for more on the subject.)

Updating Beneficiary Designations and Insurance

To update your retirement, life insurance, or payable-on-death beneficiary designations, you'll need to request and fill out a change of beneficiary designation. (You can get the forms from the company that holds the asset or issued the policy.) Make sure to keep a copy of these forms with your will, trust, and powers of attorney documents so that your family will know that you've updated them. ●

Finding a Lawyer and Help Beyond the Book

Start With Referrals 322

Do Some Research 323

Make Contact 324

Ask Questions...324

Trust Yourself...325

Read this chapter if:

- You want to work with an attorney, but aren't sure how to find one.
- You want to interview potential attorneys, but don't know what questions to ask.
- You want to do legal research and would like to learn how to do that.

Many Californians can prepare the basic estate planning documents themselves (a simple will or trust, advance health care directive, and durable power of attorney for finances), and throughout this book I show you how. But I also point out specific situations when your particular estate planning needs require professional help—for example, when you have international assets or are not a U.S. citizen, are in a blended family, need to plan for a child with special needs, own complicated assets such as a family-owned business, or want to establish a pet trust.

So, how do you go about finding the right lawyer? The process isn't really any different from what you go through to find any qualified professional—be it a doctor, a contractor, or an insurance broker. Here's what I recommend.

Start With Referrals

Ask your friends, your neighbors, colleagues, and anyone you like and respect if they've done an estate plan yet. If they have, ask them if they would recommend the person that they worked with. You might start hearing the same name from several sources; that's a good sign.

Do Some Research

Once you get a few names, see if those lawyers have websites (most do). Take a look at the websites to find out the following things:

- **What kind of information does the attorney provide about estate planning?** Is there helpful, easy-to-understand information there on estate planning? How does it make you feel? (If the information on the lawyer's site makes you feel afraid, or stupid, keep looking.)

- **What kind of information does the attorney provide about his or her services?** Can you figure out how that lawyer charges for services? By the hour? Or with a flat fee? Either one can be perfectly transparent and fair, but sometimes attorneys hide the ball here and require you to come in for an "introductory meeting" to find out the basics. I don't like that approach—it forces you to go into attorney offices just to get basic consumer information.

- **How much can you find out about the attorney's credentials and background?** Can you tell how many years of experience an attorney has, where they went to law school, whether they have any additional credentials, offer any unique areas of expertise, and specialize in estate planning? There are great estate planners who didn't go to fancy law schools, and mediocre estate planners who did. There are great estate planners who aren't certified specialists in estate planning, trust administration, and probate. That credential is meaningful: You have to pass a difficult exam to get it, but a lot of the older estate planners didn't take that exam; it's mostly for younger attorneys. Still, anyone that you want to work with should at least be open and clear about where they went to school, how long they've been in business, and whether they focus exclusively on estate planning. You want to work with someone who practices estate planning the majority of the time, not someone who dabbles in it.

RESOURCE

Nolo's Lawyer Directory is an easy-to-use online directory of lawyers, organized by location and area of expertise (including estate planning). You can find the directory and its comprehensive profiles of attorneys at www. nolo.com/lawyers. Two other useful online resources are Lawyers.com and Martindale.com. You can search on these sites by practice area and location and find detailed information on individual lawyers.

Make Contact

If you want to find out more about an attorney after checking out their website, call or email them. Trust your gut instincts here: If you don't like the way a person answers the phone (or doesn't even answer the phone), or if they don't return your messages, you probably won't like working with this particular attorney.

Ask Questions

There are two reasons to ask questions. First, pay attention to how your questions are answered. Do you feel listened to? Do you feel that your questions are being answered respectfully and honestly? The number one reason clients tell me why they aren't working with the attorney who originally drafted their documents is that they felt condescended to, disrespected, or stupid when they asked questions. There's no excuse for this: You should understand your estate plan. Period. If you don't, your lawyer isn't doing a good job. The second reason to ask questions, of course, is to get answers.

Here are some good questions to ask:

- **How much will it cost to create an estate plan?** Costs vary in California, but generally, an estate plan that uses a living trust costs about ten hours of a lawyer's time; a will about half of that. So, if lawyers charge $300/hour where you live, expect a living trust plan to cost about $3,000; a will-based plan to cost about $1,500. If a lawyer tells you that they can't predict what your plan might cost, be skeptical. Most plans fall within that 10 to 12 hour scope, and most lawyers know that. Beware of people who charge by the hour and aren't willing to provide you with an estimate of total time unless you have a large estate or a very complicated set of issues to deal with.

- **What does an estate plan include?** A plan should include a will, a durable power of attorney, and an advance health care directive. If you want to do a living trust, that, too. If you are doing a trust, does the cost include the transfer of your house to the trust? (It should.) Be wary of lawyers who charge for each document separately—that could be a bait-and-switch practice that ends up costing you too much.
- **What's the process for creating a plan?** You want to find out how many meetings to expect, what you would need to bring to the meetings, and how long the process usually takes. There's no right answer here, but you do want to get a sense for how it would be to work with that attorney.

Trust Yourself

There are lots of qualified estate planners out there. But the right one for you is someone that you feel comfortable with and trust. Many estate planners, but not all, offer a free half-hour "meet and greet" session so that you can see what it might be like to work together. If you have that opportunity, take it. But, please, don't go the meeting expecting answers to your legal questions—the introductory meeting is meant only to provide you with a chance to meet the attorney, not ask them questions for free.

Want to Do Your Own Legal Research?

California state law covers many aspects of estate planning, and I highlight these throughout this book—for example, when an estate can be administered outside of a probate proceeding, how long a custodial account can last, what kind of information trust beneficiaries are entitled to receive and when they are permitted to request it, the requirements for a legal will, the details of trust accounting, and the process of appointing a guardian for a minor child. If you want to read the actual law itself, it's easy to find. California has placed its statutes online at the California Legislative Information website, http://leginfo. legislature.ca.gov. You can search there for the law on a particular subject that interests you. Start by clicking the "California Law" tab on the top of the home page, and then go to "Probate Code," which is broken down by particular topics such as "Wills and Intestate Succession" or "Trust Law." The California Legislative Information website also has links to other useful resources, such as the California State Library.

If you want to learn about researching and understanding statutes and doing legal research, see Nolo's Laws and Legal Research page at www.nolo.com/legal-research.

How to Use the Downloadable Forms on the Nolo Website

Editing RTFs 328

List of Forms Available on the Nolo Website 329

This book comes with downloadable files that you can access online at:

www.nolo.com/back-of-book/ESCA.html

You can open, edit, save, and print the RTF files provided by this book using most word processing programs such as Microsoft *Word*, Windows *WordPad*, and recent versions of *WordPerfect*.

Editing RTFs

Here are some general instructions about editing RTF forms in your word processing program. Refer to the book's instructions and sample agreements for help about what should go in each blank:

- **Underlines.** Underlines indicate where to enter information. After filling in the needed text, delete the underline. In most word processing programs you can do this by highlighting the underlined portion and typing CTRL-U.

- **Bracketed and italicized text.** Bracketed and italicized text indicates instructions. Be sure to remove all instructional text before you finalize Every word processing program uses different commands to open, format, save, and print documents, so refer to your software's help documents for help using your program. Nolo cannot provide technical support for questions about how to use your computer or your software.

> **CAUTION**
>
> **In accordance with U.S. copyright laws, the forms provided by this book are for your personal use only.**

List of Forms Available on the Nolo Website

To download any of the files listed on the following pages go to:

www.nolo.com/back-of-book/ESCA.html

Form Title	File Name
Personal Inventory (Ch. 1)	Inventory.rtf
Net Worth Calculator Worksheet (Ch. 1)	NetWorth.rtf
Will Worksheet (Ch. 2)	Will.rtf
Trust Worksheet (Ch. 3)	Trust.rtf
Planning for Minor Children Worksheet (Ch. 4)	Planning.rtf
Interviewing Professional Trustees Worksheet (Ch. 5)	Interview.rtf
Managing Money for Minor Children Worksheet (Ch. 5)	Money.rtf
Current Beneficiaries List (Ch. 10)	Beneficiaries.rtf
Fiduciary Worksheet (Ch. 11)	Fiduciary.rtf

Index

A

A/B trusts
  blended families' estate planning and, 195–198
  income taxes and, 231–234
Accountings
  by property guardians, 150
  by trustees, 76, 135
Adoption, by stepparent, 103
Advance health care directives, 11, 280, 281–298
  constitutional right to control medical treatment, 281, 283–284
  defined, 13
  effective upon signing, making directive, 291
  execution requirements, 297
  factors to consider before filling out, 284
  failure to prepare, effect of, 286
  functions of, 282
  health care agents, duties and selection of, 291–295
  life-sustaining treatment, statement of wishes regarding, 281, 283–284, 285
  palliative care, availability of, 286, 287
  revocation of, 298, 320
  signature requirements, 297
  updating, 320
  when end-of-life instructions become effective, 282
  witnesses, 297
Affidavit procedure for small estates, 14, 21
Age
  custodianships and, 126, 129
  will, parties who may make, 44

Alternate beneficiaries, 257
Alternate executors, 54
Annual gift tax exclusion, 168, 237
Annuities, 18
Attorney-in-fact, for health care matters. *See* Health care agents
Attorneys, 322–326
  contacting, 324
  cost of estate plan, 324–325
  credentials and background of, researching, 323
  documents included in estate plan, 325
  introductory meeting with, 325
  for living trust preparation, 81–83
  procedures for creating estate plan, 325
  questions to ask, 324–325
  referrals, 322
  researching, 323–324
  website of attorney, information available on, 323
  for will preparation, 61–62
Automatic exclusions from property tax reassessment, 216–220

B

Backup wills, 89
Beneficiaries
  Current Beneficiaries List, 33, 47, 255, 256, 257
  of living trusts, 69–70, 72, 76–77
  See also Beneficiaries for life insurance policies; Beneficiaries for retirement plans
Beneficiaries for life insurance policies, 274–278

divorce, changing beneficiary after, 275–276
primary beneficiaries, 276–277
secondary beneficiaries, 277–278
selecting proper, 275
Beneficiaries for retirement plans, 255–270
charities as, 257–258, 259, 268, 270
charity along with another person, reasons to avoid naming, 268
children, naming, 266
current beneficiaries, determining, 255–258
designated beneficiaries, 263, 268
donor-advised fund as, 270
failure to name beneficiary, effect of, 264
forms for naming beneficiaries, filling out, 272–273
401(k)s, 260–261
IRAs, 260–261
multiple beneficiaries, naming, 267–268
per stirpes/Right of Representation stipulation for contingent beneficiaries, 273
Roth IRAs and 401(k)s, 261
spouse, naming, 264–265
stretch-out planning, 263
trust as, 268–269
Beneficiary designations, 21
Blended families, 180–200
bypass/survivor's trust estate plan, 195–198
children of different ages, planning for, 199–200
community versus separate property, 181, 182–190
control of assets after death, planning for, 181
gifts to children of prior marriage and, 185
guardians for minor children, selecting, 109–110

home ownership issues, 185
married couples, estate planning for, 181, 195–198
personal items, treatment of, 185–186
planning strategies for, 192–199
retirement plan/life insurance policy beneficiaries, naming, 186
statistics on number of, 3, 182
successor trustees, naming, 193–195
tax issues, 190–192, 199
unmarried couples, estate planning for, 181–182, 198–199
Bond (posting of)
for executors, 51, 172
for guardians, 108
Bypass/survivor's trust estate plan
for blended families, 195–198
income taxes and, 231–234

C

Calculators for determining amount of life insurance needed, 159–160
California Academy of Family Physicians, 290
California End of Life Option Act, 289–290
California Medical Association (CMA), 290
California Uniform Prudent Investor Act, 134
California Uniform Transfers to Minors Act (CUTMA), 126, 150, 266, 316
Capacity. *See* Mental competence
Capital gains taxes, 226, 227–234
community property and, 48–49, 190–192, 230–231
cost basis, 227
gifts of appreciated assets and, 228–229
homeowners exclusion, 227–228

step up in basis at death and, 48–49, 190–192, 228–231

tax rates, 227

Caregivers, gifts to, 239

Certificate of independent review, 239

Certification of trust, 313

Changing estate plan. *See* Revising estate plan

Charitable donations

    beneficiary, naming charity as, 257–258, 259, 268, 270

    donor-advised funds for, 270

    gifts of appreciated assets, tax implications of, 228–229

    retirement accounts, as beneficiaries of, 235

    by single persons, 247–248

Child-parent exclusion from property tax reassessment, 209–211

Children

    amount of money you have to leave to, determining, 121–122

    as beneficiaries for retirement accounts, 266

    direct monetary gifts to minors, planning for, 122–123

    disinheriting, 62

    estate plan revision for changes involving, 314–315

    Inherited IRAs and, 123

    leaving money to, 120–161

    omitted children, 62

    property guardian for, 55, 94, 107, 149–151, 152

    property tax reassessment exclusions and, 209–213

    qualification as child for purposes of property tax reassessment exclusion, 212–213

    special needs children, providing for, 125, 155, 161

    See also Guardians for minor children; Property management for children's property

Children's trusts, 131–149

    amount of control to exercise over trust, determining, 148

    control and flexibility offered by, 129, 131

    custodial accounts versus, deciding between, 124

    decisions you need to make in creating, 133

    defined, 124

    duration of trust, determining, 145–146

    interim distributions, 146–147

    limits on powers that may be exercised in, 149

    pooling trust funds, 143–44

    separate trusts for each child, using, 144–145

    setting up trust, 132–133

    trustees, role and selection of, 133–143

Cloud storage of estate plan, 310

Codicils, 317

Coexecutors, 52

Common law property states, 182

Community property, 36

    blended families, estate planning issues for, 181, 182–190

    California as community property state, 182

    characterization of property as, 183–184

    defined, 183

    discussing characterization of property with spouse, 185

    intestacy and, 63

    property agreement provisions and, 186–189

    revising estate plan when moving to common law state, 317

    source of funds and characterization as, 183

    tax advantages of, 48–49, 189–190, 230–231

unmarried couples, estate planning
for, 189–190
wages of one spouse used to pay
for real property of other spouse
and characterization as, 184
See also Community property with
right of survivorship
Community property with right of
survivorship, 36–37, 47–49
probate avoidance and, 19, 21
step-up in basis of, 48–49,
190–192, 230–231
tax advantages of, 48–49,
190–192, 230–231
wills do not override, 49
Compassion & Choices, 290
Compensation
of custodians, 130
of durable power of attorney for
finances, 304
of property guardian for children's
property, 150
of trustees, 135, 136, 140
Consent to release medical
information form, 302
Conservatorships, court appointed,
286
Consolidating IRAs, 272
Constitution of United States
medical treatment, right to
control, 281, 283–284
Contingent beneficiaries, 257
Convertible term life insurance, 157
Copies of estate planning documents,
persons who should receive, 312
Costs. *See* Fees and costs
Cotenant exclusion from property tax
reassessment, 213–214
Cotrustees, 138–139
County assessor, 203
Current Beneficiaries List, 33, 47,
255, 256, 257
Custodial accounts, 125–131

age at which custodianship ends,
126, 129
children's trust versus, deciding
between, 124
circumstances when custodial
accounts should be used, 126
cost of, 130
custodians, role and selection of,
127–128, 130
defined, 124
pros and cons of using, 127
separate custodianship for each
child, requirement for, 126
setting up account, 126
Custodians
compensation of, 130
recordkeeping requirements, 127
role of, 127–28
selection of, factors to consider in,
128
CUTMA. *See* California Uniform
Transfers to Minors Act (CUTMA)

D

Death taxes. *See* Estate taxes
Designated beneficiaries, 263, 268
Digital estate planning issues,
310–312
Disinheriting children, 62
Divorce
children's trustee or custodian
selection and, 152
durable power of attorney,
updating of, 306
estate plan, revising, 314
guardians for minor children,
stating why ex-spouse should not
be, 110
life insurance policy beneficiaries,
changing, 275–276
property guardian, requesting
ex-spouse not be named as, 152

retirement plan beneficiaries, changing, 258

DNR. *See* Do-not-resuscitate (DNR) order

Donor-advised fund, as beneficiary, 270

Do-not-resuscitate (DNR) order, 288–289

Durable power of attorney for finances, 11, 75, 280–281, 298–306

alternate agents, naming, 304

authority granted to, scope of, 300–301

coagents, reasons to avoid appointing, 304

compensation of, 304

consent to release medical information form used in combination with, 302

copies of durable power of attorney, giving agent, 312

defined, 12

discussing your choice for, 304

divorce, updating upon, 306

effective date, 301–302

execution requirements, 304–305

failure to prepare, effect of, 286

Fiduciary Worksheet, recording choice on, 304

financial institution forms for, 302

forms for, sources of, 305

incapacity, proving, 301–302

joint tenancy and, 299

liability of, 301

living trusts and, 299

notarization of, 304, 305

reasons for making, 298–300

recording of, 304, 305

revocation of, 305–306, 320

selection of, 303–304

signature requirements, 304

springing power of attorney, 301

storage of, 304–305

updating, 320

what durable power of attorney can't do, 301

witnesses, 304

E

Ed/Med exemption from gift taxes, 240

Educational expenses

Ed/Med exemption from gift taxes, 240

529 college savings plans, 241

gift tax exemptions and, 241

Educational matters, leaving guardian guidance on, 116

Electronic records, access to, 310–312

End of Life Option Act, 289–290

Estate planning, 1–8

advance health care directives, 11, 13, 280, 281–298, 320

for blended families, 180–200

California-specific issues in, 3–4

digital estate planning issues, 310–312

durable power of attorney for finances, 11, 12, 298–306, 320

getting started, 11–12

importance of, 2

international estate planning issues, 165–177

inventory, preparing, 27–34

issues and decisions required in, overview of, 5–7

keeping plan current, 313–317

life insurance policies, 13

persons who should receive copies of estate planning documents, 312–313

questions to ask in beginning process of, 2–3

real estate issues, 34–40

retirement plans, 13

revising estate plan, 308, 313–320

shopping around for estate planners, 84

storage of estate plan, 310

summary of documents in, 309–310

tax considerations, 202–248

See also Living trusts; Wills

Estate taxes, 20, 243–248, 308

assets subject to, 244–245

blended families and, 190–192, 199
countries with tax treaties with United States and, 170
deadline for filing return, 246–247
federal estate tax exemption, 167, 225–226, 237, 243
irrevocable life insurance trust (ILIT) and, 278
life insurance and, 155
marital deduction, 168, 175–176, 244
noncitizen spouse and, 175–177
nonresident aliens and, 167–169
portability of, 245–247
resident aliens and, 167–171
single persons, philanthropy strategy for, 247–248
taxable estate, 225
tax rates, 226, 243
unified gift and estate tax system, 238–239
Ethical values, leaving guardian guidance on, 116
Execution requirements
for advance health care directives, 297
for durable power of attorney for finances, 304–305
for transfer-on-death deeds for real estate, 38
for wills, 44
Executors, 42, 49–55
alternate executors, selecting, 54
California executors, 51
close friends as, 52
coexecutors, 52
communication skills and temperament of, 50
copies of estate planning documents, giving, 312
court appointment of, 51
duties of, 49–50
family members as, 52

international executors, 171–172
letter explaining will choices for, 62–63
Letters Testamentary, grant of, 51
location of will, providing executor with, 62
out-of-state executors, 51, 54
pour-over will, nomination in, 89
professional executors, selecting, 53
qualities to look for in selecting, 50–51
revising estate plan to reflect changes involving, 315–316
spouse as, 51–52
talking to your choice for, 55
Expert help, trustee's hiring of, 76, 134
Ex-spouse or partner
guardians for minor children, stating why ex-spouse should not be, 110
property guardian, requesting ex-spouse not be named as, 152

F

Facebook, 311
FBAR. *See* Report of Foreign Bank and Financial Accounts (FBAR)
Fees and costs
attorneys' fees, 324–325
custodial accounts and, 130
of living trusts, 83
of probate, 15–16, 20
professional executors' fees, 53
of trust administration, 71
Fiduciary, trustee as, 67
Fiduciary Worksheet, 10, 295, 304
Financial institutions
certification of trust, acceptance of, 313
durable power of attorney for finances forms, 302

trust, transfers of financial accounts to, 85–86
529 college savings plans, 241
Foreign assets, reporting requirements for, 169–170
Foreign trusts, 172–174
401(k) plans
  beneficiaries, selection of, 260–261
  contributions, deductibility of, 253
  distribution rules, 253, 260–261
  income taxes on inherited 401(k) plans, 234–235
  probate avoidance and, 18
  rolling over to IRA, 271–272
  spouse's rights in, 265
  See also Roth 401(k) and 403(b) plans
403(b) plans, 254
  spouse's rights in, 253
  See also Roth 401(k) and 403(b) plans
Funding, of living trusts, 84–86

G

Gift taxes, 236–243
  annual exclusion, 168, 237
  Ed/Med exemption, 240
  foreign gifts, reporting requirements for, 171
  noncitizen spouse and, 176
  nonresident aliens and, 167–169
  reporting requirements for gift in excess of annual threshold, 237, 238
  resident aliens and, 167–171
  tax rates, 237
  unified gift and estate tax system, 238–239
Godparents, as guardians for minor children, 97
Google, 311
Grandchildren
  estate plan revision to account for, 315
  grandparent-grandchild exclusion from property tax reassessment, 211–213
  leaving IRAs to, 123

Grandparents
  estate plan revision to account for grandchildren, 315
  grandparent-grandchild exclusion from property tax reassessment, 211–213
  leaving IRAs to grandchildren, 123
  as trustees of children's trusts, 139
Grantors. *See* Settlors
Green card holder. *See* Resident aliens
Guardians for minor children, 42, 55, 92–117
  annual status reports by, 96
  anxiety over nominating, overcoming, 93–94
  best interests of child standard for court determinations, 96
  both parent's wills should name same guardian, 98–99
  children from previous marriage, selecting guardians for, 109–110
  court approval and oversight of, 96–97
  day-to-day experiences of child, influence over, 95
  different guardians for different children, 109–110
  discussing guardian choice with your children, 113
  distant guardian, selecting, 108–109
  educational matters, leaving guidance on, 116
  ethical values, leaving guidance on, 116
  ex-spouse or partner should not get custody, naming guardian and explaining why, 110
  extended family relationships, leaving guidance on, 116
  family dissent to guardian choice, addressing, 111–112
  godparents as, 97
  guardians of person, 94–95
  guidance for guardians, leaving, 115–116
  ideal guardian, determining and ranking qualities and values of, 98–102

importance of nominating, 92–93, 117

international guardianships, 108, 174–175

judge's appointment of, when dying intestate or without nominating guardian in will, 66, 117

legal responsibilities of, 94–95

letter explaining will choices for, 62–63

list of potential guardians, making, 102

money management skills and, 107

multiple guardians, selecting, 97

narrowing down choices, 103–106

older person selected as, 106–107

one person in couple as guardian, naming, 107–108

out-of-state guardianships, 108

Planning for Minor Children Worksheet, 100–102, 105

pour-over will, nomination in, 89

problems and solutions in selecting, 106–113

qualities and values of ideal guardian, determining and ranking, 98–102

reevaluating choices in future years, 105

religious education and faith, leaving guidance on, 116

revising estate plan to reflect changes involving, 315–316

same-sex couples, special concerns for, 103

selection of, 97–106

talking with potential guardian prior to nominating them, 113–115

temporary guardian, naming, 108–109

written explanation of choice, leaving, 110, 111–112, 113, 115–116

See also Property guardians

Guardians of the estate. *See* Property guardians

Guardians of the persons, 94

H

Health care agents

alternate agents, naming, 291

authority granted agent, determining, 291

coagents, reasons to avoid appointing, 293

copies of advance health care directive, giving agent, 312

copy of health care directive, providing agent with, 294

discussing your wishes with, 293–294

duties of, 291–292

Fiduciary Worksheet, recording choice for health care agent on, 295

qualifications of, 292

selection of, 292–293

Health care directives. *See* Advance health care directives

Holographic wills, 44

Home, 34–39

blended family estate planning issues, 185

capital gains tax exclusion for homeowners, 227–228

deed, ordering, 35, 231

form of ownership, 35–37

living trust, transfer of home to, 86

step-up in basis at death and capital gains tax implications, 190–192, 230–231

transfer-on-death deeds, 37–39

See also Property taxes; Real estate

I

ILIT. *See* Irrevocable life insurance trust (ILIT)

Income-multiplier method, determining amount of life insurance needed, 159

Income taxes, 226–235
  A/B trusts and, 231–234
  foreign trusts, 172–174
  inherited property subject to, 234–235
  nonresident aliens, 165–166
  resident aliens, 165–166
  shift in estate planning focus to minimize, 225, 226
  See also Capital gains taxes

Individual retirement accounts (IRAs)
  beneficiaries, selecting, 260–261
  consolidating IRAs, 272
  contributions, deductibility and maximum amount of, 253
  described, 253
  distribution rules, 253, 260–261
  grandchildren, leaving IRAs to, 123
  income taxes on inherited IRAs, 234–235
  Inherited IRAs, 123
  probate avoidance and, 18
  rolling over 401(k) plans to, 271–272
  Roth IRA, advantages of converting to, 254
  spouse's rights in, 265
  See also Roth IRAs

Inherited IRAs, 123

Interim trust distributions, 146–147

International estate planning issues, 164–177
  executors and, 171–172
  foreign born residents in California, statistics on, 4, 165
  guardianships and, 108, 174–175
  noncitizen spouse and, 175–177
  nonresident aliens, taxation of, 165–169
  overview, 164–165
  resident aliens, taxation of, 165–169
  trustees and, 171–174

Interviewing Professional Trustees Worksheet, 141, 142, 143

Intestacy, 11–12, 63–64

Inventory of assets and property, 27–34
  assets owned, listing, 33
  completing, 33
  electronic access to assets, 33
  location of assets, 33
  Personal Inventory form, 27, 28–31, 255
  purpose of, 27
  safe deposit box, location of and key to, 34
  updating of, 32
  valuation of assets, 33

IRAs. *See* Individual retirement accounts (IRAs)

Irrevocable life insurance trust (ILIT), 278

IRS Form 3520 (Annual Return to Report Transactions With Foreign Trusts and Receipt of Certain Foreign Gifts), 171, 173

IRS Uniform Lifetime Table, 260–261

J

Joint tenancy with right of survivorship, 36, 47–49
  community property with right of survivorship, advantages of switching to, 48–49
  durable power of attorney for finances and, 299
  probate avoidance and, 19, 21
  wills do not override, 49

K

Kiddie Tax, 127, 128

L

Land trusts, 67
Last survivor life insurance, 157
Legal research, conducting, 326
Letters Testamentary, 51
Letter to executor or guardian
  explaining will choices, 62–63
Life insurance, 13, 153–161, 251, 252
  amount of insurance to purchase,
    determining, 159–161
  benefits provided by, 155
  blended family, beneficiary
    designations in, 186
  cash after death as benefit of, 155
  childcare/domestic services, money
    for, 155
  death benefit, 153
  defined, 153
  estate tax reduction and, 155
  income-multiplier method
    for determining amount to
    purchase, 159
  irrevocable life insurance trust
    (ILIT), 278
  lifestyle approach to determining
    amount to purchase, 160
  lost income replacement as benefit
    of, 155
  online calculators for determining
    amount to purchase, 159–160
  permanent life insurance, 157, 158
  premiums, 153–154
  probate avoidance and, 18, 155
  special needs children, providing
    for, 155, 161
  tax-free nature of, 155
  term life insurance, 156, 157–158
  types of, 156–158
  universal life insurance, 158
  work-based, 154

Lifestyle approach to determining
  amount of life insurance needed,
  160
Living trusts, 10, 11, 24–26, 66–89
  administration of, 71
  advantages of, 25
  amendment of, 318–319
  assets that should be transferred
    to, 85
  attorney, working with, 81–83
  beneficiaries, 69–70, 72, 76–77
  circumstances where it is best to
    consult with attorney, 81
  costs for attorney preparation of,
    83
  decisions you have to make in
    order to create, 72
  defined, 12, 67
  do-it-yourself living trusts, 80–81
  durable power of attorney for
    finances and, 299
  financial accounts, transfers of,
    85–86
  financial institutions must accept
    certification of trust, 313
  foreign trusts, 172–174
  funding of, 84–86
  gifts made during life, accounting
    for, 242–243
  house transfers, 86
  number of trusts to create, 73–74
  parties to, 68–70
  persons who should make, 25, 26
  pour-over wills, transfers through,
    68, 87–88
  probate avoidance and, 18, 21, 24,
    66
  property tax reassessment
    exclusion for transfers into and
    out of, 219–220
  purpose of, 67, 72
  restatements, 318–319

revocable living trusts, 68

scams, avoiding, 82

as secondary beneficiary for retirement plan assets left to children, 266

settlors, 67, 68–70

trust document, 69

trustees, 67, 68–70, 72, 74–76

Trust Worksheet, preparing, 78–80

updating, 318–319

wills used in combination with, 68, 87–89

wills versus, choosing, 13, 26, 44

Living wills. *See* Advance health care directives

M

Managing Money for Minor Children Worksheet, 151, 152

Marital deduction, 168, 175–176

Medi-Cal

nursing home coverage, qualification for, 39

transfer-on-death deeds for real estate as exempt from reimbursement of, 38

Medical expense payments made for another person, gift tax exemption for, 240

Medical treatment

conservatorships, court appointed, 286

do-not-resuscitate (DNR) order, 288–289

palliative care, 286, 287

Physician Orders for Life-Sustaining Treatment (POLST), 287–288

See also Advance health care directives

Mental competence

transfer-on-death deeds for real estate and, 38

wills and, 44

Motley Fool, 159

N

Net Worth Calculation Worksheet, 27, 122

Nonautomatic exclusions from property tax reassessment, 209–216

Nonresident aliens, 165–169

determining status as resident or nonresident alien, 167

estate and gift taxation, 167–169

income taxation, 165–166

Nonresident aliens, taxation of, 165–159

Notarization

durable power of attorney for finances and, 304, 305

transfer-on-death deeds for real estate and, 38

Notification of Death of Real Property Owner, 221

O

Omitted children, 62

Out-of-state executors, 51, 54

Out-of-state guardianships, 108

P

Palliative care, 286, 287

Parent-child exclusion from property tax reassessment, 209–211

Payable-on-death (POD) bank accounts, 18, 21

PCOR. *See* Preliminary Change of Ownership Report (PCOR)

Permanent life insurance, 157, 158

Personal inventory. *See* Inventory of assets and property

Personal Inventory form, 27, 28–31, 255

Personal property, gifts of, 185–186

Pets, 55–57

friend who will take care of pet, leaving money to, 56

pet rescue organization, leaving
  money to, 57
trust for, 56–57
Physician Orders for Life-Sustaining
  Treatment (POLST), 287–288
Planning for Minor Children
  Worksheet, 100–102, 105
POLST. *See* Physician Orders for
  Life-Sustaining Treatment (POLST)
Portability of estate taxes, 245–247
Postmarital agreements. *See* Property
  agreements
Pot trusts, 124, 143–144
Pour-over wills, 68, 87–89
  executors, nomination of, 89
  functions of, 87–89
  guardians, nomination of, 89
  methods of transferring property
    to living trust, 87–88
  party who creates, 89
Power of attorney. *See* Advance health
  care directives; Durable power of
  attorney for finances
Preliminary Change of Ownership
  Report (PCOR), 221
Premarital agreements. *See* Property
  agreements
Premiums, life insurance, 153–154
Probate, 13–22, 24
  assets subject to, 19–20
  assets that pass outside of, 16–19,
    45
  circumstances where probate
    makes sense, 20
  defined, 13
  delays caused by, 20
  fees, 15–16, 20
  length of time to complete, 15
  methods for avoiding, 18–19,
    20–21, 24, 66
  $150,000 threshold for, 14
  procedures, 14
  as public process, 20
  reasons for avoiding, 20

simple procedures for small estates,
  14, 21
value of estate assets, determining,
  15–16
Professional executors, 53
Professional trustees
  compensation of, 140
  disadvantages to using, 140–141
  finding, 141
  Interviewing Professional Trustees
    Worksheet, 141, 142, 143
  minimum investment
    requirements, 140
Property
  forms of ownership, 35–37, 47–49
  See also Real estate
Property agreements, 186–189
  estate plan challenges, as means of
    avoiding, 187–188
  express language altering
    characterization of property,
    requirement for, 186
  keeping particular property in
    family after death and, 188
  value of signing, 187–189
  written requirement, 186
Property guardian for children's
  property, 55, 94, 107, 149–151
  compensation of, 150
  duties of, 149, 150
  ex-spouse should not be property
    guardian, requesting that, 152
  recordkeeping and accounting
    requirements, 150
  selection of, 150
Property management for children's
  property, 43, 55, 122–123
  children cannot receive more than
    $5,000 directly, 120
  children's trusts, 124, 131–149
  custodial accounts, 124, 125–131
  Managing Money for Minor
    Children Worksheet, 151, 152

property guardians, 55, 94, 107, 120, 149–151, 152
property manager, 120, 122
special needs children, providing for, 125
Property taxes, 202–222
  automatic exclusions from reassessment, 216–220
  change in ownership and, 202, 204, 206–208
  co-owner transfers that don't change proportional interests, reassessment exclusion for, 217–219
  cotenant transfer reassessment exclusion, 213–214
  counties accepting base value transfers for replacement residence, 215
  county assessor, role of, 203
  exclusions from reassessment, 207, 209–220
  failure to file claim for reassessment exclusion, 222
  grandparent-grandchild reassessment exclusion, 211–213
  nonautomatic reassessment exclusions, 209–216
  parent-child reassessment exclusion, 209–211
  registered domestic partners, reassessment exclusion for transfers between, 216–217
  replacement residence purchase by persons older than 55, reassessment exclusion for, 214–216
  reporting changes of ownership, 220–221
  spouses, reassessment exclusion for transfers between, 216–217
  state law sets maximum rate of, 203
  trusts, property tax reassessment exclusion for transfers involving, 219–220
  See also Proposition 13

Proposition 13
  base year value, 204
  change in ownership of home and, 202, 204, 206–208
  exclusions from reassessment, 207, 209–220
  factored base value, 204
  historical background, 202, 203–204
  new owner's purchase price as new base year value, 205
  reassessment upon change of ownership, 207–208
  remodeling or rebuilding adjustments, 205
  situations constituting change in ownership, 206–207, 208
  2% limit to tax increases, 204, 206
  See also Property taxes
Proposition 58, 209–211
Proposition 60, 214–215
Proposition 90, 215
Proposition 193, 211–213

Q

QDOTs. *See* Qualified domestic trusts (QDOTs)
Qualified domestic trusts (QDOTs), 176–177
Quasi-community property, 183

R

Real estate, 34–40
  forms of property ownership, 35–37, 47–49
  home ownership, determining form of, 34–35
  transfer-on-death deeds, 18, 21, 37–39
  See also Home; Property
Recording
  of durable power of attorney for finances, 304, 305
  of transfer-on-death deeds for real estate, 38

Recordkeeping requirements
of custodians, 127
of property guardian for children's
property, 150
Registered domestic partners
community property and, 36–37
property tax reassessment
exclusion for transfers between,
216–217
Religious education and faith, leaving
guardian guidance on, 116
Remarriage, revising estate plan
upon, 314
Renewable term life insurance, 157
Replacement residence purchase by
persons older than 55, property tax
reassessment exclusion for, 214–216
Reporting requirements
for gifts in excess of annual
threshold, 237, 238
of guardians for minor children,
96
for property ownership changes,
220–221
of trustees, 76, 135
See also Accountings
Report of Foreign Bank and Financial
Accounts (FBAR), 169–170
Resident aliens, 165–171
determining status as resident or
nonresident alien, 167
estate and gift taxation, 167–171
income taxation, 165–166
Residue, disposition of, 78
Restatement of living trusts, 318–319
Retirement plans, 13, 250–274
beneficiaries, selecting, 258–270
blended family, beneficiary
designations in, 186
coordinating estate planning with,
250–252
income taxes on inherited
retirement plan assets, 234–235,
251

keeping track of, 252
probate avoidance and, 18
See also 401(k) plans; 403(b) plans;
Individual retirement accounts
(IRAs)
Revising estate plan, 308, 313–320
advance health care directives,
updating, 320
beneficiary designations, updating,
258, 275–276, 320
children, changes involving,
314–315
durable power of attorney for
finances, updating, 320
financial situation, changes to, 316
guardians, trustees or executors,
changes involving, 315–316
living trusts, updating, 318–319
marital status, change in, 313–314
moving out of California and,
316–317
wills, updating, 317–318
See also Revocation
Revocable living trusts. See Living
trusts
Revocable transfer-on-death deeds,
37–38
Revocation
of advance health care directives,
298, 320
of durable power of attorney for
finances, 305–306, 320
of transfer-on-death deeds for real
estate, 38
of will, 317
Rolling over 401(k) plans to IRAs,
271–272
Roth 401(k) and 403(b) plans
beneficiaries, selection of, 261–262
distributions from, 255, 261–262
income taxes and, 235
Roth IRAs
beneficiaries, selection, 261–262

contributions, 254
converting traditional IRA to, advantages of, 254
distributions from, 254, 261–262
income limitations, 254
income taxes and, 235

S

Safe deposit boxes, 34
Same-sex couples
guardians for minor children, selecting, 103
See also Registered domestic partners
Self-proving wills, 44
Separate property, 36
blended families, estate planning issues for, 181, 182–190
characterization of property as, 183–184
defined, 183
discussing characterization of property with spouse, 185
intestacy and, 63
property agreement provisions and, 186–189
source of funds and characterization as, 183
taxation of, 190
unmarried couples, estate planning for, 189–190
Settlors, 67, 68–70
Siblings
property tax reassessment exclusion for co-owner transfers that don't change proportional interests, 217–219
as trustees of children's trusts, 139
Signatures
for advance health care directives, 297
for durable power of attorney for finances, 304
for wills, 44
Single premium whole life insurance, 157
Small estate affidavit process, 14, 21

Special needs children
life insurance proceeds and, 155, 161
special needs trusts for, 125, 155, 161
Special needs trusts, 125, 155, 161
Spouse
as beneficiary for retirement accounts, 264–265
estate plan revision upon death of, 314
as executor, 51–52
noncitizen spouse, estate planning for, 175–177
property tax reassessment exclusion for transfers between, 216–217
Springing durable power of attorney for finances, 301
Stepparent adoption, 103
Step-up in basis
capital gains taxes and, 48–49, 190–192, 228–230
of community property, 48–49, 190–192, 230–231
Storage
of estate plan, 310
of wills, 62
Stretch-out planning, 263
Subjective test for U.S. domicile, 167
Successor trustees, 75, 193–195
Supplemental needs trusts. *See* Special needs trusts
Survivors/bypass trust estate plan
for blended families, 195–198
income taxes and, 231–234
Survivorship property. *See* Community property with right of survivorship; Joint tenancy with right of survivorship

T

Taxes
foreign assets, reporting requirements for, 169–170
Kiddie Tax, 127, 128
property taxes, 202–222

trust tax returns, trustee's filing of,
76, 135
See also Estate taxes; Gift taxes;
Income taxes
Temporary guardians, 108–109
Tenancy in common, 37
Term life insurance, 157–158
Traditional whole life insurance, 157
Transfer-on-death deeds for real
estate
capacity to make, 38
content requirements, 38
execution requirements, 38
for homes, 37–39
Medi-Cal reimbursement,
exemption from, 38
notarization of, 38
probate avoidance and, 18, 21
properties that may be transferred
by, 38
recording of, 38
revocation of, 38
Transfer-on-death (TOD) bank
accounts, 18, 21
Trust administration, 71
Trust document, 69
Trustees of children's trusts, 133–143
beneficiaries' interest,
administration of trust solely in,
134
compensation of, 135, 136, 140
cotrustees, 138–139
duties of, 133–136
expert help, hiring, 134
grandparents as, 139
impartiality requirement, 133
professional trustees, 140–143
prudence and diligence in
investment choices, 134
reporting to beneficiaries, 135
selection of, 136–143
siblings as, 139
tax returns, filing of, 135

Trustees of living trusts, 68–70
accountings to beneficiaries,
providing, 76
beneficiaries' interest,
administration of trust solely in,
75
blended family, strategies for
naming successor trustee for,
193–195
copies of estate planning
documents, giving, 312
duties of, 75–76
expert help, hiring, 76
fiduciary duties of, 67
impartiality requirement, 75
international trustees, 171–174
prudence and diligence in
investment choices, 75
reporting to beneficiaries, 76
revising estate plan to reflect
changes involving, 315–316
selection of, 72, 74–76
successor trustee, naming, 75,
193–195
tax returns, filing of, 76
Trust mills, 82
Trust protector, 141
Trusts, 10
A/B trusts, 195–198, 231–234
as beneficiaries for retirement
plans, 268–269
bypass trusts, 195–198, 231–234
children's trusts, 124, 131–149
defined, 67
fiduciary duties of trustees, 67
irrevocable life insurance trust
(ILIT), 278
land trusts, 67
for pets, 56–57
pot trusts, 124, 143–144
property tax reassessment
exclusion for transfers involving,
219–220

qualified domestic trusts (QDOTs),
  176–177
special needs trusts, 125, 155, 161
survivors trust, 195–198, 231–234
See also Living trusts
Trust scams, 82
Trust Worksheet
  contents of, 78
  disposition of property, 78
  personal information, entering, 78
  sample Trust Worksheet, 79
  trustee, selection of, 78

U

Uniform Prudent Investor Act, 134
Uniform Transfers to Minors Act
  (CUTMA), 126, 150, 266, 316
Universal life insurance, 157, 158
U.S. domicile, 167

V

Value of estate assets, determining, 15–16
Variable life insurance, 157
Variable universal life insurance, 157
Visa holders. *See* Nonresident aliens

W

Websites
  advance health care directive forms and
    information, 296–297
  affidavit procedure for small estates, 14
  author's blog and podcasts, 7
  for California Department of Justice
    information and complaint forms for
    trust scams, 82
  California statutes, 326
  Compassion & Choices, 290
  for Consumer Fraud Section of local
    district attorneys office, 82
  counties accepting base value transfers
    for replacement residence, 215
  digital estate planning issues, 312

for DNR forms, 290
downloadable forms, 328, 329
end-of-life options guide for family
  doctors, 290
529 college savings plans, information
  on, 241
guardianship and same-sex couples,
  information on, 103
on guardianship process, 97
inherited retirement plan assets, income
  tax consequences of, 235
legal changes affecting estate planning,
  keeping up with, 308
Motley Fool's life insurance calculator,
  159
for Nolo resources, 8
Nolo's downloadable forms, 328, 329
Nolo's Lawyer Dictionary, 324
out-of-state executors, local court rules
  on, 54
palliative care, information on, 287
pet trusts, information on, 57
for POLST form, 288
for probate procedures, 14
professional executors, finding, 53
professional trustees, finding, 141
property tax calculator, 206
Proposition 13, information on, 208
Report of Foreign Bank and Financial
  Accounts (FBAR), information on,
  169
retirement plans and IRA withdrawal
  rules, 274
for transfer-on-death deeds, 39
Wills, 10, 11, 12, 22–24, 42–64
  age and, 44
  assets that do not pass through will,
    45–49
  attorney, working with, 61–62
  backup wills, 89
  circumstances where it is best to
    consult with attorney, 61
  codicils, 317

decisions you have to make in
order to create, 42–43
disinheriting children, 62
documents required in addition
to, 45
do-it-yourself wills, 60
dying without (intestacy), 11–12,
63–64
execution requirements, 44
executors, selecting, 42, 49–55
functions of, 22–23
gifts made during life, accounting
for, 242–243
guardians for minor children,
selecting, 42, 55
holographic wills, validity of, 44
letter to executor or guardian
explaining choices, 62–63
living trusts, wills used in
combination with, 68, 87–89
mental competence and, 44
parties who should make, 23–24
pets, planning for, 55–57
pour-over wills, 68, 87–89
property guardian, selecting, 55
property management for
children's property, 43, 55
revocation of, 317
self-proving, 44
signature requirements, 44
simple wills, goals that may be
accomplished by, 43
storing, 62
survivorship property and, 47–49
trusts versus, choosing, 13, 26, 44
updating, 317–318
Will Worksheet, preparing, 58–60
witness requirements, 44
Will Worksheet
contents of, 58
disposition of property,
determining, 58
executor, choice of, 58
guardians for minor children,
nominating, 58
personal information, entering, 58
property manager, nomination of,
58
sample Will Worksheet, 59
Witnesses
for advance health care directives,
297
for durable power of attorney for
finances, 304
for wills, 44
Work-based life insurance, 154

△△ NOLO *Online Legal Forms*

Nolo offers a large library of legal solutions and forms, created by Nolo's in-house legal staff. These reliable documents can be prepared in minutes.

Create a Document

- **Incorporation.** Incorporate your business in any state.
- **LLC Formations.** Gain asset protection and pass-through tax status in any state.
- **Wills.** Nolo has helped people make over 2 million wills. Is it time to make or revise yours?
- **Living Trust (avoid probate).** Plan now to save your family the cost, delays, and hassle of probate.
- **Trademark.** Protect the name of your business or product.
- **Provisional Patent.** Preserve your rights under patent law and claim "patent pending" status.

Download a Legal Form

Nolo.com has hundreds of top quality legal forms available for download—bills of sale, promissory notes, nondisclosure agreements, LLC operating agreements, corporate minutes, commercial lease and sublease, motor vehicle bill of sale, consignment agreements and many more.

Review Your Documents

Many lawyers in Nolo's consumer-friendly lawyer directory will review Nolo documents for a very reasonable fee. Check their detailed profiles at **Nolo.com/lawyers**.

On Nolo.com you'll also find:

Books & Software

Nolo publishes hundreds of great books and software programs for consumers and
business owners. Order a copy, or download an ebook version instantly, at Nolo.com.

Online Legal Documents

You can quickly and easily make a will or living trust, form an LLC or corporation, apply
for a trademark or provisional patent, or make hundreds of other forms—online.

Free Legal Information

Thousands of articles answer common questions about everyday legal issues
including wills, bankruptcy, small business formation, divorce, patents,
employment, and much more.

Plain-English Legal Dictionary

Stumped by jargon? Look it up in America's most up-to-date source for
definitions of legal terms, free at nolo.com.

Lawyer Directory

Nolo's consumer-friendly lawyer directory provides in-depth profiles of lawyers all
over America. You'll find all the information you need to choose the right lawyer.

31901061019594   ESCA1